NORTH CAROLINA GUIDEBOOK FOR **REGISTERS OF DEEDS**

Eleventh Edition

Charles Szypszak

The cover of this guidebook features a photograph styled and taken by the Honorable J. Lee Warren, Jr., Cumberland County Register of Deeds, which was chosen as the winner of a contest that included submissions from office personnel of North Carolina registers of deeds. The author would like to thank all who submitted their ideas.

UNC SCHOOL OF GOVERNMENT

The School of Government at the University of North Carolina at Chapel Hill works to improve the lives of North Carolinians by engaging in practical scholarship that helps public officials and citizens understand and improve state and local government. Established in 1931 as the Institute of Government, the School provides educational, advisory, and research services for state and local governments. The School of Government is also home to a nationally ranked Master of Public Administration program, the North Carolina Judicial College, and specialized centers focused on community and economic development, information technology, and environmental finance.

As the largest university-based local government training, advisory, and research organization in the United States, the School of Government offers up to 200 courses, webinars, and specialized conferences for more than 12,000 public officials each year. In addition, faculty members annually publish approximately 50 books, manuals, reports, articles, bulletins, and other print and online content related to state and local government. The School also produces the *Daily Bulletin Online* each day the General Assembly is in session, reporting on activities for members of the legislature and others who need to follow the course of legislation.

Operating support for the School of Government's programs and activities comes from many sources, including state appropriations, local government membership dues, private contributions, publication sales, course fees, and service contracts.

Visit sog.unc.edu or call 919.966.5381 for more information on the School's courses, publications, programs, and services.

Printed in the United States of America

25 24 23 22 21   1 2 3 4 5

ISBN 978-1-64238-042-2

Contents

Chapter 1

The Office and Its Management

Chapter 1

The Office and Its Management

1.1 Nature of the Office

The office of register of deeds has been essential to North Carolina governance since the English first started settling the region. Although the basic nature of the register's responsibilities has remained the same, fulfilling those responsibilities has required ever greater technical expertise and managerial skill.[1] Registers perform their duties at the juncture between government service and commercial transactions, during important life moments when homes are bought, couples are married, and births and deaths occur. Every day, registers do things they have done countless times, but on most days they also see something entirely new. Despite the sometimes bewildering challenges they face, most registers would not choose any other job. They take pride in what they do as elected officials on whom others rely.

As elected officials, registers need to be attuned to their communities, but their responsibilities are unlike most who must appeal to voters. Elected officials typically are policy makers. Sometimes registers do make choices that have policy implications, such as whether to introduce new technologies into the office. But fundamentally, a register's effectiveness depends not on influence but rather on his or her ability to understand real estate instruments and record keeping procedures, pay attention to

---

1. For an analysis of the challenges that registers of deeds face and how they meet them with human traits that have always been essential for holding this important local government office, *see* Charles Szypszak, *Local Government Registers of Deeds and the Enduring Reliance on Common Sense Judgment in a Technocratic Tide*, 44 Real Est. L. J. 3 (2015).

details, and manage a busy office. Attorneys and paralegals who regularly use the office will know of such things, but most voters are unaware of the challenges that registers face or how well they meet them. Registers are therefore vulnerable to changing tides of national and regional politics. While being elected means being vulnerable to loss of the office, it also acts as a powerful incentive for registers not to take their positions for granted.

To meet their challenges, registers must know and follow many different laws that apply to recording and indexing real estate instruments, managing vital records, and issuing marriage licenses. These laws often change, and knowing all the details can be difficult. Yet registers must make decisions based on their understanding of the law, and they take an oath to follow it. This understanding may lead them to disagree with respected attorneys who represent the interests of persons seeking to record a real estate instrument or obtain a marriage license or certified vital record. To meet this challenge, registers must continually study and learn from experience. This book is intended to assist in this regard as a comprehensive reference resource. Registers also can benefit from the experience of other registers by participating in the programs of the North Carolina Association of Registers of Deeds, as discussed in Section 1.13 of this chapter, and they can take advantage of other opportunities for education and advice from such resources as the School of Government at the University of North Carolina, Chapel Hill; the Land Records Management Section of the North Carolina Department of the Secretary of State; North Carolina Vital Records within the North Carolina Department of Health and Human Services; the Government Records Section of the State Archives of North Carolina within the North Carolina Department of Natural and Cultural Resources; the North Carolina Bar Association; and other departments in county governments.

Registers' effective performance of their responsibilities also depends on their ability to work with others within their offices, in other government leadership positions, and in the public generally. They are responsible for their offices and the matters entrusted to them and can be held accountable for mistakes made by their staff members. They also are part of the broader county government and depend on the county commissioners and, ultimately, the county voters for the necessary resources to keep their offices functioning. Registers must balance a focus on meeting the pressing demands and needs of their offices with gaining the support they need to equip their offices and attract and retain high-quality employees.

Much of this book is devoted to a description of the statutes and regulations that govern the details of registers' operations. Although much of what registers do is considered performance of what the law calls "ministerial" duties that involve following clear rules, registers also exercise discretionary judgment in many ways, such as when they manage their offices and hire and supervise assistants and deputies. They also regularly must make decisions about actions for which the rules are not entirely clear. Despite the many ways in which being a register may seem to be a matter of performing mechanical acts, to perform the position well requires more than being able to follow a routine. Characteristics that make someone a good family member, friend, and neighbor—such as integrity, intelligence, and compassion—also make someone a good public official. For handling the responsibilities of a register of deeds office, some other traits are especially important. They include attention to detail, dependability, fairness, adaptability, technological competence, equanimity, humility, and responsibility for good government, which are each described in the following sections.

Attention to detail. Registers must be precise when they review and capture information. For most things in today's world, "close enough" often seems to be acceptable, but that is not true for registers. They must be accurate and complete in their inspection of presented documents and in the way they maintain them in the public record. While many records are in standard forms that registers see frequently, the information in the forms varies with each record. Registers cannot merely assume that any particular instance is the same as any other. They need to be vigilant about both human imperfection and the limitations of automation. To minimize the risk of error, registers must insist on adherence to sound procedures for accurately recording information from individual records and for continually verifying the completeness of massive collections.

Dependability. Registers are subject to strict requirements for when their offices are open to the public for business. Within these constraints they must deal with an unpredictable workflow. An instrument may be presented or a record requested at any time during office hours, and competing demands for urgency may arise in a flurry. Something that seems routine to a register may be critical to an individual who is making an important decision in a real estate transaction or otherwise in life. Unlike some offices that can allow the inflow of work to accumulate while other pending matters are addressed, registers' offices always need to be responsive to requests for new services while they carefully manage the internal processing of many other demands of the office. The public is entitled to expect that each request will be handled in a proper and timely way regardless of what other demands may have arisen for the register's attention.

Fairness. Registers are elected officials and need public approval to stay in office. Local attorneys and their assistants who do title work and present instruments for recording become familiar with registers and their assistants and deputies. But many people need the register of deeds office rarely, and maybe even only once, such as for a marriage license or to get a certified copy of a birth certificate. Everyone expects to be treated respectfully and afforded the same access and treatment as anyone else.

Adaptability. The ways in which registers function have changed in recent years. They increasingly rely on technologies to receive, record, and index real estate instruments and vital records. Registers are expected to manage databases with thousands of essential records. They also must recognize ever-changing legal details that few understand. To keep up with these demands, registers must be interested in the bigger picture and resist the tendency to stick with what is comfortable. They must keep apprised of changes around them and be ready to implement new policies and procedures.

Technological competence. Registers should be competent in the use of the basic hardware and software available for their office functions. Registers use technology for record acceptance, access, and preservation, as well as for communication with other county offices, vendors, the register of deeds community, and the public. Technological competence enables registers to make basic, ongoing decisions about what systems should be used in their counties. This competence also equips registers to make a case to their respective counties for including appropriate funds for technology acquisition and support in the county budget. An understanding of technological systems gives registers necessary background to choose appropriate vendors and manage their support, as well as to communicate these choices to the public. Technological competence is one of the most difficult challenges for registers today, not only due to the complexity and changeability of the available technological tools, but also because of the often-differing expectations that the transactional and information technology communities may have about a register's use of particular technologies. Maintaining technological competence is a critical part of the register's need for continuing education.

Equanimity. Equanimity is a word not often heard today, but it aptly describes an important trait for registers. It means maintaining composure even in stressful situations. Registers often are the face of the government in situations that are stressful for others. What might be a hundredth recording or marriage license for a register may be a singularly important event for the person with whom the register is dealing. Registers may also find themselves having to manage operations during emergencies, which in recent years have arisen from hurricanes, floods, a global pandemic, and civil unrest. Keeping one's head is a difficult challenge for anyone who is taxed with heavy burdens. Some people have this trait as a gift; others acquire it intentionally with experience and maturity.

Humility. Those in need of register services are captives of the register's receptiveness. Much may be at stake for the person who is attempting to record a document or get a marriage license or certified copy of a birth or death certificate. An effective register is able to convey seriousness about the rules without giving the impression of being a tyrant. This requires humility.

Humility is an important trait for a register for another reason: the ability to learn from others. There are many differences among the 100 counties in North Carolina. Small counties may have only two or three people who handle about 1,000 documents per year; large counties have dozens of staff members and may process 1,000 documents in a single day. Each register has an operational environment that is a unique combination of records and systems, staff, and customs of practice. But all registers are governed by the same basic state laws and regulations, and many registers have probably had experiences from which others can benefit.

Responsibility for good government. As local public officials, registers are conspicuous representatives of the government on which the public relies. Their leadership responsibilities go beyond complying with the law. Their comportment may give the public confidence in the good faith of local government. Registers' responsibility for the law's perceived legitimacy is especially important because of their unique knowledge of the laws and procedures that few others have reason to consider. The rules for how registers perform the functions of the office are not going to be improved in the public interest unless registers take responsibility for them and initiate a process for reform in standards of practice and for regulatory and legislative amendment.

1.2 History of the Office

Land registration in North America began almost as soon as settlers arrived. Towns needed local records of their settlements within land grants from the British proprietors. The first office of a register of deeds in North America was in Plymouth, Massachusetts, which provided a place to record a land transfer in a book with the names of the parties, terms of sale and payment, and descriptive bounds of the property. A law was passed in 1636 requiring all transfers to be acknowledged and recorded. In 1640, the Massachusetts legislature required all transfers to be recorded within one month or they were to be void against anyone who later acquired a deed to the same property. This is basically the same recording law that today governs real estate conveyances throughout the United States.[2]

The history of land registration in North Carolina also can be traced to the 1600s. In 1663, King Charles II executed a charter to eight Lords Proprietors authorizing them to establish a colonial government in the region that is now North Carolina and to make land grants to individual settlers. To entice settlers, the Lords Proprietors acknowledged various individual rights. Their Concessions and Agreement of 1665 provided, among other things, for the appointment of "chiefe Registers or Secretarys" to record public business and grants, conveyances, and leases. Though archaic, the language of the Concessions leaves little doubt that a function of the chief registers was to serve as recording officers with many of the same responsibilities as present-day registers:

> [A]nd to avoyde deceiptes and lawsuits [the registers] shall record and enter all Graunts of Land from the Lords to the planter and all conveyances of Land howse or howses from man to man, As alsoe all leases for Land howse or howses made or to be made by the Landlord to any tennant for more than one yeare which conveyance or Lease shalbe first acknowledged by the Grantr or Leasor or proved by the oath of two witnesses to the conveyance or Lease before the Governor or some Chiefe Judge of a Court for the time being whoe shall . . . attest the acknowledgement or proofe as aforesaid which shalbe our grant for the Registers to record the same which Conveyance or Lease

---

2. Joseph H. Beale, Jr., *The Origin of the System of Recording Deeds in America*, 19 The Green Bag 335, 335–37 (1907).

> soe recorded shalbe good and effectuall in Law notwithstanding any other conveyance deede or Lease for the said Land howse or howses or for any part there although dated before the Conveyance deede or Lease soe recorded as aforesaid.[3]

This is essentially the same law as had been adopted in Massachusetts, protecting land transfers that were recorded with the register of deeds. The land registration system was essential for a form of government that protected individual property rights and other liberties. The ability to acquire land that was protected by law enabled citizens to build homes and clear farms.

As far as can be determined, the Lords Proprietors' register of deeds office was first filled in North Carolina on November 14, 1664, when they appointed Robert Samford as "Secrytary and Chiefe Register for our County of Clarendon."[4] The earliest North Carolina statute dealing with the office of register of deeds was enacted by the Colonial Assembly in 1715.[5] This law provided that the voters of each county should elect three freeholders as nominees for the office, one of whom was then appointed to the office by the governor, acting with the advice of the Lords Proprietors' deputies. No term of office was established.

During the colonial period, registers of deeds were important officials who represented the British government. One North Carolina register became infamous as a target of resistance at the dawn of the American Revolution. Edmund Fanning, who had studied at Yale and Harvard and was a member of the bar in North Carolina, was loyal to the British government and received appointments from the British governor at the time, William Tryon. Fanning held court posts as well as the register of deeds office. He wrote to the governor and warned of local anger that was "threatening death and immediate destruction to myself and others."[6] One ominous threat Fanning was hearing came from a group known as the Regulators, who complained that Fanning was charging more to record

---

3. The Colonial Records of North Carolina I (1662–1712) 79 (William L. Saunders, ed., 1886–90).

4. *Id.* at 72.

5. 1715 N.C. Laws ch. 38.

6. Letter from Edmund Fanning to William Tryon (Apr. 23, 1768), *in* The Regulators in North Carolina: A Documentary History, 1759–1776, at 84, 84 (William S. Powell, James K. Huhta & Thomas J. Farnham eds., 1971).

a deed than was permitted and that he was using the excess for himself.[7] The Regulators demanded that the colonial government get involved and "[e]xamine the true Cost by Law for Recording and proving Deeds."[8] In 1770, the rebels took out their anger on Fanning. As a newspaper described it, a crowd confronted him in the county courthouse and "seized him by the heels, dragged him down the steps, his head striking very violently on every step, carried him to the door, and forcing him out, dragged him on the ground over stones and brickbats, struck him with their whips and clubs, kicked him, and spit and spurned at him."[9] Fanning soon left for New York and built his wealth and influence there, later commanding British troops in the Revolution as a general and becoming governor of Nova Scotia.

Things settled down for North Carolina's registers after the Revolution. No further significant change in the office was made until after North Carolina became a state. In 1777, the General Assembly provided that the justices who constituted the county court should appoint the register of deeds in each county. By the time of the Revolution, the register was therefore an established public office.[10] After 1777, the register in each county was selected by a majority of the justices of the Court of Pleas and Quarter Sessions for a four-year term. For many years, the existence and nature of the office were left to the will of the legislature because the office was not required by the state constitution. It became a constitutional office after the Civil War, when the Constitution of 1868, Article VII, Section 1, provided for the biennial election of a register of deeds by the voters of each county. The office did not long enjoy constitutional protection from legislative change, however. A state constitutional amendment, Article VII, Section 10, adopted in 1875, empowered the legislature to "modify, change or abrogate" certain constitutional provisions, including those pertaining to the register of deeds. Acting pursuant to this power, in 1935 the General Assembly set the term of office at four years in all but twenty-nine

---

7. Samuel A. Ashe, *Edmund Fanning, in* 1 Biographical History of North Carolina from Colonial Times to the Present, 272, 275 (1905).

8. Articles of Settlement and Oath of Regulators (Apr. 30, 1768), *in* The Regulators in North Carolina: A Documentary History, 1759–1776, at 97, 100 (William S. Powell, James K. Huhta & Thomas J. Farnham eds., 1971).

9. Elizabeth A. Fenn & Peter H. Wood, *Rehearsal for Revolution, in* The Way We Lived in North Carolina 94, 100 (Joe A. Mobley ed., 2003).

10. 1777 N.C. Laws ch. 8.

counties.[11] Since that time, through local acts, the register's term has been extended to four years in every county of the state.[12]

The North Carolina Constitution of 1971, in effect today, does not mention the office of register of deeds. Instead, Article VII, Section 1, states that "[t]he General Assembly shall provide for the organization and government . . . of counties." The effect of this provision is to leave all matters regarding the office and duties of the register of deeds to the General Assembly.

1.3 Election to Office

To become and remain a register of deeds, a citizen must succeed in the local government electoral process. State law prescribes the electoral qualifications and procedure, the key aspects of which are summarized in this section.

1.3.1 Qualifications

Any qualified North Carolina voter who is at least twenty-one years old is legally eligible to run for and be elected to the office of register of deeds.[13] To be a qualified North Carolina voter, a person must be a citizen of the United States,[14] a resident of North Carolina and of his or her precinct or other voting district for thirty days before the election,[15] and registered to vote.[16] A person is disqualified from holding any public office, including that of register of deeds, if he or she has been convicted of treason or any other felony, convicted of corruption or malpractice in office, or removed by impeachment from any office and has not been restored to the full rights of citizenship.[17]

---

11. 1935 N.C. Pub.-Loc. Laws ch. 362; Chapter 161, Section 2 of the North Carolina General Statutes (hereinafter G.S.).

12. 1991 N.C. Sess. Laws ch. 60.

13. N.C. Const. art. VI, § 6.

14. N.C. Const. art. VI, § 1.

15. G.S. 163-55. Article VI, Section 2(1) of the North Carolina Constitution requires residence in the state for one year, but this was declared to violate the Fourteenth Amendment to the United States Constitution in *Andrews v. Cody*, 327 F. Supp. 793 (M.D.N.C. 1971), *aff'd*, 405 U.S. 1034 (1972).

16. N.C. Const. art. VI, § 3.

17. N.C. Const. art. VI, § 8.

1.3.2 Election

North Carolina registers face election every four years.[18] As a result of the sequence in which counties' elections first occurred, in two-thirds of the counties the election corresponds with the federal presidential election and in one-third it occurs during the presidential midterm year. Almost all candidates qualify for election by becoming the nominee of the Democratic or Republican Party by winning a primary election or by becoming the party's nominee without opposition. Many registers succeed to office by becoming a candidate without having to face opposition in either the primary or the regular election. Of course, no one knows if this will be the case until the deadlines have passed for qualifying to be listed as a candidate on the ballot.

The primary is held on the Tuesday next after the first Monday in March preceding each general election.[19] To be listed on a primary ballot to become a party's candidate, a qualified citizen must file a notice of candidacy[20] (see the previous section, Section 1.3.1, about qualifications). The notice must be filed no earlier than noon on the first Monday in December and no later than noon on the third Friday in December preceding the primary.[21] The notice is filed with the county board of elections and must be signed in the presence of the chair or secretary of the county board of elections, or a candidate may have his or her signature on the notice of candidacy acknowledged and certified by any officer authorized to administer an oath.[22]

Along with filing the notice, the candidate must pay a filing fee. The fee for register of deeds candidacy is 1 percent of the annual salary of the office. By statute, "[t]he salary of any office that is the basis for calculating the filing fee is the starting salary for the office, rather than the salary received by the incumbent, if different. If no starting salary can be determined for the office, then the salary used for calculation is the salary of the incumbent, as of January 1 of the election year."[23] Accordingly, when the county does not have a salary schedule that applies to the register, the filing fee

18. G.S. 161-2.
19. G.S. 163-1(b).
20. G.S. 163-106.
21. G.S. 163-106.2(b).
22. G.S. 163-106(a).
23. G.S. 163-107(a).

for both the register seeking reelection and anyone else filing for election to the office will be based on the current register's salary.

A rarely used alternative method for getting on a ballot for a party primary is to file a written petition with the county board of elections no later than noon on Monday preceding the filing deadline. It must be signed by 10 percent of the registered voters of the election area affiliated with the same political party, or by 200 such voters, whichever requirement is greater.[24]

Someone not affiliated with a party can get on the November ballot by filing a written petition with the county board of elections on or before noon on the day of the primary election. It must be signed by qualified voters of the county equal in number to 4 percent of the total number of registered voters in the county.[25] Someone who will not be on the ballot but wishes to have write-in votes counted must file a petition with the county board of elections on or before noon on the 90th day before the general election signed by 100 qualified voters who are eligible to vote for the office, unless fewer than 5,000 persons are eligible to vote for the office as shown by the most recent records, in which case the petition must be signed by at least 1 percent of those registered voters.[26]

1.3.3 Vacancy in the Office

The office of register of deeds does not automatically become vacant when the incumbent's term expires. The register holds over and performs the duties of the office until a successor has been elected or appointed and has qualified.[27] When the office becomes vacant because of the death, resignation, or removal of the register, the board of county commissioners must appoint a person to serve the unexpired term.[28] The statute provides as follows: "If the register of deeds was elected as the nominee of a political party, the board of county commissioners shall consult the county executive committee of that political party before filling the vacancy and shall appoint the person recommended by that committee, if the party makes a

24. G.S. 163-107.1(c).

25. G.S. 163-122(a)(3).

26. G.S. 163-123(c)(3).

27. G.S. 128-7; G.S. 161-2.

28. G.S. 161-5(a1). In all but four counties (Camden, Chowan, Pasquotank, and Perquimans), the person appointed must be from the same political party as the register whose unexpired term is being filled. 1991 N.C. Sess. Laws ch. 376.

recommendation within 30 days of the occurrence of the vacancy."[29] The party county executive committee must therefore meet within thirty days after the position has become vacant to exercise its statutory right to select the replacement. The nominee must be qualified for the office, give an official bond, and take the oath in the same manner as if elected to the office. Once appointed, the new register serves out the former incumbent's term and need not stand for election until the term ends.[30]

When for any reason a vacancy occurs in the office of register of deeds, the assistants and deputies continue to serve until validly relieved of office.[31] Although the former register no longer exercises the powers of the register of deeds, the assistants and deputies continue to act under the name and seal of the former register because no one succeeds the former register until the commissioners complete the statutory appointment procedure. Should any liability arise during the vacancy, the former register's bond is to be available for that liability.[32]

By statute, the board of commissioners may grant the register a leave of absence without pay for military service, illness, or other reasons the commissioners deem satisfactory.[33] If the register takes such a leave for an extended period, the commissioners may appoint someone to be an acting register of deeds, but the register's term of office may not be extended beyond its regular expiration date because of the leave.[34] Specifically, the statute provides as follows: "If, by reason of the length of the period of absence or the nature of the duties of the official, the board of county commissioners deems it necessary, the board may appoint any qualified citizen of the county as a temporary replacement for the period of the official's leave of absence. This appointee shall have all the authority, duties, perquisites, and emoluments of the official temporarily replaced. The appointee shall possess all the qualifications required by law for holding the office for which the temporary replacement official is appointed."[35]

---

29. G.S. 161-5(a1).
30. *Id.*
31. G.S. 161-6(e).
32. G.S. 161-4(b), -6(e).
33. G.S. 128-40.
34. *Id.*
35. *Id.*

1.4 Taking Office

Once elected the register must take certain formal steps to assume the office and its responsibilities, as described in this section.

1.4.1 Oath

A register must take an oath of office to confirm a commitment to the law in carrying out the duties of the office. Usually, the register takes the oath with the other newly elected county officials on the first Monday in December following the election, although it may be taken at another time.[36] The North Carolina Constitution requires registers to take the following oath for elected officers:

> I, ______________, do solemnly swear (or affirm) that I will support and maintain the Constitution and laws of the United States, and the Constitution and laws of North Carolina not inconsistent therewith, and that I will faithfully discharge the duties of my office as register of deeds of ______________ County, so help me God.[37]

In addition, a state statute requires the following oath specifically for registers:

> I, ______________, do solemnly swear (or affirm) that I will faithfully and truly, according to the best of my skill and ability, execute the duties of the office of register of deeds for the county of ______________, in all things according to law; so help me, God.[38]

The oath must be administered by an official authorized by statute to administer oaths—a justice, judge, magistrate, clerk, assistant clerk, or deputy clerk of the General Court of Justice; a retired justice or judge of the General Court of Justice; any member of the federal judiciary; the N.C. Secretary of State; a notary public; a register of deeds; a mayor; a chair of a board of county commissioners; a member of the General Assembly; or the clerk of any county, city, town, or incorporated village.[39] After taking the oath, the register signs a document evidencing it, and this document is filed with the clerk to the board of county commissioners.[40]

---

36. G.S. 153A-26.
37. N.C. Const. art. VI, § 7.
38. G.S. 11-11.
39. G.S. 11-7.1.
40. G.S. 153A-26.

1.4.2 Bond

Before a newly elected register may be inducted into office by the board of county commissioners, he or she must tender a bond as required by statute and as approved by the board of commissioners.[41] The bond must be "with sufficient surety" and not less than $10,000 or more than $50,000; payable to the state; and "conditioned for the safekeeping of the books and records, and for the faithful discharge of the duties of his office."[42] These limits may be changed for particular counties by local act of the state legislature, but unless changed they remain the legally controlling upper and lower limits of the register's bond. The bond must also cover the acts of assistant and deputy registers, who continue to serve if the office of register becomes vacant until a successor is appointed.[43] The bond must be for the register's entire four-year term of office,[44] but the board of commissioners must examine it at least annually to ascertain its adequacy.[45] The commissioners may pay the premiums on the register's bond.[46] The clerk to the board of commissioners records its approval, and the bond is kept with the clerk of superior court.[47] In a rare case, an inability to obtain a bond can prevent someone who is elected as register of deeds from taking office. Bond companies will not agree to issue a bond in the name of someone without determining that the person is sufficiently trustworthy for the responsibilities of the office. Someone who has had serious criminal, financial, or professional conduct issues may be unable to meet this standard. In an 1887 case, the North Carolina Supreme Court held that a board of commissioners properly declared the register office vacant when the person elected to the office failed to deliver the required bond by the date set for taking the oath, and the court said that the commissioners properly appointed

---

41. G.S. 161-4(a); G.S. 58-72-5; State *ex rel.* Cole v. Patterson, 97 N.C. 360, 2 S.E. 262 (1887). In *Cole,* the person elected register of deeds was unable to tender a bond in a sufficient amount on the first Monday in December following his election, the day the board of county commissioners was to induct him into office. The board refused to grant him any delay in order to obtain a sufficient bond, declared the office vacant that day, and appointed another person to fill it. The court upheld these actions.

42. G.S. 161-4.

43. G.S. 161-4(b).

44. G.S. 58-72-10.

45. G.S. 58-72-20.

46. G.S. 58-72-15.

47. G.S. 58-72-50.

someone else to fill the office.[48] Based on this precedent, if someone elected to be the register cannot obtain a bond, the commissioners may proceed according to the vacancy rules described in Section 1.3.3 of this chapter.

If the commissioners either induct a register into office without approving the bond or approve an inadequate bond, each commissioner who voted for the action who knew or reasonably should have known of the insufficiency is liable just as though he or she were surety for the register.[49] The statute provides that any register who assumes the office without executing a bond as required by law is liable to the state in the amount of $500 "for each attempt so to exercise his office."[50]

1.4.3 Official Seal

The register must have an official seal.[51] The image made by the seal must be round and not over 1 and 5/8 inches in diameter and must contain the names of the register and the county, the letters "N.C.," and the words "Register of Deeds."[52] The seal image must be photographically reproducible.[53] It is used to authenticate certified copies of the records in the office and to attest other official acts performed by the register or by assistants or deputies in the register's name.

1.4.4 Notarial Powers

Registers have notarial powers within their counties by virtue of their office.[54] They may perform acknowledgments, verifications and proofs, and oaths and affirmations. When performing notarial duties, registers should use their register seals.[55] The notarial powers associated with the register's office extend only to the performance of official duties.[56] Fees charged for such acts must be paid to the county, and those fees are set by statute, as shown in Appendix 1.[57] As described in Section 1.6.2 of this

---

48. *Cole*, 97 N.C. 360, 2 S.E. 262.
49. G.S. 58-72-60.
50. G.S. 58-72-5.
51. G.S. 161-9.
52. *Id.*
53. *Id.*
54. G.S. 10B-21(b).
55. *Id.*
56. *Id.*
57. G.S. 10B-21(d); *see* G.S. 10B-31 (fee amount).

chapter, assistant and deputy registers have more limited notarial powers associated with their offices.

Individuals who work in registers' offices must be careful to distinguish their register responsibilities from notarial functions. For example, registers encounter notary issues *as registers* when they verify instruments presented for registration. They act *as notaries* when they perform notarial functions by virtue of the notarial powers associated with their offices or as notaries public who have completed the usual commissioning requirements. Some registers also are instructors for notary courses and have in-depth knowledge of the notary laws. When exercising register responsibilities, however, registers, assistants, and deputies must adhere to the laws applicable to those responsibilities; they are not, in their register capacities, enforcing the notary laws. This distinction commonly arises when an instrument is presented with a notarial certificate that may not comply with the notary laws for proper attestation, a condition apparent to the register because of the register's notary experience. Under the register laws, however, the instrument is sufficient for verification purposes, in which case the register must register it. The presenter may benefit from being given information about proper notarial practices, but such voluntary helpfulness should not be confused with decisions about whether an instrument may be registered.

Employees in registers' offices are sometimes asked to notarize documents that will later be registered in the office. There is no clear legal prohibition against doing so, but there are reasons to avoid it. Someone should not notarize a document that he or she also will be verifying for registration purposes. Such action could be deemed a conflict of interest and, in any event, forecloses the presenter from the benefit of an independent review of the notarial certificate for compliance with verification requirements. Even in other contexts, such as when documents to be notarized are not intended for registration, performance of notarial acts may potentially involve register personnel in private disputes and divert resources away from essential register responsibilities.

1.4.5 Restrictions

The N.C. Constitution and statutes restrict the register from simultaneously holding other elective office.[58] The N.C. Constitution, Article VI, Section 9, provides the following:

> No person shall hold concurrently any two offices in this State that are filled by election of the people. No person shall hold concurrently any two or more appointive offices or places of trust or profit, or any combination of elective and appointive offices or places of trust or profit, except as the General Assembly shall provide by general law.

By statute, the General Assembly allows someone to hold a total of two appointive offices, or one appointive office and one elective office.[59] Many registers, assistants, and deputies already hold dual offices because they are commissioned as notaries (not merely exercising ex officio notary powers that are part of the register's office). A commission as a notary public is an appointive state office. The N.C. Constitution also provides that "[t]he provisions of this Section shall not prohibit . . . any notary public . . . from holding concurrently another office or place of trust or profit under this State or the United States or any department thereof."[60] Note that this allows a notary to hold "another office," not "other offices." Consequently, an elected register or an assistant or deputy who is commissioned as a notary may not also be appointed to another state office. An elected register who is *not* a commissioned notary may hold one other appointive office. An assistant or deputy who is *not* a commissioned notary may hold one other elective or appointive office.

As described in Sections 1.4.4 and 1.6.2 of this chapter, registers, assistants, and deputies have certain ex officio notary powers.[61] *Ex officio* means by virtue of the office.[62] The vital records statutes also give registers notary powers for birth and death certificates and marriage licenses.[63] Although this vital records statute does not use the phrase *ex officio*, the power is of

58. N.C. CONST. art. VI, § 9; G.S. 128-1.1.
59. G.S. 128-1.1(a), (b).
60. N.C. CONST. art. VI, § 9.
61. G.S. 10B-21(b).
62. Pitts v. Williams, 260 N.C. 168, 172, 132 S.E.2d 329, 332 (1963).
63. G.S. 130A-100.

this nature because it is associated with the office. Ex officio duties assigned to someone in connection with an office, rather than as an individual, are part of the one office already held and not an additional office.[64]

Much of what a register does has something to do with transactions or other events with legal implications. But of course a register who is not an attorney may not practice law, and a register is specifically prohibited from the private practice of law while in office even if he or she is a licensed attorney.[65] The practice of law includes preparing or helping to prepare deeds and other legal documents for others, abstracting or advising on land titles, or giving opinions as to the legal rights of any person, whether or not the service is rendered for compensation.[66] A register should be especially careful on this point because many persons assume—correctly, in most instances—that a register knows something about real property law and the effects of various recorded instruments. Someone may naturally ask a register about the legal consequences of instruments, what type of instrument should be recorded, or what legal steps should be taken in a particular situation. A register takes two substantial risks in answering such questions. First, the answer may be wrong, thereby causing considerable difficulty for the person whom he or she advises and exposing the register to potential liability. Second, the register may face the consequences of the unauthorized practice of law. A register should not feel awkward telling someone who asks for legal advice that the matter requires an attorney. One mark of a true professional in any field is acknowledgment of one's limits—knowing what one does not know or what one is not qualified to answer. A register has quite enough to manage in the areas legislatively marked off without attempting the informal practice of law.

1.5 Register's Employment Conditions

The salary, benefits, and working conditions for registers of deeds vary widely across the state based on a number of factors, such as the county's financial resources and the office's work volume as well as the individual's seniority and working relationship with other officials within county gov-

---

64. McCullers v. Bd. of Comm'rs, 158 N.C. 75, 80, 73 S.E. 816, 818 (1911).
65. G.S. 84-2.
66. G.S. 84-2.1.

ernment. State statutes prescribe certain requirements for all registers in their status as government employees, which are summarized in the following sections.

1.5.1 Maintaining an Office

The county must provide the register of deeds with an office in the county courthouse "unless the board of county commissioners shall deem it impractical."[67] Many of the counties maintain the register's office at the county seat in a county administrative building or a separate building for the register's use. Three counties, Guilford, Iredell, and Moore, are authorized by statute to establish satellite offices at locations other than the county seat.[68] Any instrument registered at a satellite office in these counties is considered the same as though it had been registered in the register of deeds office at the seat of government.

Increasingly, those who use the register of deeds office do not have to travel to the physical office but instead can use remote methods of viewing records or filing them. In some ways the "register's office" is wherever there is an Internet connection. Registers make these methods available as a convenient and cost-saving option. The General Assembly has encouraged local public officials to provide access to services through electronic and digital means. As the statutes provide, "[a] public agency may determine, through program and transaction analysis, which of its services may be made available to the public through electronic means, including the Internet. The agency shall identify any inhibitors to electronic transactions between the agency and the public, including legal, policy, financial, or privacy concerns and specific inhibitors unique to the agency or type of transaction. An agency shall not provide a transaction through the Internet that is impractical, unreasonable, or not permitted by laws pertaining to privacy or security."[69] A register therefore must balance the efficiency and cost savings of Internet access to information against the need to manage the risks that electronic access could create for manipulation of records for wrongful purposes. Nevertheless, each register must retain a physical office open to the public for the foreseeable future, not only for making the complete records available and for instrument recordings that the pre-

67. G.S. 161-7.
68. S.L. 2012-22 (Iredell); 1989 N.C. Sess. Laws ch. 633 (Guilford and Moore).
69. G.S. 66-58.12.

senter wants to handle directly but also for the many other services that registers provide and that require a physical presence, such as applying for a marriage license.

The board of commissioners of each county is authorized to fix the hours and days of the week during which the office of register of deeds must be open, and the register or one or more deputies or assistants must be present during those hours.[70] This may include the days the office will be closed because of a holiday. The board, under its authority to establish office hours, may establish a deadline for presenting instruments earlier than the office's closing time to provide the register with time to process recordings after receipt but before shutting the doors. For example, a board might provide that no instrument will be accepted for recording after 4:30 p.m. even though the office remains open until 5:00 p.m. Registers should strive to maintain consistent public and recording hours that meet the reasonable expectations of those who depend on the office's services.

If an emergency occurs that requires closing the office temporarily without the commissioners' prior approval, the register should coordinate the action with the county manager and, if county procedure requires, obtain commissioner ratification of the action. Registers must adhere to these operating hours for real estate registration and may not make exceptions if someone asks the register to stay open late or to open during other times to accept an instrument for recording. As discussed in Chapter 3 of this book, the order of recording is important for legal rights, and no one should have an advantage over those who believe the office will adhere to its operating hours.

1.5.2 Compensation and Benefits

The salaries of the register and the register's employees are established by the board of county commissioners under their statutory authority to set the salaries of all county officers.[71] G.S. 153A-92 provides that the board of county commissioners "shall fix or approve the schedule of pay, expense allowances, and other compensation of all county officers and employees, whether elected or appointed, and may adopt position classification plans." The commissioners have the authority to revise the pay schedule as they deem appropriate. By statute, after the commissioners have adopted a pay

70. G.S. 161-8; G.S. 153A-94(b).
71. G.S. 153A-92.

plan, "the manager is responsible for . . . administering the pay plan and any position classification plan in accordance with general policies and directives adopted by the board."[72]

To protect the elected register's independence during a term, the board of county commissioners is prohibited from reducing an incumbent register's salary during the term unless the register agrees to the reduction or the Local Government Commission orders it because of a financial emergency.[73] To reduce the future salary of a register running for re-election, the commissioners must by resolution give notice of intent to do so no later than fourteen days before the last day for filing notice of candidacy for the office.[74]

This restriction applies when the commissioners "reduce the salary, allowances, or other compensation of an officer to be elected at the general election."[75] The statutes are not explicit about salary requirements for a newly elected register of deeds who was not an incumbent. The process of determining a newly elected register's salary is not the equivalent of reducing the compensation "of an officer to be elected at the general election," to whom the prior notice restriction applies. A reasonable interpretation of the statutes is that if the commissioners have set a salary schedule that applies to the register of deeds, then the county can apply that schedule to determine the salary to be paid to the new register. This interpretation is supported by the statute governing the filing fee for register of deeds election candidates. It provides that, for offices generally, the filing fee that a candidate must pay (unless the candidate goes through a written petition process to avoid paying the filing fee) is 1 percent of the first annual salary to be received by the candidate if elected, and that "the salary of the office that is the basis for calculating the filing fee is the starting salary for the office, rather than the salary received by the incumbent, if different. If no starting salary can be determined for the office, then the salary used for calculation is the salary of the incumbent, as of January 1 of the election year."[76] This recognizes that an elected office may have a "starting salary," derived from a salary schedule, that is different from the salary being paid

72. G.S. 153A-92(c).
73. G.S. 153A-92(b)(1).
74. G.S. 153A-92(b)(2).
75. G.S. 153A-92(b)(1).
76. G.S. 163-107.

to the current officeholder. A county's ability to set a new salary for a new register also logically recognizes the relevance of experience in office compared both to a predecessor register and to other county employees.

The statutes also are not explicit about whether the board of commissioners may pay a person appointed to complete an elected register's term during the remainder of the term a salary lower than that of the register being replaced. The statute prohibiting a reduction except under certain circumstances refers to "compensation paid to an officer *elected by the people*."[77] The statute can be reasonably interpreted as referring to the person actually elected, not to a person appointed to complete a term, in which case there would be no statutory restriction against adjusting the salary of the appointed person. The reasonableness of such an adjustment would be further supported if the adjustment is based on how the appointed person fits within an established salary schedule, or, if the county does not have such a schedule, the adjustment is based on experience and other reasonable criteria. The adjustment should be made before the appointed person undertakes the employment.

As described in Section 1.3.3 of this chapter, the board of commissioners may grant the register of deeds a leave of absence without pay and appoint an acting register of deeds.[78]

The board of commissioners generally is authorized to establish policies concerning workdays and holidays for county officials and employees.[79] Usually this is done through a county personnel ordinance. As an elected official, a register of deeds is not directly subject to the county's authority to set policies for annual and sick leave. However, if the register declines to be part of the county's policies, the register will not earn or accumulate vacation days or sick days, including for accumulation of unused days for which compensation might be paid at the end of employment, and there will be no possibility of accumulated sick days that will transfer to credited service for calculating retirement compensation under the Local Government Employees' Retirement System (LGERS). If the register elects to participate, with the possibility of enjoying these benefits, the register should follow the requirements of the plan and not take personal leave beyond the allocated vacation time and not take paid sick leave beyond the allocated sick time.

---

77. G.S. 153A-92(b)(1) (emphasis added).

78. G.S. 128-40.

79. G.S. 153A-94(a).

Registers are likely to be eligible to participate in retirement plans offered by or through the county. The General Assembly has authorized a pension fund to supplement local government retirement benefits to attract the most highly qualified talent available to the position of register of deeds.[80] This Registers of Deeds' Supplemental Pension Fund is administered by the North Carolina Department of State Treasurer.[81] It is funded with deposits from register receipts equal to 1.5 percent of the monthly receipts collected for recording fees, marriage licenses, and other fees, except the excise tax and the fee for use of the automated state vital records system.[82] Benefits are paid to current or future registers of deeds who will retire with ten years of service as registers. Slightly different rules apply to registers who retired before 1991. Earned benefits commence upon retirement with the LGERS.[83] The statute has special rules to determine the commencement date for registers who are not part of the LGERS if the county elects not to participate in it.[84] The amount of the benefit is 75 percent of the register's salary before retirement, limited by the total in the fund and those eligible for payments and capped at $1,500.[85] Benefits are not paid during full-time re-employment with an employer that participates in the LGERS,[86] and they cease upon death and are not paid to the retired register's beneficiaries or estate.[87]

1.6 Assistants, Deputies, and Other Office Personnel

Efficient and reliable performance of register of deeds functions depends not only on the register's abilities and effort but also on dedicated and capable assistants and deputies. Due to the unique nature of the register's work, the register has sole authority to select and supervise the office staff. This section describes the basic requirements and restrictions governing this employment.

---

80. G.S. 161-50(b).
81. G.S. 161-50.1(b).
82. G.S. 161-50.2. See Appendix 2 (examples of calculation of fee allocations).
83. G.S. 161-50.4.
84. G.S. 161-50.4(a2).
85. G.S. 161-50.5.
86. G.S. 161-50.5(d).
87. G.S. 161-50.5(c).

1.6.1 Positions and Appointment

All registers have at least one deputy, and most appoint someone as an assistant and have more than one deputy. The board of county commissioners establishes the number of salaried positions in the register's office. The commissioners must provide at least one "reasonably compensated" deputy and a second deputy if the register can make a case for needing a second one.[88] However, the register may not employ someone related by blood or marriage in a closer degree of kinship than first cousin, or a person who has been convicted of a crime involving "moral turpitude," without the commissioners' approval of the particular appointment.[89]

Once the board has set the number of positions and the salaries attached to those positions, the register has exclusive authority to hire, promote, supervise, and discharge the employees who will fill these positions.[90] This means that a county manager or other county official may not hire or terminate a register of deeds employee—only the register has this authority. Although the register makes the decision about whom to hire as an employee of the office, county human relations departments tend to have carefully developed hiring procedures aimed at ensuring fairness and compliance with nondiscrimination laws. The register may wish to follow the county personnel ordinance or policies for hiring or termination, but the register is not required to do so.[91] Even so, the register should consult the county personnel officer, manager, or attorney before discharging an employee for any reason.

The two formalities necessary in appointing an assistant or deputy are that a certificate of appointment must be completed and an oath of office administered. The register must prepare a certificate of appointment and file it with the clerk of superior court.[92] The register should sign the certificate and impress it with his or her official seal. These formalities serve as

88. G.S. 153A-103.

89. *Id.*

90. *Id.*

91. The same statute that gives register of deeds exclusive hiring and discharge authority also applies to sheriffs. In a case concerning discharge of an employee in the sheriff's department, the state court of appeals held that G.S. 153A-103(1) gives the sheriff authority to discharge an employee without complying with the county's personnel ordinance. Peele v. Provident Mut. Life Ins. Co., 90 N.C. App. 447, 368 S.E.2d 892 (1988).

92. G.S. 161-6(a).

a reminder of the importance of the responsibilities undertaken in public service. The oath is the same as that for the register set forth in Section 1.4.1 of this chapter, but with the words "assistant" or "deputy" inserted where appropriate. The oath may be administered by any official authorized to do so (as listed in Section 1.4.1 of this chapter), including the register.[93]

The employees in the register of deeds office are paid according to the salaries set by the county commissioners. However, the commissioners may not reduce the salaries of the register's employees without similarly reducing all other county salaries, unless the register consents to the reduction. If the register does not consent and the register and the board cannot resolve their differences over the salary reductions, the matter may be referred for arbitration to the senior resident superior court judge of the judicial district in which the county lies.[94]

Counties often look to apply general county personnel policies to the employees in the register of deeds office. There is no legal authority that authorizes the county to direct registers about how to manage their personnel. However, because the county commissioners fund the register's office and determine the number of positions and salaries (subject to the limitations discussed in this section and Section 1.5.2 of this chapter), they have the "power of the purse" to weigh budget decisions in a way that accounts for differences between register of deeds employees and other county employees. Registers and their employees may benefit in the long run from being included in the county's general personnel compensation and benefit programs.

The register is fully responsible for the official acts of all office employees, including assistants and deputies.[95] Thus, the register's official bond is available to those harmed by mistakes of all employees in the office. Assistants, deputies, and other employees who are likely to have in their hands more than $100 at any one time must also be covered by a separate faithful performance bond payable to the county.[96] Most counties adopt a system of blanket bonding that covers all employees who handle money rather than a system of arranging individual bonds.[97] This separate faithful

93. G.S. 11-7.1(a)(4).
94. G.S. 153A-92(b)(3).
95. G.S. 161-6(a).
96. G.S. 159-29(b).
97. G.S. 159-29(c).

performance bond protects the county against shortages in the register's office; it does not protect the county or the register against liability for negligence in recording or indexing instruments.

1.6.2 Authority

The authority and duties of assistants and deputies are legally the same as those of the register.[98] Statutory references to "the register of deeds and (or) his assistant," "the register of deeds and (or) his deputy," "the assistant register of deeds," or "the deputy register of deeds" include both subordinate offices "insofar as such reference pertains to the authority, powers, duties, privileges, or qualifications for office of assistant and deputy register of deeds," unless a contrary intent is specifically stated in the particular statutory provision.[99] The same statute authorizes assistant and deputy registers of deeds to register instruments and sign documents "in the name and under the title of the appointing register of deeds, by himself as assistant or deputy, as appropriate."[100] The statute directs that the signature be substantially in the following form:

> John Doe, Register of Deeds
> by Richard Roe, Assistant (or Deputy, as appropriate)[101]

The signature therefore shows both the register's identity and the person who performed the act. As a matter of office policy, the register may prescribe the duties of assistants and deputies and direct them to exercise their authority only for certain matters or none at all, but the assistants and deputies have the same authority as far as the public dealing with the official is concerned. In other words, an act that is within statutory authority will not become invalid simply because the register did not want the assistant or deputy to handle it.

The authority given assistant and deputy registers of deeds by statute is similar to the authority given to other public officers, and the constitutional disqualification from appointive office and multiple officeholding discussed in Section 1.4.5 of this chapter likely applies to them as well.

98. G.S. 161-6.
99. G.S. 161-6(d).
100. G.S. 161-6(b).
101. *Id.*

Similarly, assistants and deputies are also prohibited from practicing law.[102] Deputies and assistants are not elected officials, however, and the requirement that the register be at least twenty-one years old does not apply to them. They are not required to be registered voters in the county where they are employed or elsewhere. The register may as a matter of employment policy require that assistants and deputies have some level of formal education or combination of education and experience.

Assistant and deputy registers also have notarial powers by virtue of their offices, but these powers are more restricted than those of the register. Assistants and deputies may perform verifications and proofs and oaths and affirmations by virtue of their offices—but not acknowledgments.[103] They may perform acknowledgments by virtue of their offices only upon completion of a notary course approved by the N.C. Secretary of State.[104] They too use the seals of their offices when performing notarial acts under this power.[105] Fees charged for such acts must be paid to the county.[106] As noted in Section 1.4.4 of this chapter, use of notarial powers should be carefully considered.

1.6.3 Legal Restrictions on Employment Decisions

Notwithstanding a register's exclusive employment authority over the register's office employees, registers are subject to many of the same federal and state laws that govern all other supervisors of county employees. County human resource directors are charged with keeping up with these laws in general and with knowing how to obtain legal guidance about hiring, supervising, and discharging. Registers should keep themselves apprised of both the general nature of employment laws and county guidance, and they are likely to receive helpful advice by consulting with county human resource officers if a potential issue arises.

Despite the complex and sometimes surprising nature of employment law requirements, registers can take comfort that a serious law violation is unlikely to occur as long as the supervisor treats employees fairly and bases decisions on work capabilities and performance. When registers are

---

102. G.S. 84-2.
103. G.S. 10B-21(b).
104. *Id.*
105. *Id.*
106. *Id.*

asked about rights or accommodations, they should be sure to learn about the law and not simply assume what it might be.

Employment matters are the area of a register's responsibilities most likely to result in protracted dispute. Trouble usually can be avoided by keeping informed about the law and policies and keeping employees aware of them as well. Minor matters should be easily correctable and should not result in serious difficulties. More fundamentally, in a register of deeds office, just as in any other employment context, disputes are less likely to arise when employees believe they work in a supportive environment in which everyone understands his or her role in accomplishing a compelling mission.

1.6.3.1 General Statutory Prohibitions

Some of the legal restrictions on employment decisions are well known, and compliance is a matter of common sense. For example, the law prohibits county employment decisions about hiring, promotion, and discharge "because of [an] individual's race, color, religion, sex, or national origin."[107] Someone who is the victim of prohibited discrimination may have a claim for damages under federal law.[108]

A number of other laws make certain other characteristics impermissible reasons for employment decisions. The Age Discrimination in Employment Act (ADEA) prohibits discriminating against those who are forty years old or older based on their age.[109] The Americans with Disabilities Act (ADA) prohibits discriminating against individuals with a serious disability based on the disability if they can perform the essential functions of the job with no special accommodations or if they can perform such functions with "reasonable" special accommodations without an "undue hardship" on the operation of the employer's business. Factors considered in determining undue hardship include the organization's size, the nature of the job, and the costs of the accommodations. An individual with a disability as defined by the statute is someone with an impairment that substantially limits one or more major life activities, someone who has a record of such an impairment, or someone who is regarded as having such an impairment. Federal statutes also prohibit employers from asking employees about pos-

---

107. Title VII, Civil Rights Act of 1964, 42 U.S.C. § 2000e-2 (2021); G.S. 126-16.
108. 42 U.S.C. §§ 2000e-1, 2 (2021).
109. 42 U.S.C. §§ 12101–12117 (2021); G.S. 126-16.

sible disabilities, except when such questions are asked in connection with the employee's ability to perform specific job functions. Employers may make a job offer contingent on a medical examination if it is required of all entering employees in similar jobs. This may be appropriate, for example, if the employee's functions involve lifting boxes or heavy books.

The Uniformed Services Employment and Reemployment Rights Act (USERRA)[110] prohibits any employer from denying employment or discriminating in pay or benefits because of federal military service obligations. In general, the law requires employers to reinstate veterans who serve in the military not more than five years. Qualified veterans must be reinstated in the same or comparable jobs with the same benefits they would have attained if they had not left for service.

Another law that restricts a register's employment decisions is the anti-retaliation or "whistleblower" law that prohibits employers from firing or taking other adverse action against an employee because the employee pursued a legally protected right, such as making a workers' compensation claim or disclosing truthful information reasonably believed to concern a violation of a law or regulation.[111] An employee who believes that a decision has been made in violation of this law may file a written complaint with the North Carolina Commissioner of Labor alleging the violation. The complaint must be filed within 180 days of the alleged violation.[112]

1.6.3.2 Political Affiliation

Most registers are affiliated with political parties and stand for election as a party's nominee. When a register resigns or otherwise leaves office before an election, by statute the former register's party has the opportunity to designate the successor for the rest of the term. Despite this conspicuous role of party politics in a register's accession to office, in general the register may not fire or hire employees based on their party affiliation. Public employees have a constitutional right to their own political views, including what party they wish to support, and their employment cannot be made conditional on party affiliation, with one exception that is unlikely to apply. Party affiliation may be considered only when it is required for effective job performance. This would exist only if the register can establish that

110. 38 U.S.C. §§ 4301–4334 (2021).
111. G.S. 95-240 to -244.
112. G.S. 95-242(a).

the employee is effectively a spokesperson for the register's policies and is privy to confidential information in this regard.[113] As the United States Supreme Court explained, "the ultimate inquiry is not whether the label 'policymaker' or 'confidential' fits a particular position; rather, the question is whether the hiring authority can demonstrate that party affiliation is an appropriate requirement for the effective performance of the public office involved."[114]

A register's discretion to consider political affiliation in making employment decisions can be informed by cases involving the sheriff's office. The North Carolina Supreme Court has held that a deputy sheriff is not a county employee for purposes of this state's statute prohibiting employment decisions based on political activity.[115] In that case, the deputy alleged that she was not reappointed to her position because she did not contribute to the sheriff's reelection campaign. The court said that under state law a sheriff "has singular authority over his or her deputies" and is considered the employer even though the county provides the funds for the employment. The sheriff's authority includes the exclusive statutory right to hire and fire employees in the sheriff's office, authority also given to a register of deeds under the same statute. The court also said that sheriffs are entitled to expect loyalty from their deputies, who are entrusted with confidences and may act in their sheriffs' names and with their sheriffs' authority.[116] The state supreme court noted with approval a North Carolina Court of Appeals case in which the court held that a register of deeds had the same employment authority as a sheriff and was entitled to the same loyalties. The court of appeals held that a register could "without violating the United States and North Carolina Constitutions" dismiss his second-in-command when she announced her plan to run against the register.[117] Therefore, the statute prohibiting certain kinds of political influence[118] was deemed inapplicable. Accordingly, based on these recent cases, a register of deeds may when making employment decisions consider a deputy's or assistant's political activity that is related to the office, at least to the extent that the

113. Branti v. Finkel, 445 U.S. 507 (1980).
114. *Id.* at 518.
115. Young v. Bailey, 368 N.C. 665, 781 S.E.2d 277 (2016).
116. G.S. 153A-103(1).
117. Sims-Campbell v. Welch, 769 S.E.2d 643 (N.C. Ct. App. 2015).
118. G.S. 153A-99(e).

register's deputy or assistant is similar in relationship to the register as a sheriff's deputy is to the sheriff.

1.6.3.3 Protected Speech

Register assistants' and deputies' First Amendment rights extend to being able to express personal views on matters of public concern in public without fear of employment retaliation, but this right is limited with respect to matters related to their jobs. The U.S. Supreme Court explained that "the First Amendment does not prohibit managerial discipline based on an employee's expressions made pursuant to official responsibilities."[119] As the Court said, a restriction on speech that relates "to a public employee's professional responsibilities does not infringe any liberties the employee might have enjoyed as a private citizen. It simply reflects the exercise of employer control over what the employer itself has commissioned or created."[120] Accordingly, for example, a register may prohibit an employee from making off-duty public statements about register operations but not about tax rates, presidential candidate preferences, or school board policies. Of course, registers may restrict activities while on duty to the extent reasonably necessary for office functioning.

G.S. 51-5.5(b) provides the following:

> Every assistant register of deeds and deputy register of deeds has the right to recuse from issuing all lawful marriage licenses under this Chapter based upon any sincerely held religious objection. Such recusal shall be upon notice to the register of deeds and is in effect for at least six months from the time delivered to the register of deeds. The recusing assistant or deputy register may not issue any marriage license until the recusal is rescinded in writing. The register of deeds shall ensure for all applicants for marriage licenses to be issued a license upon satisfaction of the requirements as set forth in Article 2 of this Chapter.

This election is not limited to any particular religion or religious practice and applies to assistants and deputies, not to registers. If the right is exercised, it applies to "issuing all lawful marriage licenses" and is irrevocable

---

119. Garcetti v. Ceballos, 547 U.S. 410, 424 (2006).
120. *Garcetti*, 547 U.S. 410.

for six months. It remains in effect after the six months until the assistant or deputy rescinds it in writing. The law does not require that the assistant or deputy be excused or refrain from other aspects of managing marriage records. The law is unclear about whether an election not to issue marriage licenses is a matter of public record. Given this uncertainty a reasonable approach would be to treat any information about the electing deputy's or assistant's election as part of the confidential personnel record under G.S. 153A-98 until the law has been otherwise clarified either through legislation or judicial decision. Although the law does not explicitly say that the election may be in writing, a reasonable interpretation is that a register may require a signed notice in order to make a record of the election. If it is required it would appropriately contain a declaration that the assistant or deputy is electing not to issue any marriage licenses for at least six months, that this election is based on a "sincerely held religious objection," and the date of the election.

1.6.3.4 Employee Rights to Compensation and Benefits

The laws regarding employee compensation and benefits are complex and can be surprising. They often change. Registers should consult with county human resources managers to be aware of requirements and restrictions that may apply to employment practices or decisions. Counties typically have policies in place for other county employees to ensure compliance, and following the same policies is therefore likely also to ensure compliance within the register of deeds office. Only a brief summary of some of the important laws is possible here.

The federal Fair Labor Standards Act (FLSA)[121] requires a minimum wage to be paid, which includes time-and-a-half pay or compensatory time off for hours worked after forty in a week. The overtime pay requirements do not apply to elected registers and may not apply to an employee who is paid on a salary basis and has executive or significant managerial responsibilities. The ADA, discussed in Section 1.6.3.1 of this chapter, may require accommodations for employees with disabilities. The federal Family and Medical Leave Act (FMLA)[122] requires up to twelve weeks of unpaid leave per year for childbirth, for a serious health condition, or to care for a family member with a serious health condition. Entitlement to leave arises with

---

121. 29 U.S.C. §§ 201–219 (2021).
122. 29 U.S.C. §§ 2601–2654 (2021).

the birth of a child for care within one year of birth; for care upon adoption or foster care within one year of placement; for care of the employee's spouse, child, or parent who has a serious health condition; for a serious health condition that makes the employee unable to perform the essential functions of his or her job; and for any qualifying exigency arising out of the fact that the employee's spouse, son, daughter, or parent is a covered military member on active duty. Additional requirements apply to a covered service member with a serious injury or illness if the eligible employee is the service member's spouse, son, daughter, parent, or next of kin.[123]

1.7 Contract Administration

Registers of deeds are likely to rely on commercial vendors to support the office's essential services. These services are likely to include a document management system for recording, scanning, indexing, and preserving land records, and an e-recording management platform that connects trusted submitters to the register's recording system. The register's county will be the contracting party, and the compensation due under the contract will be part of the commissioner's approved budget. The register must therefore look to the commissioners or manager for approval to bind the county, according to the county's particular procedures for such approvals. But as the official responsible for delivering the office's services, the register should be directly involved in determining the terms and conditions of the vendor contracts and in administering their performance. As manager of a public office, the register's primary objective in administering a vendor contract is to benefit the public. This includes protecting the public's rights in the records.

Choosing the best contractual partner is an important responsibility. When entering into system vendor contracts, registers and other responsible county officials should carefully consider the implications of the terms to which they agree. For example, registers must ensure that contracts with system vendors comply with the regulation requiring that the system must "store data using open standards and architecture and each data set and table shall be well-documented, enabling conversion to a different system at the register of deeds' sole discretion without need for proprietary soft-

123. 29 U.S.C. §§ 621–634 (2021).

ware, licenses, or approvals to which the register does not have full and irrevocable rights and access as part of the use agreement for the system."[124]

An obvious goal of a contract is to establish a legal mechanism for enforcing promises. Entering into a contract is also a way to reach a clear agreement and avoid dispute. Registers should not assume that contract language is nonnegotiable or that a contract must have magical language that only attorneys can understand. In many consumer transactions there is no realistic opportunity to negotiate the terms of a contract, and purchasers trust assumptions they make about their contractual rights. Even if the consumer tries to read the contract that accompanies a purchase, he or she will find mysterious language and will not likely get a response to any request for an explanation or chance to negotiate for changes. Registers should not follow this approach with vendor contracts for which they are responsible. These are not contracts that are written for mass consumption, and registers are responsible to the public to ensure that terms and conditions are reasonable. Vendors who can be trusted with the public's records should be willing to discuss the meaning and intent of all aspects of the contract and to address concerns about troubling issues or lack of clarity.

An important goal of any contract is to express the parties' intentions clearly. This is best accomplished when the parties understand the terms to which they are agreeing. Insisting on clarity in a contract can illuminate issues that are important and could result in a dispute. Failing to address an issue means that if disagreement arises, the parties' rights and obligations will be determined by application of legal principles of which the parties may be unaware and to which they would not have wanted to agree. Formalizing an agreement can focus attention on ambiguity and can result in a better agreement. Committing to a contract without understanding its terms invites problems. The importance of clarity does not end once a contract is signed. Contracts involve performance that is to occur in the future, and things change. To avoid disputes the parties should clarify their agreement whenever they depart from the original contract. During performance, registers should discuss expectations with the vendor and insist that issues be addressed as they arise. They should stay alert for signs

---

124. North Carolina Association of Registers of Deeds (NCARD) Land Records Committee, *Minimum Standards for Indexing Real Property Instruments*, NCARD, 13 (2012), https://www.sosnc.gov/documents/forms/land_records/Minimum_Standards_Indexing.pdf. (Section 7.02).

of trouble and have a contingency plan in case a vendor stops performing the services as needed. If disagreements arise, the parties should revisit the contract. Parties risk worsening problems if they allow their eagerness to complete a project obscure the need for adjustments.

The county may, but is not required to, use a request for proposal (RFP) process for contracts to provide information technology services, such as office systems, software, and related information technology support.[125] This type of process opens the possibility of engaging a vendor who may be able to provide better services than a company that does not need to compete for the contract. This process involves advertisement of contract requirements and review of submitted proposals based on price and performance factors that the county determines it will use. After receiving proposals, the county may negotiate with any proposer to obtain a contract that "best meets the needs" of the county as long as the changes to the RFP do not deprive other possible vendors of a fair opportunity to compete for the contract or result in an award to a different company.[126] Regardless of whether the county uses an RFP process, registers should consider whether there are suitable vendors other than those with which the register is already most familiar and choose the most promising proposal. However, successful experience with a vendor is among the most valuable considerations, as well as a recommendation from another trusted register about such an experience.

The following are among the important points that registers should consider when looking at a possible contract or reviewing a contract already in place:

- To what extent does the vendor seek a right to transfer rights or obligations to someone else? If such rights are reserved, the register is at risk of later having to rely on someone whose experience and qualifications were not considered at the time of contracting.
- What is considered to be a breach of the contract, and what happens if this occurs? Contracts should not include language that could result in a situation in which the register's office is rendered unable to be fully operational if the vendor for any reason ceases to provide the services described in the contract. Language for

125. G.S. 143-129.8.
126. G.S. 143-129.8(c).

concern includes a claim that the vendor has exclusive rights to software needed for access to the data that might not be available to a different vendor, that the vendor can assign its rights and obligations without the county's approval, or that the vendor has unilateral rights to terminate the agreement without notice. An important question to ask when reviewing a proposed contract is if the vendor disappeared, how long would it take to obtain full access to the records and indexes and to be able to add documents and indexing entries to the database?

- What measures will the vendor use to ensure that the system is secure and backed up? These measures should include a way to overcome breaches of security or technology failures and should include assurances of promptness in responding to trouble with the system.
- What is the procedure for changes to the contract, including how price adjustments will be figured if there is a need for changes? Technology tends to change quickly, as do the support personnel for technology support companies. If the register is relying on particular features or particular support personnel, the contract should make clear the indispensability of these features and support.
- Does the contract give assurances against claims by a third party? The vendor should be willing to give assurances that it has all intellectual property rights needed and can give the register a license to use them.
- Does the contract attempt to disclaim or limit the vendor's liability for breach of the contract? Nothing in the contract should be a barrier to holding the vendor responsible for fulfilling the contract and standing behind the promises made in it.
- Does the contract attempt to apply the laws of some jurisdiction other than North Carolina, or require dispute resolution there? Provisions in consumer contracts often state that the consumer must seek remedies in some distant forum according to unfamiliar laws.

1.8 Official Accountability and Ethics

As public officials, registers of deeds are accountable to the people of North Carolina for executing their duties faithfully and honestly. It is a Class 1 misdemeanor for a register to fail "to perform any of the duties imposed or authorized by law," and the potential penalties include removal from office.[127] It is also a Class 1 misdemeanor for a register to "fail, neglect or refuse to make, file, or publish any report, statement or other paper, or to deliver to his successor all books and other property belonging to his office, or to pay over or deliver to the proper person all moneys which come into his hands by virtue or color of his office."[128]

Registers are subject to other restrictions and prohibitions in their conduct that apply to public officials generally. The N.C. Constitution provides that funds raised through taxation may be used "for public purposes only."[129] The North Carolina Supreme Court instructed that "for a use to be public its benefits must be in common and not for particular persons, interests, or estates; the ultimate net gain or advantage must be the public's as contradistinguished from that of an individual or private entity."[130] In most cases there is no question that a proposed purpose, such as personnel costs and costs of operations, is public. But in a modern environment, a wide variety of less obviously public expenses are incurred in connection with such things as educational programs and consultation with other officials and policy makers. Expenses for participation in educational programs and associational activities related to the registers' offices are appropriate for registers and their employees. This includes participation in the North Carolina Register of Deeds Association, which is described in Sections 1.12 and 1.13 of this chapter. Although each register's participation and support of individual initiatives may vary, the law recognizes that each county has an appropriate role in an association of this nature.[131] For instance, each county benefits from its register's participation in statewide policy initiatives. Expenses for meeting as an association to discuss such things as reg-

---

127. G.S. 14-230, -231, -241.

128. G.S. 161-27; G.S. 14-231.

129. N.C. Const. art. V, § 2(1).

130. Martin v. N.C. Hous. Corp., 277 N.C. 29, 43, 175 S.E.2d 665, 673 (1970).

131. Horne v. Chafin, 62 N.C. App. 95, 302 S.E.2d 281 (the N.C. Court of Appeals upheld the appropriateness of county and city expenditures for a reception for state and local officials, noting that local officials have a duty to represent their constituents in influencing state policy), *aff'd*, 309 N.C. 813, 309 S.E.2d 239 (1983).

ister operations, educational requirements, and legislative issues, including necessary associated expenses such as travel, lodging, and meals, also are public matters and fall squarely within traditional notions of appropriate use of public funds.

Registers are prohibited by state statute from personally benefiting from contracts entered into on behalf of the county and from accepting a gift in exchange for influencing an award of a contract. Under the statute, a personal benefit is received if an official or his or her spouse personally derives income or property from the contract or has more than a 10 percent ownership in the vendor.[132] In addition, the statute provides that "no public officer or employee may solicit or receive any gift, favor, reward, service, or promise of reward, including a promise of future employment, in exchange for recommending, influencing, or attempting to influence the award of a contract by the public agency he or she serves."[133] A register therefore may run afoul of this statute if he or she receives a gift from a vendor with whom the register's county has or will have a contract.

The law does not prohibit gift exchanges among employees and their relatives as part of their personal relationships rather than in connection with the office's business.[134] A statute provides, however, that "all such gifts knowingly made or received are required to be reported by the donee to the agency head if the gifts are made by a contractor, subcontractor, or supplier doing business directly or indirectly with the governmental agency employing the recipient of such a gift."[135]

A statute known as the "gifts and favors" statute generally prohibits public officials from accepting a gift from a vendor who has a contract or is anticipated to bid on a contract if the register is or anticipates being involved in defining, awarding, or administering the contract.[136] The statute makes exceptions for certain kinds of gifts or donations.

A public official may accept honorariums for participating in meetings. These are payments made to an individual for fees that are not legally or technically required, such as a speaker fee. The statute also allows receipt of "advertising items or souvenirs of nominal value, or meals furnished at

132. G.S. 14-234(a1)(4).

133. G.S. 14-234(a)(3).

134. G.S. 133-32(d).

135. *Id.*

136. G.S. 133-32(a), (b).

banquets."[137] A souvenir can be understood as a token that marks the occasion. Something would have nominal value if it has no trading or market value. Individuals may also accept plaques or other mementos recognizing individual services or achievement. For example, a cup or tote bag given at a conference with the donor's logo is unlikely to have any resale value and therefore would be allowable under the statute, but a marketplace gift card or a voucher for a future hotel stay may be deemed a cash equivalent and therefore impermissible under the statute.

1.9 Liability

The county is immune from liability for the negligence of its officers and employees in the exercise of governmental functions, unless the government waives the immunity.[138] Immunity for register functions is waived to the extent of the bond required by statute, which is discussed in the next section. Immunity also is waived to the extent that the county has liability insurance coverage for the act or omission alleged to have caused the harm, which is discussed in Section 1.9.2.

Claims on the bond, on the insurance, or against someone in the register of deeds office may arise from a variety of acts or omissions, including the kinds of things that occur in any office, such as personal injuries resulting from negligent maintenance. The registration and indexing of real estate instruments are activities that are special to the register's office and may affect transactions involving a lot of money. But there are few reported cases in which a register has been alleged to have been the cause of a loss in connection with a real estate transaction. Usually, a problem is attributable to circumstances that have nothing to do with the register—drafting mistakes, confusion about intent, conflicts between legal descriptions and physical features, oversights in recording or in reviewing the indexes or records, and sometimes outright fraud. The remedy for these kinds of problems rests with the parties, their counsel, and assurance mechanisms—not with the register or the county.

---

137. G.S. 133-32(d).

138. Robinson v. Nash Cnty., 43 N.C. App. 33, 257 S.E.2d 679 (1979) (holding that register of deeds is a governmental entity with associated sovereign immunity).

Registers do have important responsibilities and potential liability, especially if harm is caused by an intentionally wrongful act or an obvious failure to execute a clear-cut duty, such as losing an instrument presented for registration or failing to index a conspicuously identified party to an instrument. Even in these cases, the register will be potentially responsible only if, among other things, the register's act or omission was the proximate cause of the harm and no one else is found to be more legally responsible. Under North Carolina law, for example, a plaintiff cannot recover for negligence if the plaintiff's own negligence also was a proximate cause of the harm. This is likely to be the case when a defective instrument, such as one with an incomplete notarial acknowledgment, is recorded. But registers should also keep in mind that eventual legal liability is not the only concern. The costs of litigation can be a drain even when the register succeeds in the litigation. Good risk-management practices are an important part of modern officeholding.

1.9.1 Bond

A bond is a guarantee issued by a surety, such as an insurance company, to pay the loss of those who are defined as beneficiaries. In essence, the bond enables someone to recover a loss up to the maximum amount of the bond without having to file litigation. The surety company issues a bond based on its assessment of risks and charges a premium, usually based on a percentage of the coverage amount. Bonds require that the surety be given notice within a reasonable time after discovery of any loss covered by the bond.

As discussed in Section 1.4.2 of this chapter, before taking office a register must provide a bond in a sum approved by the board of county commissioners in the amount of not less than $10,000 or more than $50,000, payable to the state and "conditioned for the safekeeping of the books and records, and for the faithful discharge of the duties of his office."[139] Although the statutory language concerning the scope of the register's bond—"conditioned for the safekeeping of the books and records, and for the faithful discharge of the duties of his office"—might appear to be rather narrow, in fact another statute[140] and case law[141] have broadened the scope of the bond to include all actions and omissions of the register in performing official duties.

---

139. G.S. 161-4.

140. G.S. 58-72-10.

141. State *ex rel.* Kivett v. Young, 106 N.C. 567, 10 S.E. 1019 (1890).

If a person alleges injury by an action or omission of the register and makes a claim against the register's bond, the surety on the bond may—after investigating the claim—decide that it is meritorious and pay it. If the surety refuses to pay the claim, the injured person may sue the register on the bond in the name of the state.[142] Recovery on the bond is, of course, limited to the amount of the bond.

If the surety on the register's bond must, under the bond, pay a person injured by the register's actions, the surety is then subrogated to all of the rights of the claimant against the register and has a right of action against the register to recover all sums paid pursuant to the surety contract.[143] This is true whether the payment is made pursuant to an allowed claim or pursuant to a judgment in a suit on the bond. The register's official bond thus protects members of the public who may be injured by the register's actions or omissions, and if recovery is had on the bond, the surety may attempt to recoup its losses from the register personally. The bond neither protects the register from personal liability nor serves as insurance against that liability. The time limit for making a claim on official bonds is three years.[144] The time begins to run when the error or omission occurred.[145] If someone recovers on a bond, the bond company has three years after it pays a claim to bring an action against the register to recover what was paid.[146]

1.9.2 Insurance

Someone harmed by an act or omission in a register of deeds office may bring a claim to the extent that the county provides liability insurance for acts or omissions in connection with such functions.[147] The insurance coverage paid for by the board of commissioners likely will be for at least $2 million, which will be the limit for all claims against the county during the policy period, not just claims against the register. Each county is required to provide liability insurance to the register to the same extent

142. G.S. 58-76-5.

143. G.S. 26-3.

144. G.S. 1-52(1a).

145. *See* State *ex rel.* Bank of Spruce Pine v. McKinney, 209 N.C. 668, 184 S.E. 506 (1936).

146. G.S. 1-52(1); Am. Nat'l Fire Ins. Co. v. Gibbs, 260 N.C. 681, 687, 133 S.E.2d 669, 674 (1963).

147. G.S. 153A-435(a).

that it provides such insurance to other county officers and employees.[148] If a county does not provide liability insurance to any officers and employees, the chairman of the board of commissioners is required to inform the register of that fact before the first Monday in December each year.[149]

Many registers are covered by their county's blanket liability policy, which for many counties is the North Carolina Public Officers and Employees Liability Insurance policy authorized by the Public Officers and Employees Liability Insurance Commission. This policy is an "occurrence" policy: it insures the register against liability for any error or omission occurring during the time the policy is in effect, regardless of when a claim for loss is made. Some registers are covered by another type of policy, a "claims made" policy, which insures the register against liability for errors or omissions only if the claim for loss is made during the policy period. Claims made policies usually specify the number of years during which the error or omission must have occurred (the retroactive period) in order for the claim to be payable if it is made during the policy period.

1.9.3 Personal Liability

Under North Carolina law, a public official may not personally be held liable for damages that are claimed to have resulted from official actions that involve deliberation, discretion, and judgment.[150] A public official is not protected against suits for actions outside the scope of duties or for actions that are malicious, corrupt, in bad faith, deliberate, or a violation of constitutional rights.[151] For example, a register could be personally liable for misappropriation of funds or sexual harassment.

If a register or an employee of the register's office is sued because of a negligent act or omission, the county is authorized to pay for the legal defense and to pay all or part of any judgment or settlement.[152] A county may not appropriate funds to pay for a claim or judgment based on a register's or employee's fraud, corruption, or actual malice.[153]

---

148. G.S. 161-4.2.

149. *Id.*

150. Pigott v. City of Wilmington, 50 N.C. App. 401, 273 S.E.2d 752, *cert. denied,* 303 N.C. 181, 280 S.E.2d 453 (1981).

151. Craig v. New Hanover Cnty. Bd. of Educ., 363 N.C. 334, 678 S.E.2d 351 (2009); Reid v. Roberts, 112 N.C. App. 222, 224, 435 S.E.2d 116, 119 (1993).

152. G.S. 153A-97; G.S. 160A-167.

153. G.S. 153A-97; G.S. 160A-167(b).

A register or employee should give immediate notice to the county manager of any claim, lawsuit, or threat of litigation in connection with the register's office, and the county should comply with notice requirements in bonds or insurance policies. The time limit for bringing suit against a register or employee is three years.[154] This period begins to run when the act or omission occurred, which could be at the end of the register's term of office if the act or omission is continuing at that time.[155]

1.9.4 Contract Liability

Vendor contracts may involve substantial long-term financial commitments. There may be difficult practical complications in trying to terminate such arrangements, especially when the office depends on unique or specialized services, systems, programs, or databases. Of course, registers and other county officers must ensure that any commitment of county funds is accounted for in the budget and that all required approvals have been obtained before agreeing to a contract. By entering into a contract, the county implicitly consents to be sued if the contract is breached. The sovereign immunity from liability discussed in Section 1.9 of this chapter does not apply to suits for breach of contract.[156]

In general, contracts are enforced as they are written, and contracts typically include provisions that address potential liability. Among other important provisions, waivers, releases, and indemnification clauses may affect both the county's liability for breach of the contract and the county's ability to recover from the other party for its breach. Waivers and releases are promises not to hold another responsible in the event of a loss. Indemnification clauses, sometimes called "hold harmless clauses," are promises to protect another party from liability to others. Registers

---

154. G.S. 1-52(2) (liability based on statute); G.S. 1-52(16) (injury or damage not provided by statute). *See also* Shackleford v. Staton, 117 N.C. 73, 23 S.E. 101 (1895). If the action is for recovery of a statutory penalty or forfeiture (as provided in G.S. 51-17 and -19, for example), it is subject to a one-year statute of limitations. G.S. 1-54(2).

155. *Shackleford*, 117 N.C. 73, 23 S.E. 101 (in a suit against a superior court clerk personally for his failure to index, the North Carolina Supreme Court stated that because of a continuing duty, the clerk could have indexed the judgment at any time during his term; therefore, the statute of limitations did not begin to run until his term had ended).

156. Smith v. State, 289 N.C. 303, 222, S.E.2d 412 (1976).

should be sure to understand the meaning of all of a proposed contract's clauses and should obtain the advice of the county attorney if necessary.

1.10 Registers of Deeds and County Government

Registers of deeds fit into the government of North Carolina in ways that are not typical of other local government officeholders. Their organizational role is most closely aligned with that of the sheriff than with any other office. They both are elected by county voters, take an oath, have important responsibilities involving the public on a daily basis, and have exclusive authority to choose their employees and direct their work. Much of what they do is done independently of other county operations. However, while others may readily understand the need for careful attention to providing the sheriff with resources and discretion to carry out the responsibilities of that office, the same understanding may not exist for the register of deeds. The register will accomplish the office mission most successfully if the register has a collaborative working relationship with other county officers that enables those officers to understand the register's functions and the demands of the office. These other officers include the county commissioners, county manager, finance officer, human resources director, chief information officer, and county attorney.

Each county is governed by an elected board of county commissioners, which varies in size among the counties from three to eight commissioners. In most counties, commissioners serve four-year terms, while in some counties the term is two years. The board adopts a budget, sets the tax rate needed to fund it, and organizes many of the county boards and agencies. As the county's legislative body, the board enacts ordinances pursuant to authority given to counties by the General Assembly.

The commissioners hire a professional county manager to oversee day-to-day operations. The manager is responsible to the board for administering the county departments, with the exception of the elected sheriff and register of deeds. Powers delegated to the manager by the commissioners may include the hiring of county employees. A manager also prepares a proposed budget. The North Carolina statutes require that counties have a balanced budget, which means that county expenditures must meet county revenues, raised mostly through property taxes.[157]

157. G.S. 159-8(a).

The county finance officer, who can be the same as the county budget officer, has day-to-day responsibilities for keeping the county's accounts, making payments and deposits, and maintaining records of bonded debt and other obligations. The register works with the finance officer in managing the office's receipts and expenditures and in preparing the office's annual budget requests.

Registers regularly work with several other county officers who manage county functions that support register office operations. Counties typically have a human resources department, with a human resources director, that manages employee hiring and development and employee pay and benefits. Although, as explained in Section 1.6 of this chapter, the register of deeds has exclusive hiring authority over the employees in the office, human resources personnel are a valuable resource for compliance with federal and state employment laws and for following sound employment and supervision policies. Another important county office is the information technology department, managed by a chief information officer. The county information technology department typically supports register of deeds operations with countywide services, including internal office systems, email, Internet, and an office webpage, as well as with training and support for the use of these services. The county information technology department also plays a central role in the connectivity of the county's internal system with external vendors who provide recording and e-recording systems, and in the security of all these systems.

Registers may also have occasion to consult with the county attorney. The typical county attorney is an independent practitioner or a member of a law firm who works for the county on a contract basis. Larger counties may have at least one full-time attorney who is a county employee. County attorneys usually are available for reviewing and preparing contracts and for consultation when legal issues arise with employees, vendors, or the public. The county attorney represents the county's interests, and communications within the scope of that representation are protected by the attorney-client privilege. If a matter arises that involves the individual interests of a register or register employee, that individual should consider having separate attorney representation.

1.11 Budgets, Fees, and Accounting

Register of deeds operations involve substantial public funds. In some counties millions of dollars flow through the register's office in a single year. Registers are entrusted with receipts for services and with managing expenses for personnel, vendor contracts, and operations. Their budgeting and accounting are part of a county finance system, and many of the register's financial responsibilities are carried out with policies and practices that are clearly established and monitored. This section describes the basic laws and procedures for handling budgets, fees, and accounting.

1.11.1 Budget

Registers are part of county government and function within its financial environment. Although registers are responsible for office operations and have exclusive hiring and supervisory authority over their employees, the office's revenues and expenses are part of the county budget. With the exception of funds restricted for the Automation Enhancement and Preservation Fund, as described in the next section, regardless of how much a register collects in recording fees and excise taxes, the funds for personnel, equipment, and operations depend on allocations by county commissioners. Commissioners, managers, and finance officers must rely on registers to predict receipts and expenses for current personnel and operations and for enhancements to meet the public's needs. Consequently, effective register of deeds office operations depend not only on the register's knowledge about the office's budget but also on a cooperative working relationship with other county officials.

The county budgeting process is governed by the Local Government Budget and Fiscal Control Act.[158] When the county adopts its budget, including allocations for register operations, it is known as a *budget ordinance.* The adoption process is administered by a budget director in some larger counties and by a finance officer in the medium and smaller counties. Under the law, the county's budget officer prepares a budget ordinance with a balanced budget and presents it to the county commissioners no later than June 1.[159] A budget is balanced when the estimated net revenues and appropriated fund balances are equal to appropriations. A budget message provided with the proposed budget contains an explanation of the goals

158. G.S. Ch. 159, Art. 3.
159. G.S. 159-11(a), (b).

of the budget; important features of the anticipated activities; reasons for changes in goals, programs, and appropriation level; and any major changes in fiscal policy. Before adopting the budget ordinance, the board holds a public hearing at which anyone who wishes to be heard may appear.[160] The ordinance must be adopted not earlier than ten days after the budget is presented to the board and not later than July 1. It may later be amended provided the budget remains balanced, but there are severe restrictions on changes that would require increases in the tax rate.

To collect the necessary information for the county's budget, the register and other department heads submit their budget requests and revenue estimates by April 30.[161] The requests must comply with the budget officer's direction regarding form, detail, supporting information, and justifications. Each request needs to include a complete statement of the estimated expenses and revenue in the current year through the end of that fiscal year. To develop this request, the register considers the actual revenues and expenses for the previous year and anticipated changes and needs. The budget officer likely has provided preliminary information about what to expect in allocated revenues for the next year and whether proposals for new major expenses might be accommodated. The register typically meets with the budget officer to discuss the proposal and how well it fits within the county's full budget.

Typically, budget components are organized into three general categories. A major expense is *personnel,* which includes salaries, Social Security, health insurance, retirement contributions, and other benefits. This typically accounts for half or more of the budget. Budgets need to consider adjustments for cost-of-living and merit pay increases, health-care and workers' compensation changes, and increases or decreases in the number and level of positions. *Operations* includes such items as technology, equipment leases, maintenance and repair, telephones, supplies, and travel and training. These can vary widely based on the activity within the county and the history of investments already made. *Capital outlays* are items planned in the budget for such things as new equipment.

North Carolina's county governments can have very different fiscal circumstances, as can their register of deeds offices. In large counties, revenues from recording fees and excise taxes likely exceed the register's

160. G.S. 159-12(b).
161. G.S. 159-10.

requirements and therefore supplement the county's general fund. In small counties, recording fees and excise taxes may be too limited to pay for even the few personnel needed to keep the register's office functioning, and registers therefore must compete with other departments for revenues from the general fund.

The register's revenues are highly dependent on excise tax receipts—counties that have more valuable real estate and more real estate activity have more revenue received from excise taxes as well as from fees. Therefore, register revenues are also dependent on the state of the economy. Downturns in real estate sales can cause a severe decrease in revenue. Registers must consider these trends when they prepare a budget. But no one can predict with complete accuracy what the next year's budget cycle will bring, and counties must keep in mind that markets can speed up as well as slow down. They must also be prepared to handle increases in demand for services that require sophisticated technologies and expertise and experience.

All registers face challenges in preparing their budgets and working with the budget officers and county commissioners to retain experienced and knowledgeable personnel, keep up with technological demands, and maintain the level of service expected by the transactional community and the general public. Registers' financial circumstances can be very different—but all registers face difficult challenges working within the county budget. In a small county, a register must compete for meager resources to provide the same kind of basic services as any other county in the state. In a large county, a register is expected to continue to operate in a way that generates the revenue needed for the many other services a county must provide in a metropolitan area. To deal with these challenges, registers must be both knowledgeable about their offices and able to communicate well about their offices' requirements in the next year and thereafter. Register of deeds offices must be supported adequately to perform their functions reliably and efficiently in a modern environment, but everyone also must understand the constraints of the county revenues and the competing demands for support of other county services.

1.11.2 Automation Enhancement and Preservation Fund

The North Carolina General Statutes (hereinafter G.S.) require counties to have an "Automation Enhancement and Preservation Fund" (AEPF) for register of deeds offices as follows:

> Ten percent (10%) of the fees collected pursuant to G.S. 161-10 and retained by the county, or six dollars and twenty cents ($6.20) in the case of a fee collected pursuant to G.S. 161-10(a)(1a) for the first page of a deed of trust or mortgage, shall be set aside annually and placed in a nonreverting Automation Enhancement and Preservation Fund, the proceeds of which shall be expended on computer or imaging technology and needs associated with the preservation and storage of public records in the office of the register of deeds. Nothing in this section shall be construed to affect the duty of the board of county commissioners to furnish supplies and equipment to the office of the register of deeds.[162]

Fees "collected pursuant to G.S. 161-10" to which the 10 percent retention requirement applies include all fees *retained by the county* for real estate instrument recording, marriage licenses, vital record fees, and other fees but do not include what the register collects for forwarding to the state, nor do they include excise taxes. As the statute provides, the percentage retained is separately calculated for fees for deeds of trust and mortgages.

This statute was intended to ensure that a portion of the register's receipts be available for the implementation and maintenance of technologies supporting the register's functions. It does not give specific direction about how this fund interrelates with other county funds necessary for the register's budget. The statute's intent clearly would be violated if the AEPF amount were merely blended into the county's general fund and applied indiscriminately to general county expenditures. Although the statute does not require that funds be collected for more than one year, the logic of a nonreverting fund is to address a register's need to accumulate funds from year to year for expenses that cannot be met from the recurring operating budget.

The AEPF earmark for "needs associated with the preservation and storage of public records" is broad. Information technology has since become

162. G.S. 161-11.3.

central to register operations, with demands not only for imaging and data processing but now also for Internet facilities to enable online access and filing. To honor the statutory intent and to fulfill the register's and the county's responsibilities to county citizens, the register and the county finance officer should work together to develop a multiyear technology plan that includes how the fund is to be applied. The AEPF is a tool for ensuring that resources are accumulated and made available for upgrades and enhancements that require more than the usual operating budget allocation.

The county can account for the AEPF, tracking the additions and withdrawals, as a reserve in the general fund or as a special revenue fund. The balance of the AEPF can be invested to earn interest. Like interest on any other fund, the interest earned from the AEPF is tied to the AEPF and must be used only for its purposes. As a recommended best practice, for greater transparency and ease in tracking and reporting, the county should consider showing the AEPF on its own separate page within the county budget. The AEPF does not have to be balanced annually; the funds' nonreverting nature allows registers to accumulate a fund balance to pay for large capital expenses that likely would not be funded through the annual operating budget. Neither does the statute require that the funds accumulate from year to year. The county should consider showing the year-end fund balance for the previous five years to show the change in fund balance over time.

1.11.3 Fees

The recording fees charged by registers are prescribed by the Uniform Fee Schedule in G.S. 161-10, which covers all real property instruments as well as a variety of services performed by the office (see Appendix 1). The register may not impose different or additional fees or charges that are not authorized by the statute. The statute makes no exception from the fee requirements for instruments registered by other county or governmental offices or by nonprofit organizations.

An exact amount is specified for almost all services. For services not specified, the statute provides as follows: "For performing miscellaneous services, such as faxing documents, providing laminated copies of documents, expedited delivery of documents, and similar services, the cost of the service."[163] This enables registers to recover the costs of providing a

163. G.S. 161-10(a)(19).

service that is not specifically addressed with a fee, which may vary somewhat from county to county. To justify the amount of a miscellaneous fee, a register should be able to show a rough calculation based on the actual costs of providing a service. The statute does not exclude consideration of personnel costs that can be directly tied to the service.

All fees must be collected before an instrument is recorded or any other service is performed.[164] A register cannot accept a recording if less than the full amount is paid and is not obliged to accept checks with overpayments from which an amount is refunded from the register's account. A register is not authorized to allow presenters to maintain charge accounts for which statements are later mailed periodically. A register may enable presenters to keep prepaid accounts from which the register deducts fees as they are incurred, because this is the equivalent of payment in cash.

Registers are responsible for the handling of all funds they receive, and they must ensure that receipts are deposited into the appropriate accounts. Fees and excise taxes are deposited into the county general fund, except as otherwise allocated by statute. Portions of fees and excise taxes that are payable to the state are deposited according to the instructions of the State Treasurer and likely handled through the county finance director. Allocations include a portion of instrument recording fees for use in state accounts[165] and a portion of marriage license fees for state funds related to children and domestic violence.[166] The register also works with the finance director to ensure that required deposits are made into the Automation Enhancement and Preservation Fund, discussed in Section 1.11.2 of this chapter, and the Registers of Deeds' Supplemental Pension Fund, discussed in Section 1.5.2 of this chapter. Fees and their allocations frequently change, so registers and finance officers should regularly check current statutes.

The collection of excise taxes is discussed in Section 3.2.6 of this book. One half of the excise stamp tax proceeds are to be paid into the county general fund; the remaining half, less an administrative charge not to exceed 2 percent of that half (meaning that the county may retain 51 percent), must be forwarded to the state Department of Revenue.[167]

---

164. G.S. 161-10(c).
165. G.S. 161-11.5.
166. G.S. 161-11.1, -11.2.
167. G.S. 105-228.30(b).

All funds collected by the register must be deposited in the county's official depository as selected by the board of commissioners.[168] The deposits must be made daily, unless the commissioners give the register permission to make a deposit only when the funds on hand amount to $500 or more.[169] The deposit may be made directly with the official depository, in which case it must be reported immediately to the finance officer by means of a duplicate record, or it may be made with the finance officer, who then makes the deposit in the official depository.[170]

The county finance officer may audit the register's accounts at any time, and they must be audited at least once a year by an accountant.[171] The register should keep separate accounts for general recording fees, marriage license fees, excise tax, and any other receipts that require allocation or otherwise warrant special treatment. A receipt should be issued for every transaction involving a fee, even a small copying charge. Registers must follow good practices intended to account accurately and fully for all receipts and expenditures. Practices may be defined in a particular county by Local Government Commission regulations, the finance officer, or the board of commissioners. In any event, registers should establish and follow practices with internal controls that do not enable anyone—including the register—to mishandle county funds without immediate detection. Such practices may include dividing cash handling duties into receiving, depositing, and reconciling, and regular audits of receipts and deposits by someone other than the person who handles them.

1.11.4 Credit Cards and Electronic Payments

State law authorizes units of local government to accept an electronic payment for any tax, assessment, fee, or charge.[172] An "electronic payment" is defined by statute to include payment by credit cards, debit cards, and electronic fund transfers.[173] The statute further provides that a local government may pay any discount or transaction fee imposed by a credit card

168. G.S. 159-31(a), -32.
169. G.S. 159-32.
170. *Id.*
171. G.S. 159-32, -34.
172. G.S. 159-32.1.
173. G.S. 147-86.20(2a).

company or bank for handling the electronic payment and then impose a surcharge on the maker of the payment to recover this cost.[174]

The register determines when the appropriate fee has been paid and what medium is acceptable as payment. Consistent with the statute, a register could accept credit card, debit card, and electronic fund transfers as payment and absorb any discounts or transaction fee. Whether a register can pass this charge onto the person making the payment is not entirely clear. As noted above, the general local government statutes authorize a surcharge for electronic payment, but the register fee statute requires that charges by registers be uniform statewide and states that these charges are exclusive.[175] However, the register fee statute also allows a charge for a "miscellaneous service" equal to the cost of the service.[176] The ability to make the payment with a credit or debit card or an electronic funds transfer seems to be a service. Passing this payment charge onto the requester seems consistent with the intent of this statute as long as the same service is available without the surcharge if payment is made by other means.

1.12 Continued Learning

North Carolina registers of deeds should be dedicated to learning about subjects relevant to their responsibilities. Registers play an important role in sophisticated and complicated financial transactions. They manage records that are essential for individual and community matters. They also select and supervise employees who are entrusted with interacting with professionals and other citizens on these important matters. How these responsibilities are performed changes with technological developments and evolving business and individual expectations. Becoming an expert in office functions and staying abreast of change are especially personal responsibilities for registers, because there is no knowledge or experience qualification for taking office except in the minds of voters, and no governing authority that ensures registers become and stay experts. Registers are entrusted with taking the initiative to educate themselves about what they do and to continually learn about developments going on around them.

---

174. G.S. 159-32.1.
175. G.S. 161-10.
176. G.S. 161-10(a)(19).

There are various venues offering education that is valuable for registers. The North Carolina Association of Registers of Deeds regularly hosts educational sessions at conferences and regional workshops. The School of Government at the University of North Carolina, Chapel Hill, offers basic and advanced programs for registers of deeds, as well as an array of educational programs aimed at local government officials that are relevant to register responsibilities, such as courses on leadership and employment law. State departments, including the N.C. Secretary of State, State Archives, and Vital Records, offer training opportunities in matters for which registers are responsible. Registers also can organize programs in their counties or districts with invited speakers, such as attorneys, surveyors, bankers, human resources experts, and information technology experts.

Registers' continued learning should be broader than about specific register functions. Being an informed and effective register also requires knowledge of subjects that generally apply to managers in today's transactional environment, who work with sophisticated technologies, interact with the public, and supervise diverse employees. North Carolina community colleges and other college extension programs offer a wide variety of such courses, and universities throughout the world offer online courses, some of them at no charge. The subjects in which registers should continually seek opportunities include the following:

- basic computer science;
- basic cybersecurity;
- basic database structure and use;
- basic spreadsheet design and use;
- basic web design;
- digitization and preservation of records;
- office management;
- cross-cultural management;
- effective social media management for business;
- communication skills;
- basic public employment law;
- professional writing;
- basic real estate law;
- basic mortgage lending;
- foreign language study (in any language commonly encountered with the public); and
- leadership.

1.13 North Carolina Association of Registers of Deeds

North Carolina's registers of deeds began formally associating as a group in 1931 to share their knowledge and experience, when Professor Albert Coates founded the Institute of Government at the University of North Carolina, Chapel Hill (hereinafter the Institute), to help public officials and citizens understand and improve state and local government. He and a group of registers agreed about the need for more collaboration and the potential benefits to the public of formulating statewide standards of practice. One of the Institute's earliest publications was the first edition of this guidebook, published in 1933, an effort that was led by Charles T. Boyd, an attorney from Greensboro who worked with Professor Coates as chief of the instructional staff for the registers of deeds division.

The Institute brought registers together for meetings at which they could share their experiences and participate in educational sessions presented by their own members, Institute faculty, and other officials. In December 1952, W. C. Bumgarner, a faculty member at the Institute, convened a meeting at which the North Carolina Association of Registers of Deeds was first constituted. William Massey, the Johnston County Register of Deeds and first treasurer of the association, noted that "the purpose of organizing is not limited to augmenting the welfare of the officials as a group but extends to increasing their individual effectiveness as public servants."[177] The association adopted a constitution and bylaws and has now been bringing registers together in collaboration for more than sixty years.

Since its formation, the association's objectives have been to study, discuss, and recommend more efficient methods of operation and legislative changes for better administration and to provide educational opportunities and promote the ideal of service. The association's first president was Forsyth County Register of Deeds Eunice Ayers, who was widely recognized for employing and advocating newly efficient techniques for a land records system. She became president of the National Association of County Recorders and Clerks and received that association's Public Official of the Year award. She showed how a local government's register of deeds can have an impact far beyond the county's borders. Since 1984, the association has given the Eunice Ayers Award for extraordinary service to dozens of registers from dozens of North Carolina counties.

---

177. *Officials Meet in Chapel Hill*, Popular Gov't, Jan. 1953, at 13–14.

Membership in the association is open to all registers and includes educational opportunities for the registers' assistants, deputies, and other employees. Almost all registers are active participants. The association does much of its work through committees formed from across the state. A legislative committee studies current law, solicits input from the membership, and makes recommendations for legislative and regulatory reform to address issues of concern and further improve the operations of the register of deeds office. Its work has led to many changes in the law to keep register operations aligned with developments in real estate transactions and technology. A land records committee develops uniform indexing rules that are approved by the N.C. Bar Association and adopted by the N.C. Secretary of State and works with registers on implementation of indexing systems. An education committee delivers conference sessions and regional workshops to several hundred participants annually, at which many experts provide training and insights. A certification committee administers a program that recognizes completion of education about the operations of register of deeds offices. Basic certification is awarded upon completion of the School for Registers of Deeds at the School of Government and a prescribed number of hours at other office-related seminars, workshops, or short courses. Additional certifications are based on completion of other programs. Other association standing and special committees work on reforms and programs pertaining to register operations and consult with government offices, the bar, and other professionals and groups on matters of mutual concern.

Chapter 2

Records Management

Chapter 2

Records Management

2.1 Record Keeping Generally

Recorded information is all around in various forms and for various purposes. Archivists, librarians, and records managers are among the professionals whose mission is to manage this information. When the records involve government activities, their management implicates principles that go to the heart of a representative government. The United States National Archives (NARA), which is the nation's record keeper and holds in trust historic documents and billions of federal records, says that record keeping "serves American democracy by safeguarding and preserving the records of our Government, ensuring that the people can discover, use, and learn from this documentary heritage. We ensure continuing access to the essential documentation of the rights of American citizens and the actions of their government."[1] The laws of North Carolina recognize that state officials share in this responsibility.

The official in charge of any government office is the legal custodian of its public records.[2] For most government employees, record keeping is something in the back of their minds that only occasionally becomes a focus of their attention. Registers of deeds are different. Their mission is public record keeping. They safeguard essential information recorded with them on which people rely to protect property rights and to prove the occurrence of important life events. In addition to being the keeper of information entrusted to them by others, registers receive and generate internal records that may have only temporary value but that are sub-

---

1. *About the National Archives*, U.S. NAT'L ARCHIVES AND REC. ADMIN., www.archives.gov/about/info/mission.html.

2. Chapter 132, Section 2 of the North Carolina General Statutes (hereinafter G.S.).

ject to rules for retention, public access, and disposal. This chapter covers North Carolina's general record keeping laws and practices. Other chapters provide more details about particular kinds of primary records: Chapter 3 covers real estate instruments, Chapter 6 covers marriage licenses, and Chapter 7 covers vital and other records.

2.1.1 General Record Keeping Responsibility

Today's registers handle records in various formats. For many years their records were all paper—either original, signed instruments delivered to them, or papers onto which they had transcribed the contents of what was presented. Many years ago, registers began maintaining copies of records that began as paper but were converted into other forms, first with duplication machines, then with microfilm and microfiche, and more recently, digitally generated images stored in local computer systems, portable disks, and "clouds" hosted in massive digital storage networks. Now many records never exist in paper form—they are "born digital," created, presented, recorded, and maintained in purely electronic form. Registers' custodial responsibilities therefore require that they be aware of the requirements both for accepting records in various formats and for preserving these formats for future public access. Realizing the opportunities and addressing the challenges of the digital age have required rethinking how best to manage public records. Regardless of format, the register must know the condition of the records, take steps to protect them from loss or degradation, and restore any records that are in such a condition that they could become inaccessible.[3]

Increasingly, records exist only in electronic form as the law now allows. State law provides that any record or signature required by law may be satisfied with an electronic record or an electronic signature that complies with the statute.[4] Any requirement that a document be a paper "original" is met with "information that is . . . [i]nscribed on a tangible medium or that is stored in an electronic or other medium and is retrievable in perceivable form,"[5] if such documents comply with standards established by the North Carolina Secretary of State.[6] Real estate instruments are subject to

3. G.S. 132-7.
4. G.S. 66-317(a), (c), (d).
5. G.S. 47-16.2(1).
6. G.S. 47-16.4, -16.5.

special considerations because registers must verify certain components of their originality before accepting them for registration. Chapters 3 and 4 discuss these requirements.

Registers also are authorized to convert paper documents submitted for recording into electronic form.[7] By statute, the board of county commissioners may require the register to "transcribe" records whose condition warrants it.[8] The transcribing required by this statute should be read broadly to include any reliable method of copying the records and not just copying by hand, the technique available to registers when the statute was enacted in 1868. Statutes authorize use of electronic media to reproduce and store county records if the medium is not subject to erasure or alteration.[9] Registers of deeds must first obtain approval from the Government Records Section of the North Carolina Department of Natural and Cultural Resources before destroying paper originals that have been digitized.[10] Although papers routinely are converted into digital form, registers are subject to requirements that may prohibit having records in only digital form. As discussed in Section 2.4.3 of this chapter, the policy of the Government Records Section may require that registers have backup copies of essential records in a nondigital, human readable form—paper or filmed images. This may change as digital storage methods evolve, and registers should consult the Government Records Section about current requirements and best practices.

Technology has enabled custodians to handle voluminous records more efficiently in some important ways, including by reducing the need for public building storage space. The Internet provides an opportunity to give the public the convenience of being able to file and retrieve information directly from their offices and homes. The registers' responsibility for safeguarding public records is essentially the same regardless of the record format: to protect them against loss and keep them available for public access as the law requires. Registers are ultimately responsible for the maintenance of information contained in electronic systems.

---

7. G.S. 47-16.4(b)(5).

8. G.S. 161-18.

9. G.S. 153A-436(f).

10. *Records Retention and Disposition Schedule, Register of Deeds*, N.C. Dep't of Nat. & Cultural Res., Gov't Rec. Section, at vii, 74 (2012), https://archives.ncdcr.gov/media/778/open.

Basic responsibilities for keeping records are the same regardless of their format, but the challenges are changing along with rapidly changing technologies. Registers must rely on expert support for important aspects of their services. They cannot fairly be expected to acquire the technical expertise to write programming codes or assemble complex computer systems, but they must understand these programs and systems well enough to make choices about their implementation, supervise those who function with them, and foresee the risks posed to security of the records. In addition to the support available from contract vendors, the Government Records Section of the N.C. Department of Natural and Cultural Resources is a source of guidance about general record keeping and about best practices specific to various formats. To carry out its functions, the office is authorized by law to examine the condition of any public records and advise the custodian about preservation methods and availability for public inspection.[11] In support of registers, its personnel publish reference materials, hold workshops, and answer questions.

2.1.2 Emergency Preparation

As officials responsible for safeguarding important public records, registers of deeds must include in their practices precautions against threats of severe damage. Some of North Carolina's registers of deeds have had recent experiences with hurricanes, floods, tornadoes, and fires. Those who live in areas prone to severe weather are painfully aware of the dangers extreme conditions pose to life and property. Others in areas in which officials have no recent memory of disasters may not give much thought to what they would do if one was imminent. But no one is immune from suddenly having to deal with a severe risk to records and systems and with having to restore access to them after a danger has passed. Every register should think about these possibilities and have a plan for how to deal with them.

Some disaster preparation results from complying with the rules and best practices for duplication of records. As noted in Section 2.4.4 of this chapter, registers must have a backup "preservation duplicate," and it should be stored at the N.C. Department of Natural and Cultural Resources or another remote location at a safe distance from the register of deeds office. Digital files also should exist in more than one place in case a medium is corrupted or a system fails. Typically, a vendor providing automated

11. G.S. 132-8.

recording and filing systems has a practice of maintaining both a current version and some prior digital versions of the records so that if the current version is lost or corrupted, the majority of the files can immediately be restored while recent additions are re-entered. This enables the public to resume using the records with minimal disruption.

In addition to adherence to sound backup procedures, disaster preparation involves a continuous process of identifying risks to the collections, taking steps to eliminate or reduce the risks, and being aware of the proper steps for containing damage to the records if a disaster occurs. Just as avoidable loss can result from lack of prior planning, it can also occur from unsuitable treatment of items after they have become exposed to the elements. Registers should develop and regularly revisit a plan for what happens before, during, and after a severe condition.

An important early and ongoing part of disaster preparation is to identify the records that are most important to protect from loss. Priorities for removal of records are based on the need to preserve them. Any original documents with historical value should be among those identified for protection or quick removal to a safer location, along with the records most necessary to resume operations. Registers also should consider which records would require the most time and money to reconstruct.

Careful consideration should be given to how records are physically arranged and the condition of the space and furnishings. By statute, public records must be kept "insofar as possible" in a fireproof vault, safe, or room that is fitted with noncombustible materials and easily accessible.[12] Few of today's registers are able to keep all records in such a thing as a fireproof vault, but they can take steps to make other kinds of spaces safer from fire and water damage than the typical storage room. Records should be kept off floors and out of basements or attics that are subject to flooding or leaks. Shelves should be adequately supported and attached to the floor or walls so that they will not topple over. Registers should consult experts in record storage and building safety for advice about these matters as well as such things as appropriate fireproof materials, ventilation, and sprinkler systems. The disaster preparation plan should include instructions about personnel responsibilities during an extreme condition. These instructions should be clear and simple and readily accessible not only to office employees but also to responders during an emergency. All employees of the office should be

12. G.S. 132-7.

aware of their roles for their own safety as well as for minimizing damage by covering windows, moving items to secure locations, and turning off electric power as a severe storm approaches. Also, registers should identify and store supplies that might be needed, such as plastic trunks to carry and store records, waterproof sheeting, flashlights, buckets, and waterproof markers.

Everyone in the office also should be educated about proper procedures to protect records for salvage after they have been subjected to the elements. For example, if papers become wet, the proper action to protect them may be to freeze them rather than attempt to wipe them dry. Wiping wet documents may inflict further damage. Experts have methods for removing water with vacuums and other techniques that minimize damage.

Responsible emergency preparation also involves having a contingency plan for continuing office operations if access to the office becomes restricted or if personnel are unable to be in the office, which happened in North Carolina when the COVID-19 pandemic began in early 2020. Emergency considerations figure in office configuration; registers should coordinate with the county to have some physical access to the office and a place to deliver essential services, even if public entry to county buildings is restricted. Also important is cross-training of personnel, so that staff members can assume the responsibilities of others who become unavailable for work. While register officers can draw on their experience with the COVID-19 pandemic to be prepared for the possibility of a similar emergency in the future, that experience also shows the impossibility of predicting the nature of future emergencies. Registers should therefore strive not only to have a general emergency preparedness plan that would enable the office to continue to function operationally in a wide variety of circumstances that can be envisioned, but also to be alert to entirely new threats and ready to improvise as circumstances may demand.

2.2 Access to Public Records

Under North Carolina law, all documents and other records, "regardless of physical form or characteristics, made or received pursuant to law or ordinance in connection with the transaction of public business" by a government office, are "public records" and are "the property of the people."[13] This public right to information reflects the fundamental rule of law notion that the people have a right to know about their government's activities so that they can make informed decisions and hold officials accountable. As described later in this chapter, a few types of records or certified copies of them are restricted and may be provided only to certain categories of individuals or entities. But as the public records statutes provide, "[n]o person requesting to inspect and examine public records, or to obtain copies thereof, shall be required to disclose the purpose or motive for the request."[14]

In general, the public records laws are concerned with content, not format. The right to know applies to the information in a record, which does not depend on whether the record is in paper or digital form. A record that addresses public business is a public record regardless of whether it is on paper or in an email or text message, and regardless of whether it is communicated through a device supplied by the county or one that is owned personally. This includes public business messages and other postings on social media platforms. Conversely, a record that is about a purely personal matter is not a public record regardless of the format by which it is communicated. While the basic laws governing public access have stayed the same as new information technologies have emerged, managing public records has become increasingly demanding as the use of email, texting, social media, and other digital formats has proliferated. A public business email or text message once sent or received is considered to be among the office's records as long as it is accessible to the office, including in individual device folders as well as in network archives. These records may be permanently deleted consistent with retention requirements, which are described in Section 2.4 of this chapter, and the register's public records management program should include protocols about retention and deletion of these types of communications.

The law presumes that every record related to public business is open for inspection and copying unless there is a law specifically restricting access to it.[15] For the purpose of considering questions that might arise about public access, registers' records can be grouped into three general categories:

13. G.S. 132-1.
14. G.S. 132-6(b).
15. G.S. 132-1.

- Records that individuals file to make a public record, which principally include real estate records, birth and death certificates, marriage licenses, and military discharge records. In this chapter, these records will be referred to as *primary records.*
- Records that the register generates for finding or managing public records, such as indexes. In this chapter, these records will be referred to as *operational records.*
- Internal records, such as correspondence and interoffice memoranda. In this chapter, this material will be referred to as *internal office records.*

Only a few of the register's records are restricted. Usually the restriction is not on public inspection; it is on getting a certified copy. Certified copies are used for many important purposes, some of which are described in the next sections. Occasionally, copies of real estate instruments are needed in court. When authenticated by the register's certificate and official seal, they are as admissible as the original documents.[16] Restrictions apply to certain documents likely to be used as proof of identity or to gain access to someone's records or accounts. For example, a certified copy of a birth certificate may be used to get a driver's license, and a certified copy of a death certificate may be used to withdraw a deceased person's accounts. These rules are intended to protect against fraud.

For records that are not subject to a restriction, anyone may see it upon request and, as noted above, need not give any reason for the request. By statute, public records custodians must permit inspection of the records "at reasonable times" during business hours.[17] What is reasonable depends not only on the public's need for the record but also on the custodian's other responsibilities. Modern technology makes it a simple matter to make records easily accessible. The Electronic Commerce in Government Act specifically encouraged public agencies, including county governments, to use the Internet "to maximize citizen and business access to their services."[18] Registers commonly make at least relatively recent real estate instrument records viewable on the office's Internet site and enable the public to use the indexes on the site to identify other kinds of primary

16. G.S. 8-18; G.S. 8C-1, Rule 902(4); G.S. 1A-1, Rule 44(a).
17. G.S. 132-6(a).
18. G.S. 66-58.12.

records. These services add another level of complexity to managing the records in the office.

2.2.1 Primary Records

The register's basic mission is to record primary records and make them available for public use. The vast majority of these records comprises real estate instruments, marriage licenses, birth and death certificates, and military service records.

2.2.2 Operational Records

Operational records are generated and maintained to enable the public to identify relevant primary records. The real estate index is an operational record. It exists for the public's use, and a current version should always be accessible. As discussed in Section 2.3.2 of this chapter, registers must keep a record of all databases they create, which would include electronic indexes.

The real estate index changes every time an entry is made in it. Obviously, registers cannot be expected to retain a copy of an index as it has existed at every point in time. However, there may be instances in which a register should have a record available to the public showing that a change was made. For example, if a corrective or additional index entry is made for a real estate instrument that had been on record for some time without the entry, there should be a record showing this fact. This can be done with some sort of administrative notice that is available to the public that shows when the later entry was made and what the index previously showed, rather than giving the impression that the corrective or additional entry had been part of the index since the instrument was recorded.

2.2.3 Internal Office Records

State law defines public records to include all documents, recordings, and electronic data "made or received pursuant to law or ordinance in connection with the transaction of public business."[19] The content is what matters; not the format or the device on which the record is generated. For example, with respect to electronic files, it does not matter whether the computer or other device or account in which it can be found is what is considered by the employee to be "personal." It is a public record if *the content* has to do

---

19. G.S. 132-1(a).

with the transaction of public business. However, state law excludes from public access certain types of information generated or kept for internal office purposes. A register who receives a request from the public for access to a document that is not kept for the public in the ordinary course should review current laws to determine whether a restriction applies. The following sections describe the general exclusions to the public records disclosure requirements that are most likely to be encountered. When in doubt, the register should consult with the county attorney.

2.2.3.1 Personnel Records

Statutes protect from disclosure some of the information in public employee personnel files.[20] The statutes permit the employee and the employee's supervisor to have access to almost everything, and they permit certain others access to some of the file in limited circumstances. Public information includes such things as the employee's name, age, current salary, salary history, title, current position, original employment date, and date and reason for promotions, demotions, transfers, suspensions, and separations with that county. If an employee was dismissed, a copy of the dismissal document noting the basis of the discharge is public record.[21] The law governing public access to personnel records changes frequently. Current law should be checked whenever a request is received. Registers should consult with the county human resources office regarding requests for information from an employee's personnel file.

2.2.3.2 Legal Materials

Communications between a register and an attorney in connection with legal advice may be protected from compelled disclosure as privileged information. Communications from an attorney to a government body are protected if they involve a claim by or against the government or a judicial or administrative proceeding to which the public body is a party or by which it may be directly affected. This protection expires three years after the date the public body receives the communication.[22] Also protected from disclosure are certain kinds of trial preparation materials, such as documents showing the mental impressions or legal theories of an attor-

---

20. G.S. 153A-98.
21. G.S. 153A-98(b).
22. G.S. 132-1.1.

ney or reports from consultants to be used at trial or in support of trial. Requests for information involving legal representation should be reviewed with the county attorney.

2.2.3.3 Trade Secrets

Material that was designated as confidential or a trade secret when it was shared with the government is subject to an exception to the public records disclosure requirements.[23] For example, this might arise in connection with a contract vendor's proprietary secrets. The code in software programs used in the register's record keeping is not likely to be considered a public record and is likely protected from copying or disclosure. Requests for this type of information should be reviewed with the county attorney.

2.2.3.4 Records Involving Public Security

Public records statutes restrict material related to public security concerns, such as plans and drawings of public buildings and infrastructure. The statutes also exempt from public access the security features of a government's electronic data-processing systems, information technology systems, telecommunications networks, and electronic security systems.[24] Requests for this type of information should be reviewed with the county attorney.

2.3 Copies of Unrestricted Records

The right of access to public records extends to obtaining a copy of an unrestricted record when the fee prescribed or allowed by statute is paid. Requests for copies of public records must be met "as promptly as possible."[25] There is no specific time limit. What would be considered prompt depends on the public's legitimate need for the record as well as the record keeper's other office responsibilities. A simple request for a readily available record should be met within a few hours, but a register may take longer to furnish copies of records that require special treatment.

Registers provide a copy of a record specifically identified by the requesting party. They do not search for records in response to a general request

23. G.S. 132-1.2.
24. G.S. 132-1.7, -6.1(c).
25. G.S. 132-6(a).

for information about a subject. For example, a register provides a copy of a real estate instrument identified by book and page as can be found in the index, but does not conduct a search of the records for a deed by which a named individual acquired title. Similarly, a register of deeds would not cull death certificates to provide only those showing a particular cause of death. Undertaking such a search or collection is not only beyond the register's statutory custodial responsibilities but also under some circumstances could be deemed the unauthorized practice of law. A register who receives a request in connection with litigation by subpoena or otherwise should consult with the county attorney about an appropriate response.

2.3.1 Copies of Single Records

The previous section describes access, including restrictions on certified copies. Otherwise, the public has a right to a copy of a public record in any medium requested if the custodian is capable of generating it in that medium, including digital files.[26] An office is not required to create files in different formats or to acquire additional equipment to comply with a request for a record in a medium that the register does not usually maintain.

For most kinds of copies, a posted charge applies. The statutes set a specific charge for a certified copy of certain types of documents, and the fee schedule sets a charge for a certified copy of any other document.[27] For uncertified copies, a register is to charge a reasonable fee that must "bear a reasonable relation to the quality of copies supplied and the cost of purchasing and maintaining copying and/or computer equipment."[28] This county-specific fee must be posted in the office. There is no simple formula for determining this amount. It should be an estimate that takes into account the actual cost of acquiring, maintaining, and operating equipment—including the cost for personnel whose time is specifically attributable to the copying, such as overtime to complete a request.

The ease of access to records made available on the Internet has caused some concern about the public's use of this feature to misrepresent a printout as a certified copy. Nothing in the statutes prohibits registers from configuring their systems to place a mark on uncertified copies or Internet downloads to indicate that an image is uncertified, but those who need

26. G.S. 132-6.2.
27. G.S. 161-10(a)(9).
28. G.S. 161-10(a)(11).

the records may have reasonable objections when the mark is so large and conspicuous that it obliterates the contents or makes the copy simply seem suspicious. Those who require a certified copy should not be easily fooled by an uncertified one. Anyone who requires a certified copy should check for the register's seal and certification and not conclude that a document is certified without it.

There are companies that solicit members of the public to pay a fee for a copy of a deed, vital record, or other public record that is already available in the register of deeds office for the usual copy charge. The mailings or other communications may use language intended to mislead that paying the fee provides access to a record not already available. G.S. 75-43 requires anyone soliciting a fee in exchange for a copy of a record available in a register of deeds office to include a conspicuous notice in the communication that the solicitation is not from a state agency or unit of local government; no action is legally required; and the register has the record. The communication must also include the fee for obtaining the record from a register and the contact information for the person doing the soliciting. There are also limits on the amount that can be charged. A violation of these requirements is an unfair trade practice and subject to enforcement and penalties.

2.3.2 Copies of Databases

Registers occasionally receive requests for a copy of an entire database. As noted above, the public has a right to a copy of a public record in any medium requested if the custodian is capable of generating a copy in that medium.[29] A register must pull from a database a public record specifically identified, but he or she need not sort the database to generate uniquely arranged information. Of course, anyone relying on a copy of a database runs a risk that it will be incomplete or incorrect because it is not constantly updated as is the database that the register currently maintains.

Registers sometimes receive requests for continuing delivery of records in a database. For example, a commercial company that collects and sells information about real estate conveyances might want the register to regularly forward copies of all deeds to the company. To fulfill this request would require the register to redirect limited public resources to serve a particular commercial enterprise, while those records are already made publicly available according to the responsibilities the North Carolina Gen-

29. G.S. 132-6.2.

eral Assembly has assigned to registers. The North Carolina public records laws provide that a register is not required to supply bulk records in this manner, nor is a register required to provide the operability of a database. A statute provides that the required access is satisfied "by making public records in computer databases individually available online in a format that allows a person to view the public record and print or save the public record to obtain a copy."[30] The availability of an online database does not alter the register's duty to allow access to the same records in paper form if they are kept in the office.[31]

The law is not entirely clear about a right to a database of vital records even if none of the information in it is restricted. A statute provides as follows: "The following birth data, in any form and on any medium, in the possession of the Department, local health departments, or local register of deeds offices shall not be public records pursuant to Chapter 132 of the General Statutes: the names of children and parents, the addresses of parents (other than county of residence and postal code), and the social security numbers of parents."[32] This provision, if interpreted literally, would exclude from public records information essential to the birth certificate: the names of the child's mother and father. A more plausible interpretation of this confusing restriction is that it is intended to exclude certain information from requests for copies of databases. The restriction on parent information was added to the vital records statutes in 1997, just two years after the statute was enacted to require offices to provide copies of databases in general. The General Assembly may reasonably be deemed to have amended the statute to give some protection to vital records collections from the database disclosure requirements.

2.4 Records Disposal and Archiving

A right of public access to information would mean little if the government custodian was not required to keep the records in which the public can be expected to be interested. The law requires custodians to maintain records of their activities in a manner in which the records can be retrieved and

30. G.S. 132-6.1(a1).
31. *Id.*
32. G.S. 130A-93(b).

not to dispose of them except according to the statutes and applicable retention schedules. Some kinds of records that have historical value or that provide useful information about decisions may be required to be maintained indefinitely, while documents routinely generated or received that have only transitory value may be authorized for disposal on an ongoing basis. The following sections explain the rules that govern the retention and disposal of register of deeds records.

2.4.1 General Retention Practices

Registers' responsibility for retaining real estate, vital records, marriage, and other primary records is simple: they must ensure their permanent availability. This means keeping the records readily available and maintaining a required backup. With respect to other records within the office, state statutes, regulations, and local policies address not only what records a register must keep and make available to the public but also what records may be transferred to the state archives or destroyed and when this action may be taken. Some records may be disposed of, transferred, or copied onto other media after a certain period has expired.

The obvious first question for registers to consider about retaining a record is whether there might be a need for it. If the register envisions a future need for the record, it likely should be retained regardless of whether disposal technically is permitted. Nonetheless, registers' ability to manage records effectively is related to their volume, and records management best practices include a periodic review of the collection to determine whether disposal or transfer to another format may enhance operations. Disposing of paper and electronic records that are no longer useful or transferring little-used records out of the office is not only good records management but also frees valuable space for the increasing quantity of current records. If a register determines that there is no apparent need to retain a record, the second question is whether the state laws and rules allow its destruction or transfer to the N.C. Department of Natural and Cultural Resources. The following section summarizes these rules.

2.4.2 Retention Requirements

The N.C. Department of Natural and Cultural Resources has statutory authority to issue policies for local government management of public records. The statutes direct that no one "may destroy, sell, loan, or otherwise dispose of any public record without the consent of the Department of Natural and Cultural Resources" except as authorized by statute. The department's Government Records Section receives many records that may not be destroyed but that registers may no longer deem useful to official business in their offices. G.S. 121-5(d) authorizes county officials to turn over "public records no longer in current official use" to the department, and G.S. 153A-436(f) provides that "nonerasable, computer-readable storage media may be used for preservation duplicates, as defined in G.S. 132-8.2, or for the preservation of permanently valuable records as provided in G.S. 121-5(d)." Transfer of these permanent records must be arranged with the Government Records Section and comply with its directions about packaging and documenting.

Primary records and records with historical value are permanently retained. The Government Records Section describes "historical records" as records that "document significant events, actions, decisions, conditions, relationships, and similar developments. These records have administrative, legal, fiscal, or evidential importance for the government or its citizens."[33] Some documents have obvious historical value, such as old plats that are not in the land records system, and should be safeguarded for posterity. Historical value may be obvious based on a document's age and subject, such as an old document related to a public figure's role in county history. The older a document, the more likely it will have obvious historical value. Before disposing of any record that might have special significance, the register should first consult with the Government Records Section. Often, even though a record is not required to be maintained by statute or rule, the section may have an interest in acquiring the record for permanent preservation. Therefore, consulting with the Government Records Section not only ensures compliance but also ensures that the section has the chance to acquire any records it deems valuable to its collection.

No record may be disposed of unless its destruction complies with the instructions given by the N.C. Department of Natural and Cultural Resources. Pursuant to its statutory authority, the department has approved registers' destruction of records according to the Government Records Section's records retention and disposition schedules if the register recommends adoption of the schedule and the board of county commissioners

33. *Records Retention and Disposition Schedule, General Records Schedule for Local Government Agencies*, N.C. Dep't of Nat. & Cultural Res., Gov't Rec. Section, at v (2019), https://archives.ncdcr.gov/media/807/open.

approves it with a vote as shown in their minutes. Once schedules have been adopted by a county, the register may transfer or dispose of records according to the schedule. However, in addition to the retention requirements in the schedules, registers, like any other custodians, may have other retention requirements, such as those that arise in connection with litigation. Registers should consult with their county attorneys if they have received subpoenas or requests for documents in connection with litigation or if they are otherwise involved in proceedings regarding their records.

The records retention and disposition schedules have lists of record categories, known as *series,* and information about whether and when each series may be destroyed or transferred. If the record is not of a type that appears on the schedule, it may be destroyed only with the Government Records Section's approval, which can be requested on a form for "disposal of unscheduled records" provided in the schedule.[34] Registers of deeds records are addressed in schedules. The General Records Schedule for Local Government Agencies[35] is intended to address the types of records that are associated with local government offices generally. For example, this schedule addresses work schedules and assignments, educational records, travel reimbursements, and citizen complaints. The Records Retention and Disposition Schedule, Register of Deeds,[36] is intended to address records particular to a register of deeds office. Most of the record types listed in this schedule are primary records that must be retained permanently. Others are record types that have a limited retention period. For example, the register schedule addresses a temporary index, supporting proofs for marriage licenses, and transmittals for notary commissions when the notary has not appeared to take the oath. These schedules are subject to revision periodically, and some types of register records may be addressed in other schedules.

The records retention and disposition schedules note that some types of records have only "short-term value" and need not be kept any longer than their reference value.[37] These kinds of routine items are not listed on

34. *Id.* at iii, 87.

35. *General Records Schedule for Local Government Agencies, supra* note 33 Registers should check for a current version of the schedule.

36. *Records Retention and Disposition Schedule, Register of Deeds, supra* note 10. Registers should check for a current version of the schedule.

37. *Id.* at iii.

the schedule. Examples include routing slips, fax cover sheets, reference copies, memory aids, and reservations and confirmations.[38] Some kinds of records that have been identified as having more lasting importance are listed as eligible for disposal when "administrative value ends." The schedules define administrative value as "the usefulness of records to support ancillary operations and the routine management of an organization."[39] The schedules direct that the custodian "must establish and enforce internal policies by setting minimum retention periods for the records that the State Archives of North Carolina has scheduled with the disposition instructions, 'destroy when administrative value ends'" as part of adoption of the schedules.[40] The register should recommend a policy that weighs expectations about how long administrative material can be expected to be retained against the burden of storing and managing such records. The locally adopted policy could be to retain administrative value records for a certain limited time measured in months or years.

The following sections describe retention and disposition requirements for the most common kinds of records in the register of deeds office.

2.4.2.1 Primary Records

Most of the register's public records fall within what the Government Records Section defines as "program operational records." These are received, recorded, and created according to statutory requirements and are principally real estate records, vital records, marriage licenses, notary public commissions, armed forces discharges, and indexes. In general, all of these records are to be permanently retained, and the only instance in which any such records will be destroyed is if they have been duplicated into another format according to an approved method. If a register digitizes paper records and intends to retain the electronic copy as the primary, permanent record, the register must first obtain the approval of the Government Records Section before destroying the paper original.[41]

---

38. *Id.*
39. *Id.* at ii.
40. *Id.*
41. *Id.* at vii, 74.

2.4.2.2 Operational Records: Indexes

The register of deeds retention and disposition schedules require registers to retain the "index" permanently. Registers' primary duties include keeping complete, up-to-date indexes for the public's use. With respect to new entries for newly recorded documents, registers are required to make this information available to the public within twenty-four hours of registration.[42]

What does it mean for registers to *retain* an index for archival purposes? The index of recorded instruments is constantly evolving. Entries are added for newly recorded documents, and occasionally information is corrected or added for documents already indexed. Each time new information is added or changed, the index is different than before. Keeping every version of the index would be an absurdly onerous obligation. A more reasonable interpretation is that registers must retain both a current index and a record of when changes were made to indexing information that had already been in use, as described in Section 2.2.2 of this chapter.

A statute requires that registers who maintain indexes electronically at least monthly obtain "a printed copy on paper or film, or a tape or disk, of all index entries made since the previous printed or filmed copy, or tape or disk, was obtained."[43] This can be understood as intended to ensure that registers can quickly produce a useable index if electronic data are lost.

2.4.2.3 Internal Office Records

Some internal office records may be destroyed when their reference ends or routinely destroyed according to the local policy for such records, as described in Section 2.4.2 of this chapter. Some internal office records are subject to other, specific retention requirements. For instance, records of employee certification must be retained for five years after the date of separation, whereas educational records for specific employees must be kept or transferred to the county personnel office.[44] Other personnel records, such as applications and performance files, are subject to various retention requirements in the schedule.[45]

---

42. G.S. 161-22(a).

43. G.S. 161-22(f).

44. *General Records Schedule for Local Government Agencies*, *supra* note 33, at 53, 64 (Standard 6, Items 9, 42).

45. *Id.* at 50–66 (Standard 6).

Before disposing of any office record as to which direction is not given in the records retention and disposition schedules, the register should contact the Government Records Section for advice.

2.4.3 Digital Preservation

The public records with which the register of deeds is entrusted, as well as the information on which the register relies to manage the office, are typically created and accessed in digital form. Unlike paper records, the composition of the digital file that produces the image of a record is not apparent to the user. Anyone who has substantial experience with digital files appreciates how unexpectedly a file can become unusable. While computers in many ways greatly advance information storage and access, the technical complexity that makes this advancement possible adds new risks and requires careful practices to ensure record integrity.

With digital files, information access depends on the usability of the digital media and the integrity of the stored data. Advances in digital preservation strategies, tools, and methodologies make it possible to minimize the risk of storage in digital form while enabling reliable access to the content.

Registers need not personally necessarily have the technical knowledge to carry out digital preservation practices. They may look to others on their staff, or rely on county information technology experts or vendors, to have the expertise and tools needed to manage digital files in current use as well as those that are in storage as backups or archives. But a register should be sufficiently familiar with digital preservation strategies, tools, and techniques to supervise others in performing these functions and to ensure that the office's goals are being met. The following is a general description of some of the most important aspects with which registers should be familiar.

A primary concern with digital preservation is ensuring that files will be usable when needed. One risk to usability is the potential for corruption of the files. Files can be corrupted when there is a problem during the saving process, such as a computer crash or loss of power. Corruption can also occur if the hardware or storage media is damaged. Another cause of corruption is intrusion by viruses or malware. When a file is corrupted, the code that is in the saved file may not be the same as what was received. In some cases, the problem can be fixed and at least most of the record can be recovered; in other cases, the information in the record can become for practical purposes entirely inaccessible. Whenever an important file is saved, it should be checked to ensure there were no problems in the process. Accordingly, the first step in a sound digital preservation practice is paying careful attention to files as they are received. Some other aspects of this step may include scanning for missing files, viruses, and malware.

File formats are an important consideration in preserving digital files. This can be an issue, for example, if current hardware can no longer run the software that was used to create a record. Particular file formats may require particular software for readability, as is true even for some common formats, such as PDF. For preservation purposes, different file types vary in the complexity of their data encoding. Not all file types are migrated to a newer version, and there can be error or data loss even when there is mostly successful migration. Some types that have been used over the years have become practically obsolete with today's common software applications. The risks of format obsolescence are greatest with formats that are used for software specially developed for particular users or uses, as may be the case with vendors who promise unique features for recording applications. Preserving data encoded in a format that has become obsolete, or that cannot be migrated successfully into newer versions, may involve a preservation method that will not allow access in the ordinary course. At least for now, formats that are in common use promise greater resistance to obsolescence, such as PDF, TIFF, JPEG, XML, and CSV files. Just as with receipt of any paper material, the preservation of which is important, there should be a verifiable and constantly updated inventory of files that are part of the record. The information on this list includes file names, locations, sizes, and format types.

When arranging for storage of electronic records, registers should consider the presence of metadata that may not be contained in a mere image of the document, such as a printout. Metadata are most simply understood as data about data; it is information that describes, explains, or locates an electronic record. A record's metadata can be contained within the same file as the record, or the record may contain information that points to metadata distributed elsewhere within a computer system. In some cases, without its metadata the full nature of a record may be incomprehensible. For example, a spreadsheet often displays the results of calculations. A printout or screen image of the spreadsheet would only show the output of the calculations, not the formulas. However, the formulas used to calculate the output may be an important part of the record. Other metadata that may be necessary for understanding a record may include the header that shows the path a message took or the date or creator of a record, like in the case of email. Due to the potential importance of metadata, when making duplicates, registers should consider the necessity of including metadata in the copying process. The Government Records Section has issued a document describing best practices for handling metadata as well as other informative material.[46]

An additional important consideration in a sound digital preservation practice is ensuring that what is stored digitally keeps its integrity over time. A common technique for ensuring that a digital file contains all of the original data is the use of something called a *checksum*, which uses something called a *hash algorithm*. This is a function that generates a unique value that is the sum of all of the data. A program puts the data through a computation that produces a string of numbers and letters of fixed length. This checksum would be different if any bit of the data is different, which alerts the user that something has either been altered or corrupted. These kinds of preservation tools make it easier to have confidence in the integrity of digital records in ways not possible with paper storage.

The availability of sophisticated tools to protect the integrity of digital records should not cause a record keeper to overlook sound daily practices based on common sense. Good housekeeping practices include keeping multiple copies of important files on storage media that are not subject to the same risks as the copies in current use and periodically checking those files to ensure that no damage has occurred. Diligent staff management is equally important. Those who input and manage digital records should be technically competent and worthy of trust. Well-trained employees are an important defense to prevent and address risks to digital preservation. Security management also involves setting the appropriate system and folder privileges within systems to those who have a needed access in performance of their responsibilities.

2.4.4 Required Duplication

The statutes direct the N.C. Department of Natural and Cultural Resources to cooperate with local governments to identify "public records considered essential to the operation of government and to the protection of the rights

46. *Metadata as a Public Record in North Carolina: Best Practices Guidelines for Its Retention and Disposition*, N.C. Dep't of Nat. and Cultural Res., Gov't Rec. Section (2010), https://digitalpreservation.ncdcr.gov/Metadata_Guidelines.pdf.

and interests of persons" and to have a program for making and keeping "preservation duplicates" of them.[47] The department identified land records and marriage licenses among examples of documents for which preservation duplicates are required.[48] The statute describes suitable preservation duplicates as records that are "durable, accurate, complete and clear" and "made by a photographic, photostatic, microfilm, micro card, miniature photographic, or other process which accurately reproduces and forms a durable medium."[49] The statute further provides that "such preservation duplicates shall be preserved in the place and manner of safekeeping prescribed by the Department of Natural and Cultural Resources."[50] In the retention schedule the department instructs as follows: "The preservation security duplicate of permanent records must be either on paper or microfilm."[51] The department bases this human readability requirement on a concern that digital files can become corrupted and the programs for using them have changed over time. As the department explains, "[m]icrofilm can be read with nothing more sophisticated than a magnifying glass. There is no software to keep current. Usually, deterioration in the film itself can be detected by visual inspection."[52] As a service to local government entities, the Government Records Section stores copies of microfilmed records.

If a record that must be retained is destroyed, the register may bring an action in superior court to have a copy ordered to be recorded based on the register's certification.[53]

Since 1868, a state statute has authorized the board of county commissioners to direct a register to "transcribe and index" the books in the office when necessary due to "decay or other cause." It also authorizes payment of compensation for the transcription.[54] A reasonable interpretation of

---

47. G.S. 132-8.2.

48. *Public Records Requiring Human-Readable Preservation Duplicates*, N.C. Dep't of Nat. & Cultural Res., Gov't Rec. Section (undated), https://archives.ncdcr.gov/media/39/open.

49. G.S. 132-8.2.

50. *Id.*

51. *Records Retention and Disposition Schedule, Register of Deeds*, *supra* note 10, at ix.

52. *Id.* at x.

53. G.S. 98-1.

54. G.S. 161-18.

this statute is that it is meant to apply to a *transcription* as it was understood before modern technology: that is, a hand-written copy. At that time transcription was a major undertaking, and requiring that commissioners first approve it made sense. According to this interpretation, commissioner approval would not be necessary when a register is duplicating a record in a modern sense, such as by converting photocopies to digital images. When the records are such duplicates of duplicates—not copies of original documents—no commissioner approval requirements would seem to be implicated. On the other hand, if the register intends to dispose of original documents—such as deeds, plans, or other instruments—prior consent of the N.C. Department of Natural and Cultural Resources should first be obtained, and the department may direct that the documents should instead be transferred to the department for permanent retention.

2.4.5 Destruction

The Government Records Section provides guidance about the proper method of complete destruction of a public record. Approved destruction methods include burning, shredding, and tearing so as to destroy the record's content.[55] Records to be destroyed may be sold as wastepaper, provided that the purchaser agrees in writing not to resell the paper as documents or records.[56]

An electronic record that has only very short-term value may be destroyed according to the same disposition schedule as would apply to such a record in paper form. To destroy an electronic record, registers must take steps to ensure complete destruction. Merely deleting a file from an operating system does not necessarily finally dispose of it; utilities exist to recover such files. If the device or media on which the file is stored is not being physically destroyed, additional steps may be needed to wipe clean the drive or other device on which the file was stored. The Government Records Section provides guidance for complete erasure of electronic records.

---

55. *Records Retention and Disposition Schedule, Register of Deeds*, *supra* note 10, at vii.

56. *Id.*

2.5 Archived Records No Longer Recorded

Over the years, registers of deeds have maintained various kinds of local public records that are no longer recorded with the register. In some cases, the record is no longer generated or has become obsolete; in other cases, the record is recorded elsewhere. For records that no longer have any legal significance and no reference or historical value, the register need not be concerned with their retention. The register should consult the register records retention and disposition schedules[57] and the Government Records Section to determine if records are considered permanently valuable before disposing of them. The following are some of the records that registers may have but are no longer among the records that they must maintain.

Public officials often are required to obtain a bond that gives someone harmed by their actions a right of financial recovery. In North Carolina's counties, *official bonds* given to the board of county commissioners were for years kept in a book at the register's office. The register no longer keeps copies of these bonds. They are deposited with the clerk of superior court.[58] According to the records retention and disposition schedules, any bonds already on file may be destroyed six years after termination.[59]

The statutes formerly provided for a procedure by which the owner of a North Carolina farm could register a *farm name* with the register of deeds in the county in which the farm was located. The farm owner first had to complete a process with the clerk of superior court and then record the name in a book kept by the register with a description of the land to which the name applies. This procedure has been discontinued in practice for many years. Under current law, rights to farm names can be protected the same as other assumed business names.[60]

Historically, the register was the custodian of the *jury list* prepared by the county jury commission. The register no longer performs this function and is not responsible for keeping jury lists. The records retention and disposition schedules do not require the register to retain jury lists.[61]

---

57. *Id.*

58. G.S. 58-72-50.

59. *Records Retention and Disposition Schedule, Register of Deeds, supra* note 10, at 56 (Standard 7, Item 6).

60. See Chapter 8 of this book for a discussion of assumed business name registration.

61. *Records Retention and Disposition Schedule, Register of Deeds, supra* note 10, at 61 (Standard 7, Item 18)

Some registers have what are known as *slave deeds*, which were bills of sale and other records for the ownership and sale of slaves. The people who were the subject of these records were sometimes identified by name and age and other times identified only by number. These records are used by historians and genealogists. Universities and other collecting institutions collect this information and enter it into databases to provide a searchable reference resource. Registers should not dispose of these records without prior approval from the Government Records Section.

For many years, the statutes provided a method for an individual who impounded *stray livestock* to comply with public notice requirements by providing information to the register, who then posted the information at the courthouse. The register is no longer involved in this procedure. Notice of impounded stray livestock is to be given to the sheriff.[62] Registers are required to obtain the approval of the Government Records Section before disposing of these records.[63]

Timber dealers may adopt trademarks under North Carolina law, a process that includes filing notice of the adopted mark with the North Carolina Secretary of State. The statutes used to require a special notice to be filed in the register of deeds office when a *timber mark* was adopted. The register no longer registers timber marks separately. Such a notice may be recorded the same as any other real estate–related instrument.

County clerks prepare the minutes of governing board meetings and maintain them in a set of minute books. They are a permanent record of board deliberations and actions, including the adoption of ordinances. In some counties registers have copies of these minutes from meetings over the years. Registers are not required to keep these copies. Before disposing of them, the register should confirm that the county clerk has the same record.

In addition to the above examples, registers may have in their offices various other records or materials that at one time were deposited with their offices. These may include such things as maps that were not recorded but that were deemed of historic value by someone, genealogical compilations, or local histories. Nothing in the law compels registers to keep such material or to dispose of it if it is not part of the required public record nor

62. G.S. 68-18.1.

63. *Records Retention and Disposition Schedule, Register of Deeds, supra* note 10, at 67 (Standard 7, Item 35).

required to be kept by the records retention and disposition schedules. The choice of keeping, returning, or destroying this material often depends on the demand for space within the register's office. After consulting with the Government Records Section, and before destroying this material, registers may wish to consult with local historical societies and the county library about their possible interest in having it.

Chapter 3

Real Estate Instrument Registration

Chapter 3

Real Estate Instrument Registration

3.1 Conveyances and Instruments

The role of the register of deeds in maintaining public records is vital to property ownership and finance. Registers do not practice law while in office and do not advise those who use real estate records about how to prepare legal instruments or consummate a transaction. Nonetheless, those who work in registers' offices handle many types of legal instruments, and basic knowledge about real estate law and the instruments employed in real estate transactions provides a useful framework for understanding the nature and purpose of important documents of which registers are custodians.

3.1.1 Conveyances

For centuries the law has required that those claiming an interest in real estate have some written evidence of the conveyance. This rule stems from the English "Statute of Frauds," which was imported into the American legal system and is firmly embedded in North Carolina law.[1] But documents

1. Chapter 22, Section 2 of the North Carolina General Statutes (hereinafter G.S.) ("All contracts to sell or convey any lands, tenements or hereditaments, or any interest in or concerning them, and all leases and contracts for leasing land for the purpose of digging for gold or other minerals, or for mining generally, of whatever duration; and all other leases and contracts for leasing lands exceeding in duration three years from the making thereof, shall be void unless said contract, or some memorandum or note thereof, be put in writing and signed by the party to be charged therewith, or by some other person by him thereto lawfully authorized."). Courts have made limited exceptions to the rule requiring written evidence to enforce a real estate transaction. These exceptions generally have arisen under circumstances involving obvious injustice, such as in a constructive trust, when one party wrongfully attempts to keep property transferred for someone else's benefit.

can be forged and used as a tool to commit fraud as well as to prevent it. The law therefore imposes formality and authenticity requirements on real estate instruments.

Relatively little is required for a document to prove a real estate conveyance—only enough to identify the property and the parties and a signature by the person making the conveyance. A document is accorded an added presumption of authenticity when its execution is acknowledged by a third party with official capacity, which usually is a notary but can be one of certain other officials authorized by statute. The official verifies the signer's identity based on the official's personal knowledge, reliable identification such as a driver's license, or recognition by someone else known to the official. The official then makes a record of the acknowledgment on the document with a certificate. Registers must verify compliance with this requirement for certain kinds of instruments, which is an added safeguard of the public record's reliability.

The register's role, however, is far more limited than it once was, a change that has important implications for understanding the nature of the registration process. Until 2005, registers were obliged to evaluate the notarial certificate on a presented instrument by determining whether it was in "due form" and "duly proved or acknowledged,"[2] and, if so, by placing a certification on the instrument. These responsibilities were a remnant of eighteenth-century law, when those who wished to register their real estate ownership were required to complete a court procedure. This process can be traced further back to early land ownership, when many real estate instruments were not recorded and were competing claims derived from different proprietors. As a kind of validation, instruments were required to be "probated" in a court, which would determine if the instruments had been "duly acknowledged."[3] When the court had judged the instruments to be duly acknowledged and the certificates to be in due form, it ordered the instruments to be recorded by the register. In 1967 the burden of probating was shifted to registers[4] and remained with them until 2005. Now registers are directed only to verify the existence of certain components of a notarial certificate if one is required.[5]

---

2. G.S. 47-14(a) (2005).
3. N.C. Rev. Stat. ch. 37 (1837).
4. 1967 N.C. Sess. Laws ch. 639, § 1.
5. G.S. 47-14(a).

3.1.2 Purpose of Registration

The documentation and acknowledgment requirements for real estate instruments of conveyance are intended to prevent false claims about real estate interests. Fraud also can occur with multiple transfers, each of which involves a document that is properly signed and acknowledged. To illustrate this risk, consider the following scenario:

> Seller agrees to convey a lot to First Buyer, who pays Seller for a deed but knows nothing about any register of deeds. Second Buyer approaches Seller and purchases the same property. Second Buyer's deed is recorded before First Buyer's deed.

Who should be the rightful owner?

The recording system is intended to provide a mechanism for a buyer to confirm the rights of someone offering to sell and for those who legitimately acquire real estate interests to protect themselves against wrongful claims. Recording a real estate instrument is deemed to notify the public of the contents of what is recorded. This is called *constructive notice*, which means everyone is held accountable for knowing it whether or not they actually look to find out. Elaborate rules have evolved based on the notion that those who first make a public record of their ownership and give this constructive notice have priority over those who do not. A potential buyer can protect against fraud and verify the seller's rights by examining the public record for prior conveyances. Someone who fails to record risks having someone else acquire a superior right by recording the conveyance first. In the sample scenario, First Buyer could have avoided the problem by registering the deed, a step that Second Buyer took. If Second Buyer knew nothing about First Buyer's deed, in all states Second Buyer would be the rightful owner of the property.

Although recording priority may seem straightforward, the rule is complicated by concerns that arise when someone had actual knowledge of a prior conveyance that was not yet recorded. If someone conveys the same real estate twice, and only recording matters, a second buyer who knew of the prior conveyance is rewarded by recording first, which may seem unfair, because the rule could reward someone who knew someone else was being defrauded. Most states address this problem by subordinating the rights of a buyer who had actual knowledge of a prior transfer to the person who, in good faith, purchased first. In our scenario, in most states if Second Buyer knew about First Buyer's then-unrecorded deed, First Buyer rather than Second Buyer would be the rightful owner of the property.

The registration laws are different in North Carolina. North Carolina is one of only three states with a "pure race" recording statute, which is characterized simply as "first to record, first in right." Section 47-18(a) of the North Carolina General Statutes (hereinafter G.S.) provides that no deed or other instrument of conveyance "shall be valid to pass any property interest as against lien creditors or purchasers for a valuable consideration from the donor, bargainor or lessor but from the time of registration thereof in the county where the land lies."[6] This has been interpreted to mean that those who record first will have title even if they knew someone else was already conveyed the same property. In other words, according to the North Carolina statute, Second Buyer prevails regardless of whether Second Buyer knew about First Buyer's deed, unless a court employs an equitable remedy to override the effect of the registration statute.

North Carolina's present recording law originated in the nineteenth century. Prior to 1885, an unregistered deed was considered a legal conveyance, and courts looked to the situational equities to determine whether someone who knew of a prior competing conveyance should be denied ownership despite being the first to record.[7] Actual notice was as important as recording. In 1829, North Carolina began to require that a security instrument, such as a deed of trust, be registered before a party could claim a lien on real estate.[8] In 1885, the same rule was applied to deeds by a statute providing that no deed "shall be valid to pass any property interest as against lien creditors or purchasers for a valuable consideration from the donor, bargainor or lessor but from the time of registration thereof in the county where the land lies."[9] This law was known as Connor's Act, named

---

6. G.S. 47-18(a). The same language is used in different statutes for deeds [G.S. 47-18(a)], security instruments (G.S. 47-20), and easements (G.S. 47-27). Delaware also has such a statute. Del. Code Ann. tit. 25, § 153 (2021). Louisiana, with its unique legal system, is the third state with what is still described as a "pure race" recording statute. La. Civ. Code Ann. § 3338 (2021).

7. *See* Ray v. Wilcoxon, 107 N.C. 514, 526, 12 S.E. 443, 447 (1890) (remanding title dispute "for an equitable adjustment of the rights of the parties").

8. 1829 N.C. Sess. Laws ch. 20.

9. Connor's Act, 1885 N.C. Sess. Laws ch. 147, § 1 [codified at G.S. 47-18(a)]. In 1943, the same race recording language was added to a statute specifically applying to easements. 1943 N.C. Sess. Laws ch. 750 (codified at G.S. 47-27).

for the state senator and judiciary committee chair, Henry Groves Connor, who sponsored it.

Although the recording laws were intended to make the public record a complete statement of real estate ownership interests, the law governing real estate rights is in reality far more complicated. There are potential claims to real estate that are not shown by the public records; the recording laws apply to third parties as well.[10] Failure to record is not a defense against a grantee's enforcement of an instrument against its grantor.[11] Also, a deed obtained fraudulently[12] or without valuable consideration is not protected by the recording laws.[13] The courts have made exceptions to recording priority that are not reflected in any statute's text. An owner will be held subject to rights described in an unrecorded instrument if this instrument is incorporated by reference into the owner's deed or another recorded instrument in the chain of title. Parties' relative rights have been realigned based on other theories of equity as well.[14] Ownership rights to real estate can be acquired without a deed by adverse possession based on open and continuous occupation to the exclusion of others, without permission, for at least twenty years.[15] Easement rights can be enforced based on a development plan to which a deed refers.[16] There are also a number of exceptions to the recording requirement based on other statutes. A lis pendens, or litigation lien, which binds later purchasers and creditors to the outcome of the pending proceeding, is indexed in the superior court

---

10. *See, e.g.,* Bowden v. Bowden, 264 N.C. 296, 302, 141 S.E.2d 621, 627 (1965) ("The registration of deeds is primarily for the protection of purchasers for value and creditors; an unregistered deed is good as between the parties and the fact that it is not registered does not affect the equities between the parties.").

11. Patterson v. Bryant, 216 N.C. 550, 553, 5 S.E.2d 849, 851 (1939).

12. Twitty v. Cochran, 214 N.C. 265, 268, 199 S.E. 29, 30 (1938) (explaining that the statute did not give priority to recorded deed over unrecorded deed when the former was "a voluntary one made for a fraudulent purpose").

13. *Patterson,* 216 N.C. at 553, 5 S.E.2d at 851 (holding that the first to record prevails "in the absence of fraud or matters creating an estoppel").

14. Hice v. Hi-Mil, Inc., 301 N.C. 647, 273 S.E.2d 268 (1981) (deed reformed because individual shareholders' knowledge was imputed to a corporation).

15. G.S. 1-40; Locklear v. Savage, 159 N.C. 236, 237–38, 74 S.E. 347, 348 (1912) (discussing adverse possession in North Carolina). North Carolina shortens the required possession period to only seven years when someone occupies the property under color of title. G.S. 1-38.

16. Green v. Miller, 161 N.C. 24, 76 S.E. 505 (1912).

records, not in the register of deeds records.[17] A judgment affecting real estate also is docketed in superior court, and it can have priority over any subsequently acquired security interest in the real estate that is recorded with the register.[18] Statutes also grant parties who provide labor or materials for improvement of real estate a lien on the property perfected with an action in superior court.[19] A lien for municipal and county real estate taxes attaches when the property is listed for taxes annually and has priority over other liens.[20] Competing claims based on inheritance are determined according to the governing estate planning instruments and laws of succession.[21] Because of these and other ways to acquire property rights without recording an instrument, those who examine real estate titles must look beyond registers' records to assess the nature of various claims to ownership. Nevertheless, the records in the registers' office provide the foundation for real estate ownership rights and are thus essential evidence of conveyance transactions.

Although most ownership and lien rights must be registered to be valid against subsequent purchasers and lenders, not every document that is recorded is entitled to the priority benefits of the statute. North Carolina's recording laws state that instruments are entitled to protected priority status "from the time of registration thereof."[22] The North Carolina Supreme Court has consistently held that completion of the recording process is not enough to secure protection from subsequent claims; an instrument is denied the benefits of the statute if it lacks any of the required components of a *proper* registration. The following rule, as stated by the supreme court, causes much concern to those relying on the records:

> Taking the acknowledgment or proof of a deed or admitting it to probate is a judicial or quasi judicial act, and, if the acknowledgment or proof or probate is defective on its face, the registration of the instrument imparts no constructive notice and the deed will be treated as if unregistered.[23]

---

17. G.S. 1-118.
18. G.S. 1-234; Moore v. Jones, 226 N.C. 149, 36 S.E.2d 920 (1946).
19. G.S. 44A-8, -10, -12.
20. G.S. 105-355, -356.
21. *Bowden*, 264 N.C. 296, 141 S.E.2d 621.
22. G.S. 47-18(a), -20(a), -27.
23. McClure v. Crow, 196 N.C. 657, 659–60, 146 S.E. 713, 714–15 (1929); *see also* Cnty. Sav. Bank v. Tolbert, 192 N.C. 126, 130, 133 S.E. 558, 560 (1926) (citing cases).

In a number of cases, courts have held that deeds acknowledged or probated before unauthorized officials were not entitled to protection under the recording laws.[24] However, a court will not necessarily invalidate an instrument's registration merely because the instrument includes a mistake in the probate or acknowledgment form. The North Carolina Supreme Court once quoted from a legal encyclopedia: "'The courts uniformly give to certificates of acknowledgement a liberal construction, in order to sustain them if the substance be found, and the statute has been substantially observed and followed. It is accordingly a rule of universal application that a literal compliance with the statute is not to be required of a certificate of acknowledgement, and that, if it substantially conforms to the statutory provisions as to the material facts to be embodied therein, it is sufficient.'"[25] The cases show that the courts' real concern has been with instruments whose legitimacy is in doubt—not with errors in the form of certificates describing the events.[26] The statutes confirm this interpretation: "Technical

---

24. *E.g.*, Norman v. Ausbon, 193 N.C. 791, 138 S.E. 162 (1927) (clerk could not probate instrument to which he was a party); Woodlief v. Woodlief, 192 N.C. 634, 135 S.E. 612 (1926) (recorded deed that was not probated was not admissible as evidence); Buchanan v. Hedden, 169 N.C. 222, 85 S.E. 417 (1915) (invalidating deed signed by a power of attorney that was not probated and that lacked a proper signature); Scranton and N.C. Land & Lumber Co. v. Jennett, 128 N.C. 3, 37 S.E. 954 (1901) (deed probated by the grantee's heir and relative); Bernhardt v. Brown, 122 N.C. 587, 29 S.E. 884 (1898) (conveyance for a corporation executed by an individual for whom there was no evidence of corporate authority); Long v. Crews, 113 N.C. 256, 18 S.E. 499 (1893) (acknowledgment by a notarial officer who was a preferred creditor of the signatory); White v. Connelly, 105 N.C. 65, 11 S.E. 177 (1890) (clerk who probated his own certificate).

25. Freeman v. Morrison, 214 N.C. 240, 244, 199 S.E. 12, 14 (1938) (quoting 1 C.J. *Acknowledgment*, § 183, p. 841).

26. *E.g.*, Consolidated Realty Corp. v. Houston, 213 N.C. 628, 197 S.E. 144 (1938) (obvious transcription mistake in notarial certificate that indicated notary was from West Virginia rather than North Carolina held not to invalidate the instrument); Roberts v. Saunders, 192 N.C. 191, 194, 134 S.E. 451, 453 (1926) ("[T]he mere fact that no seal appeared upon the records in the office of the register of deeds is not conclusive as to whether or not a seal was actually affixed to said deed."); *Tolbert*, 192 N.C. 126, 133 S.E. 558 (finding certificate said it was completed in South Carolina when it was actually completed in North Carolina; the court held that the error was not patent and therefore did not invalidate the registration); Mfrs.' Fin. Co. v. Amazon Cotton Mills Co., 182 N.C. 408, 109 S.E. 67 (1921) (holding that an instrument which was "subscribed and sworn to before" a notary public was equivalent to its being acknowledged); Smith v. Ayden Lumber Co., 144 N.C. 47, 56 S.E. 555 (1907) (holding

defects, errors, or omissions in a notarial certificate shall not affect the sufficiency, validity, or enforceability of the notarial certificate or the related instrument or document."[27] "Technical defect" is defined to include such things as errors in a certificate's depiction of the notary's commission date, technical noncompliance of the notary's seal, or minor inconsistencies in the way in which the notary's name appears on the instrument compared to the notary's commission.[28]

These rules reflect that the land records maintained by registers are vital to real estate transactions. The enforceability of someone's claim to ownership depends both on the validity of the instrument by which the ownership was acquired and the rights that follow from having properly recorded with the register.

3.1.3 Basic Nature of Instruments

Real estate instruments are usually prepared by legal professionals. Many instruments follow standard forms, such as those provided to attorneys by bar associations, which were developed over time to ensure that the instruments address all appropriate aspects of conveyance law. Increasingly, real estate instruments, especially those used in connection with institutional financing, are prepared according to a standard form used nationally, to ensure compliance with federal regulations and accommodation to secondary mortgage market considerations. Even when standard forms are used, however, some parts of the instruments—such as descriptions of the parties and the property being conveyed—are carefully tailored to suit a particular circumstance. The register does not review the instrument contents to ensure that the instrument is legally effective or will accom-

---

that omission of signatures by register's transcription did not invalidate registration); Hatcher v. Hatcher, 127 N.C. 200, 37 S.E. 207 (1900) (holding that proper execution and acknowledgment of a grantor's signature, in the absence of any acknowledgment on the instrument, could be proved by testimony of the justice of the peace who performed the acknowledgment); Quinnerly v. Quinnerly, 114 N.C. 145, 19 S.E. 99 (1894) (distinguishing between when "the probate was in fact insufficient," in which case "the registration was invalid and of no effect," and a shortcoming in the manner in which the probate was depicted on the instrument); Matter of Hess, 104 N.C. App. 75, 407 S.E.2d 594 (1991) (rejecting a contention that an instrument was defective because its certificate did not state that the affiant personally and voluntarily made the acknowledgment).

27. G.S. 10B-68(a).

28. *E.g.*, G.S. 10B-37(f), -67, -68(c).

plish the parties' intent, nor should a register provide advice to the public about such matters—these responsibilities belong to the parties and their attorneys. Nonetheless, in accomplishing their proper role of registering and indexing instruments presented to them, registers can benefit from a general understanding of the nature of common real estate instruments.

The most common real estate instruments include deeds, deeds of trust, and satisfaction instruments. A *deed* is an instrument of conveyance in which real estate owners, or *grantors*, convey property interests to others, or *grantees*. The most common type of deed is a *warranty deed*, which contains warranties about the title and the grantor's obligation to defend it. Less common is a *special warranty deed*, which limits the grantor's warranty to defects arising because of, through, or under the grantor, and a *quitclaim deed*, which simply transfers the grantor's interest without any warranties. All deeds should contain the names of the parties and the grantees' mailing address, words of conveyance, a description of the property being conveyed, the signature of all grantors, and notarial certificates for each signature. Deeds commonly do not include the grantees' signatures. A document does not have to be entitled "deed" or be in any particular form to constitute one; it is the intended legal effect that makes it a deed.

Title to real estate may be held by an individual or by a legal entity, such as a corporation. Property owned by a husband and wife together is usually owned in the form of *tenants by the entireties*, in which one spouse becomes sole owner upon the other's death, and neither spouse may convey or mortgage the property without the other's consent. A similar form of common ownership is *joint tenants with rights of survivorship*, in which a survivor becomes sole owner upon the other's death. With a *tenancy in common*, each of multiple owners has a full right of possession, but each has an interest that may be transferred separately. The choice of form of ownership usually is expressed in the deed with an explicit reference to these kinds of well-established terms, but sometimes the entire instrument, and perhaps other circumstances, may need to be examined and interpreted according to real estate law principles.

A *deed of trust* and a *mortgage* are security instruments given by a property owner to a lender as security for repayment of a loan. Deeds of trust, which are more common than mortgages in North Carolina, involve three parties—the borrower, who conveys the property to a third party, known as the *trustee*, as security for the *beneficiary*, who is the lender, or the lender's nominee. A mortgage involves only two parties—the *mortgagor*, or property owner and borrower, and the *mortgagee*, who is the lender, or the lender's nominee. Both deeds of trust and mortgages give a lender the right to foreclose and sell the property if there is a default. Both types of documents will contain the owner's name, the terms and conditions of the security instrument, a reference to the loan or obligation being secured, a description of the subject property, the signature of all grantors, and notarial certificates for each signature. Parties to loan transactions sometimes use other security instruments in their arrangements. An *assignment of leases and rents*, for example, gives the lender rights in rental property if the borrower defaults. For registration and satisfaction purposes, these instruments are treated the same way as deeds of trust.

Termination of a deed of trust, mortgage, or other security instrument, which usually occurs when the loan has been paid from a sale or refinance, is reflected by a *satisfaction* instrument. In other regions these instruments are sometimes called a *discharge*, a *release*, or a *termination*. A typical satisfaction instrument identifies the parties to the deed of trust or mortgage and the deed's or mortgage's recording data, and it will be signed and acknowledged by the secured lender or trustee. There are other methods by which a record of satisfaction can be made, such as with an attorney's affidavit, as described in Section 3.2.7.4 of this chapter.

3.1.4 Closings

The event by which a transfer of real estate interests from one party to the other is consummated is called a *closing*. The typical closing involves at least three parties: an owner who is conveying real estate, a buyer who is acquiring it, and a lender who is providing the buyer with financing and getting a security interest in the real estate. Others also may have a substantial interest in the closing, such as a broker expecting a commission. In the typical sale transaction, two key instruments will be prepared by professional legal representatives, signed before a notary, and immediately recorded with the register: a deed of transfer and a deed of trust. Many other papers will be prepared before the closing and signed during it, including a *settlement statement*, which will calculate and attribute costs and allocate funds, as well as other forms used to comply with disclosure or documentation requirements or intended to prevent later disputes about the transactional details. Similar activities are involved in other kinds of real estate transaction closings. In a refinancing, for example, a new loan is made and a deed of trust is prepared, executed, and recorded, but there is no deed of conveyance for a transfer of title to the real estate to a different owner.

In some jurisdictions, closings are held at the register's office, historically a focus of real estate transactions and a convenient location for attending to recording requirements. Today a closing is more likely to occur at an attorney's office or a bank. A register plays no role in a closing other than to provide the mechanism for parties to conduct searches of the public records and to record instruments for the conveyed interests. The use of the records involves a series of interrelated steps—a complex process that contributes to the obvious stress involved as the parties' representatives conduct searches and present instruments for registration.

As described in the preceding section, a security instrument, which in North Carolina can be a mortgage or a deed of trust, is recorded with the register at the time the loan is made to give the lender rights in the real estate, including the right to foreclose upon default. Usually, when a new loan is made, the real estate will be subject to a prior security instrument, which will be satisfied with the proceeds from the new loan. The title search conducted before a closing is intended to disclose not only the extent of the seller's interest in the real estate and whether anyone else might have a competing claim to it but also the existence of any security instruments still giving lenders potential rights as security to enforce unpaid loans made to the seller or the seller's predecessors in title. Lenders want to make certain that the record shows satisfaction of all such security instruments in order to prevent problems if the lender must later foreclose. To avoid future problems for themselves, borrowers also want to be certain that the record does not indicate the existence of any other security interests in the property that have in fact been discharged.

The instrument showing satisfaction is therefore extremely important to real estate conveyances and financing. In almost all cases it is not possible, however, to record a record of satisfaction instrument until after the new lender has disbursed the loan, because the loan proceeds are necessary to satisfy the prior mortgage. The new lender will not want to make the new loan until the buyer has title and can convey a security interest to the new lender. The closing therefore essentially involves simultaneous exchanges of funds and interests, and each step of the process depends on completion of another step.

The law requires a lender to provide a satisfaction instrument if a security interest has been satisfied. A new lender is usually therefore willing to disburse a loan for a purchase as long as that lender is assured that the funds are being applied to pay off all existing security interests, because the new lender knows that the prior lender must eventually provide the satisfaction instrument and leave the new lender with the only effective security instrument on record.

Those who handle a closing must ensure that these events proceed as planned and that the registration of the deed, the deed of trust, and the satisfaction instrument occur in proper sequence without anything intervening on the record that might affect the rights of the parties involved. Consequently, any delay in recording, such as might occur if new information appears on the record or if there is a problem getting an instrument accepted for registration, may be perceived as a substantial risk by those responsible for the closing.

3.2 Registering Real Estate Instruments

Registration refers to the act by which an instrument that has been presented becomes a permanent part of the real estate records. This section discusses the register's duty to register instruments and the prerequisites.

3.2.1 General Duty to Register Instruments Presented

North Carolina law provides that "[a]fter the register of deeds has determined that all statutory and locally adopted prerequisites for recording have been met, the register of deeds shall immediately register all written instruments presented to him for registration."[29] The prerequisites involve such things as payment of recording fees and excise taxes and the register's verification that instruments required to be acknowledged by a notarial officer have the basic elements of such an acknowledgment. The statutes expressly provide that the register "is not required to verify or make inquiry concerning . . . the legal sufficiency of any proof or acknowledgement, . . . the authority of any officer who took a proof or acknowledgement, [or] . . . the legal sufficiency of any document presented for

29. G.S. 161-14(a).

registration."[30] The register only checks to see that required components have been completed; the decision to register a document is not a determination that the instrument has any legal effect.

After all prerequisites to registration have been satisfied, the instrument is registered. The statute governing the first step in this procedure—the endorsement of registration—provides that after the register determines that recording prerequisites have been met,

> the register of deeds shall immediately register all written instruments presented to him for registration. When an instrument is presented for registration, the register of deeds shall endorse upon it the day and hour on which it was presented. This endorsement forms a part of the registration of the instrument. All instruments shall be registered in the precise order in which they were presented for registration.[31]

The endorsement consists of the day and the hour the instrument was presented, although to indicate the order of recording more precisely the recording information typically will show a more specific time.[32] The register's signature image is customary, but it is not required for the registration to be effective. Although the register's endorsement indicating the day and hour of presentation does not conclusively establish the time of registration, it will control in the absence of convincing evidence showing a different time.[33] The time will determine the order of registration, unless more than one instrument indicates the same time. In that case the statutes create a presumption that priority will be based on the document number or, if there is no document number, on the sequential book and page numbers provided on the registered instrument.[34]

If a person delivers two instruments for registration and requests that one be registered first, the register may comply and register the instruments in the order specified. This routinely occurs when a deed and a purchase money deed of trust on the property conveyed by the deed are presented for registration together. The presenter may ask that the deed

---

30. G.S. 47-14(a).

31. G.S. 161-14(a).

32. *Id.*

33. Cunninggim v. Peterson, 109 N.C. 33, 13 S.E. 714 (1891).

34. G.S. 47-18(a) (conveyances, contracts, leases); G.S. 47-20(a) (deeds of trust, mortgages).

be recorded first to show that title to the property was held by the grantor when the deed of trust was recorded. Lenders also are concerned about the handling of purchase money deeds of trust, as they seek to protect themselves against statutory liens in connection with construction. According to the doctrine of "instantaneous seisin," the beneficiary of a purchase money deed of trust has a first lien on the property based on the theory that title to the property passes instantly through the grantor in the deed of trust to the trustee. Although some attorneys have a practice of requesting that the recording time for both the deed and the deed of trust be shown as the same, the protection afforded purchase money mortgages is given to them because they are presented and recorded as part of the same transaction, not because of any notion of simultaneity.[35] In any event, registers cannot comply with a request that an instrument be given a filing time different from the time it is actually presented.

Once a document has been registered, it becomes a matter of public record available for anyone's viewing. There is no such thing as "unrecording" a public record. Recorded instruments are copied into backup files and may be duplicated and retained by any member of the public. Once a record becomes public, there is no way of knowing who may have seen it or who may have a copy of it that can be further disseminated.

A natural first inclination by someone who encounters a document that is objectionable—for example, because of fraudulent or malicious intent—is to want to remove the document from the record, but the problem rarely can be addressed so simply. Problems with records are addressed by corrective documents that provide indexing cross-references to the problematic records. The statutes contain two provisions that require registers to take action upon previously recorded documents. As described in Section 3.2.10 of this chapter, if a register is presented with a court order declaring that a filed lien or encumbrance is false, the register must conspicuously mark on the first page of the original record previously filed a specified statement about it being false. This seems to require that any digital image of the false document addressed by the order, which is or may become available to the public, be replaced with an image containing this legend, which would include both in-office and Internet versions. Also, as discussed in Section

35. Smith Builders Supply, Inc. v. Rivenbark, 231 N.C. 213, 56 S.E.2d 431 (1949); Carolina Builders Corp. v. Howard-Veasey Homes, Inc., 72 N.C. App. 224, 324 S.E. 2d 626 (1985).

3.3 of this chapter, personal identification numbers can be redacted from Internet images.

3.2.2 Instrument Format and Required Contents

As the following sections describe, some kinds of instruments must have certain components to be recordable, and instruments are subject to a surcharge if they do not comply with statutory format requirements.

3.2.2.1 Nonconforming Features

Registers make permanent records of registered documents. It is in the presenter's best interest to provide instruments in a format that can be easily converted into images in the volumes of records. When instruments with certain nonconforming features are presented, the register collects a surcharge for all documents except Uniform Commercial Code forms, which represents the added cost of handling a document.

In order to avoid the surcharge, instruments presented for recording must meet all of the following statutory requirements:

- "Be eight and one-half inches by eleven inches or eight and one-half inches by fourteen inches."
- "Have a blank margin of three inches at the top of the first page and blank margins of at least one-half inches on the remaining sides of the first page and on all sides of subsequent pages." This space is for the register's use for recording information, excise stamps, and notations. For a document that does not have a three-inch margin on its first page of text, a presenter can attach a cover page with the required document type and drafter's name if required to be on the first page. Customarily registers do not charge the fee when the three-inch margin violation is a result of a cover page attached to a certified copy by the office issuing the copy.
- "Be typed or printed in black on white paper in a legible font. A font size no smaller than 9 points shall be considered legible. Blanks in an instrument may be completed in pen and corrections to an instrument may be made in pen." Note that the presumption that a 9-point font is legible does not mean the register must reject an instrument with a smaller font if the register deems it legible. Note also that nothing requires signatures or pen entries to be only in black ink.

- "Have text typed or printed on one side of a page only."
- "State the type of instrument at the top of the first page." The purpose of this requirement is to provide information that the register can include in the index. As described in Chapter 5, Section 5.3 of this book, registers will have a list of recognized document types in the local rules. Presenters will facilitate useful indexing by choosing one of these types. But there is no requirement that drafters use a document type from the register's list, nor is there a prohibition against listing more than one type on the document. In such a case, a register may reasonably use the first listed type for the index or show something such as "see instrument" in the index.[36]

3.2.2.2 Drafter's Name

A deed or deed of trust executed after January 1, 1980, must show "the name of the drafter of the deed or deed of trust" on the first page; otherwise, the register should not accept the document for registration.[37] The name can be for an individual or an entity. Although someone who drafts a real estate instrument for someone else may be required to be a licensed attorney, the name information on the deed or deed of trust does not need to indicate that the name is of an attorney or law firm for the instrument to be registered. The statute also provides, "[t]he register of deeds shall not be required to verify or make inquiry concerning the capacity or authority of the person or entity shown as the drafter on the instrument."[38] By local act in several counties, a person who cannot identify the drafter or obtain the drafter's signature can petition a court for an order of registration, in which case the document will refer to the order.[39]

3.2.2.3 Mailing Name and Address

By statute, the board of county commissioners may require that the register not accept for registration any instrument affecting real property that is not submitted electronically unless the face of the instrument shows the

---

36. G.S. 161-14(b).

37. G.S. 47-17.1.

38. *Id.*

39. This option applies in Alamance County, 1957 N.C. Sess. Laws ch. 1290, and in Caldwell, Camden, Chowan, Currituck, Pasquotank, Rutherford, and Vance counties, 1955 N.C. Sess. Laws chs. 273, 575.

name and address of the person to whom the instrument is to be returned and the grantee's or owner's permanent mailing address. In counties where the commissioners have exercised this authority, the register must determine that the required names and addresses are on the instrument before recording it.[40]

3.2.2.4 Grantor Signatures

The verification requirements for instruments of conveyance do not generally include verification of the grantor's signature, and a register should not be legally faulted for registering an instrument without a grantor's signature if the verification elements are present. If in reviewing the required verification elements the register notices that the instrument was not signed by one or more grantors, the register could reasonably reject the instrument on the basis that "the execution of the instrument by one or more signers" obviously was not in fact acknowledged, contrary to what is stated in the certificate.[41]

The statutes governing satisfaction instruments contain an additional verification requirement not applicable to instruments of conveyance generally. Satisfaction instruments require an acknowledgment or proof and are thus subject to the register's verification of the officer's signature, official seal, and commission expiration date. In addition, a satisfaction of security instrument must be signed by a secured creditor,[42] a trustee's satisfaction of a deed of trust must be signed by the trustee or substitute trustee,[43] a certificate of satisfaction must be signed by the owner of the note or other indebtedness,[44] a notice of satisfaction must be signed by a secured creditor or trustee,[45] and an affidavit of satisfaction must be signed by a satisfaction agent.[46] The register does not verify actual authority of the signatory and may rely on information in the instrument or certificate to determine that a signature appearing on the signature line is that of an authorized party. The party's name or capacity need not be indicated separately at the signature line.

---

40. G.S. 161-30.
41. G.S. 47-14(a).
42. G.S. 45-36.10(b)(2).
43. G.S. 45-36.20(e)(2).
44. G.S. 47-46.2.
45. G.S. 47-46.1.
46. G.S. 45-36.18(c)(2).

3.2.2.5 Real Estate Tax Certifications

By statute, the board of county commissioners may require the register to refuse to record any instrument conveying an interest in real property—other than a mortgage or a deed of trust—unless it contains a notation by the tax assessor that the instrument has been presented to the assessor and the necessary information has been obtained from it.[47] Some counties use this procedure; others elect to follow a different procedure authorized by statute that requires the register to furnish certain information to the tax assessor after the instrument is recorded.[48] Counties may use either method to supply the tax assessor with the necessary information, and a few counties require both that the instrument be presented to the assessor before registration and that the assessor be furnished a copy after registration.

Additionally, statutes authorize the boards of commissioners of specified counties to impose by resolution a prerequisite to registration of a deed that the county tax collector certify that there are no delinquent taxes that are a lien on the subject property.[49] More than two-thirds of the counties have this authority.[50] The boards of commissioners of those counties may specify the content of the certification.[51] If the commissioners adopt such a requirement by resolution, a register must nonetheless accept a deed for registration without the tax collector's certification if the deed contains the following statement: "This instrument prepared by: ________, a licensed North Carolina attorney. Delinquent taxes, if any, to be paid by the closing attorney to the county tax collector upon disbursement of closing proceeds."[52]

Several counties that are not authorized by the statute to adopt their own resolutions regarding certification of no tax delinquencies have been separately authorized by local acts of the General Assembly to require that all delinquent property taxes be paid on a parcel of land before a deed to that parcel may be recorded.[53] Registers in these counties may not record

---

47. G.S. 105-303(a)(2).
48. G.S. 105-303(a)(1).
49. G.S. 161-31.
50. G.S. 161-31(b).
51. G.S. 161-31.
52. G.S. 161-31(a1), (b).
53. *See, e.g.,* S.L. 2010-24 (Duplin County and municipal taxes in the county); S.L. 2005-433 (Ashe and Alleghany counties); S.L. 1999-326 (Mitchell County, Town of

a deed unless it bears a certification from the appropriate tax collectors that no delinquent taxes are owed. Some local acts require certifications about municipal taxes as well as county taxes. The statutory exception for a closing attorney's statement, which applies to tax certifications required by county resolution, does not apply to most of the certifications required by these local acts. Registers should consult any local acts pertaining to their counties for details about applicable requirements.

3.2.2.6 Parcel Identifier Number

Once parcel identifier numbers (PINs) have been assigned to land parcels in a county, the board of commissioners is authorized to direct the register not to accept any real property instrument for recording unless the PIN either is on the face of the instrument or is part of the legal description in the instrument and is verified by the county.[54] This authority is important to counties implementing land-records management systems that use property maps and PIN indexes. In a county adopting an ordinance pursuant to this section, the PIN need not be verified by the register, but before recording the instrument, the register must ensure that the instrument bears a PIN that has been verified by the responsible county department (often the mapping department).

3.2.3 Originality Requirements

The basic nature of North Carolina's real estate instrument registration system allows the public to record any document that the presenter considers pertinent to real estate in the county as long as appropriate fees are paid and the document meets minimal format requirements. The register does not check to see if the person recording the document has the legal authority to do so. However, the statutes do require registers to check certain kinds of documents to ensure that they appear to have been signed and acknowledged before a notarial officer or that they have been previously recorded or are certified copies of recorded documents. If such a requirement applies and the instrument does not comply, the register informs the

---

Spruce Pine and Town of Bakersville); S.L. 1998-73 (Avery County, Town of Newland and Town of Banner Elk); S.L. 1997-410, S.L. 2012-51 (Avery County, Town of Newland; Mitchell County, Town of Spruce Pine; Alleghany County, Village of Spruce Pine; Ashe County); 1993 N.C. Sess. Laws ch. 657 (Ashe County); 1975 N.C. Sess. Laws 175 (Watauga and Stokes counties).

54. G.S. 161-30(b).

presenter of the discrepancy and does not accept the instrument for registration. If no such requirement applies to the particular kind of instrument presented, it may be recorded regardless of whether it is acknowledged, is an original, or is unsigned.

3.2.3.1 Instruments Requiring Verification

Registers must verify the presence of certain notarial officer components on instruments that require notarial certificates, which include most commonly recorded real estate instruments, such as deeds, deeds of trust, satisfaction instruments, leases, contracts to convey, and powers of attorney, as described more particularly in the following sections. For paper instruments, the register's verification requirement involves confirmation that a presented document is the same document that was signed before an authorized official and not a copy, unless a statute specifically allows a copy to be recorded. Verification is different for electronic recording; as described in Chapter 4, Section 4.5 of this book, the trusted submitter is responsible for ensuring compliance with the originality requirements, and the register looks for completion of the required elements and the submitter's certification of compliance with originality requirements. When a copy of an instrument requiring a proof or acknowledgment may be recorded in place of the original, the registration statutes expressly provide for this alternative.[55] Therefore, when the statutes speak of procedures for registering a "deed" or a "deed of trust," it should be understood that they are referring to the instrument with an original signature.

Verification in its present form is a continuation of a long-standing practice with two principal functions, both of which protect the interests of bona fide grantees of real estate interests. The first function reflects the historic requirement that presented transactional instruments must appear to have basic elements of genuineness in a process known as *probate.* Most real estate instruments are presented for registration not by the grantors who executed them, but by the grantees to whom the instruments were delivered or their representatives. Possession and presentation of a document that bears direct evidence of the grantor's execution are some assurances of authenticity. Registers enable grantees to make a public record of

---

55. *See, e.g.,* G.S. 47-29 (copy of federal bankruptcy records); G.S. 47-31 (certified copy of an instrument recorded elsewhere); G.S. 1-228 (certified copy of judgment affecting title to land).

such bona fide conveyance instruments. Originally, someone who wished to register a document was first required to establish before the clerk of superior court that the document was duly acknowledged. If the clerk adjudged the document to be duly acknowledged and its certificate to be in due form, it was ordered to be recorded by the register. In 1967, the burden of probating was shifted to the registers of deeds. After confirming that a presented instrument complies with the registration requirements, registers make a record of that instrument. Historically, this was done by transcription, and more recently it is accomplished through a scanning process. The original document is returned after it has been examined. Once the document is registered, the presence of the document on the public record is an indication that the presenter satisfied the authenticity prerequisites for recording. Verification is a link in authentication of the record of a real estate transaction.

The second principal function that verification performs is confirmation that an instrument submitted for registration has a completed acknowledgment, which is a requirement for instruments of conveyance to be properly registered and for them to be effective against third parties claiming competing interests. Purchasers' and creditors' compliance with the recording requirements is therefore essential to protection of their interests, and verification is one means of preventing omissions for which the submitters are responsible.

Assessing whether a particular presented instrument requires verification may be difficult. The answer ultimately rests within the register's exercise of reasonable judgment based on information apparent in the instrument itself. For example, the statutes require that the signatures on a "contract" be the subject of a notarial certificate, subjecting it to register verification.[56] A document entitled "agreement" would generally be understood to be a contract. A register thus would likely reasonably conclude that an instrument entitled "agreement" is a contract requiring a notarial certificate for verification purposes. What happens if a document's title or contents make it difficult for a register to determine whether acknowledgment is required under North Carolina law, and a register decides to accept a presenter's insistence that none is required? In this case the presenter takes the risk that the document could later be deemed unenforceable

56. G.S. 47-17.

due to the absence of a notarial certificate, and the register should not be expected to challenge this decision.

The statutes provide that the following instruments must be acknowledged, proved, or the subject of an oath or affirmation, and they must therefore meet verification requirements to be registered:

- affidavit accompanying deed executed before 1920 (deed not subject to verification) (G.S. 47-19);
- affidavit of satisfaction [G.S. 45-36.16(8)];
- certificate of satisfaction of deed of trust, mortgage, or other security instrument (G.S. 47-46.2);
- contract (G.S. 47-17);
- curative affidavit (G.S. 47-36.1);
- deed (G.S. 47-17);
- deed of trust (G.S. 47-17);
- document of rescission of satisfaction instrument or affidavit [G.S. 45-36.6(f)(3)];
- lease (G.S. 47-17);
- marriage settlement (G.S. 47-25);
- memorandum of lease or option (G.S. 47-120);
- mortgage deed (G.S. 47-17);
- notice of preservation of interest in real property (G.S. 47B-4);
- notice of satisfaction of deed of trust, mortgage, or other security instrument (G.S. 47-46.1);
- power of attorney (G.S. 32C-1-105, G.S. 47-28);
- power of attorney termination (G.S. 32C-1-110(g));
- release deed (G.S. 45-41);
- renunciation under a will [G.S. 31B-1(c)];
- request for copies of notice of foreclosure [G.S. 45-21.17A(a)];
- satisfaction of security instrument [G.S. 45-36.10(b)(2)];
- statement of authority as to real property by nonprofit association (G.S. 59B-6(d)); and
- trustee's satisfaction of deed of trust [G.S. 45-36.20(e)(2)].

Specific types of affidavits are in the above list because a statute prescribes the requirement. Any instrument stating it is an affidavit must have a notarized jurat for it to meet the legal requirements for such an instrument. Registers should consult the statutes for unintentional omissions from this list or for additions or changes to this list as a result of new legislation.

3.2.3.2 Previously Recorded Instruments

Once a document requiring verification has been verified and recorded, there is no logical reason to subject that same document to a second verification if it is submitted for rerecording. Someone may wish to record the same document in another county or to rerecord it in the same county to put it in a different sequence of recording with other documents. The logic of the exception from verification does not apply if the presented document is different from what was previously recorded. For example, if a previously recorded document has been altered to describe different or additional real estate, or different parties or interests, the presented document expresses a different conveyance and logically requires verification in the same manner as any other document not previously recorded. If the previously recorded document incorrectly expressed the grantor's intent, it is the grantor who must express the correct intent on the record, with a newly signed and acknowledged corrective instrument or a re-signed and re-acknowledged altered instrument, both of which are subject to verification. Without the grantor's signature and an acknowledgment, the instrument may be legally invalid as a conveyance.[57]

To rerecord an original document without verification, the presenter must mark it on its first page as a "rerecording," which is a representation that it is the same unaltered document as previously recorded. This mark is a representation on which the register may rely. The register checks for it and for recording information that shows that the document is a previously recorded document. The register has no responsibility to check for alterations on such pages.

Occasionally, someone wishes to record something to give notice that an error was made in a previous recording. This may be appropriate, for example, if a minor technical mistake is made in a deed that does not

---

57. *See, e.g.,* Moelle v. Sherwood, 148 U.S. 21 (1892) (deed with altered property description not valid against subsequent purchasers); *In re* Hudson, 182 N.C. App. 499, 642 S.E.2d 485 (2007) (foreclosure petition dismissed when property description was added to deed of trust after its execution); William A. Campbell, *Correction Deeds and Deeds of Trust*, Land Rec. Bull. No. 6 (UNC School of Government, Sept. 1984) ("To summarize, changes in a recorded instrument should be made by preparing and recording a correction deed. An attempt to short-cut this procedure by altering the original instrument results in a new instrument that the register of deeds should not record unless it is re-executed and re-acknowledged. If it is recorded anyway, the recording is invalid and does not give constructive notice.").

materially change the grantor's expression of intent, such as a minor error in a property description. The purposes of giving notice of a minor error can be accomplished with an *affidavit of correction*, also known as a *scrivener's affidavit*. Information about errors identified in an affidavit clearly is attributable to the affiant. Registers have no role in reviewing an affiant's capacity to give the affidavit. Anyone can submit an affidavit of correction (the person need not be an attorney) to make a record of typographical or minor errors, and those who give affidavits can attach any exhibits they want to explain or show the correction, including marked-up copies of the corrected document. Registers verify the notarial certificate the same as any other affidavit. If an affidavit is conspicuously identified as a corrective or scrivener's affidavit in its title, the register indexes the affiant's name, the names of the original parties to the document described in the affidavit, and the recording information for the document being described, if and as this information is provided in the affidavit.[58]

Registers should not give advice to the public about how to address a problem with the contents of a registered instrument or even about whether such a problem should be addressed. As described in Section 3.1.2 of this chapter, the sequence of registration determines the priority of competing interests, and in North Carolina only properly registered instruments are entitled to the registration statute's protection. When there is a potential problem with a registered instrument's contents, the interested parties should determine whether the problem is sufficient to cast doubt on the registration's effectiveness. If so, they may decide that a new recording is necessary, and in that event they must consider whether the new recording will conflict with other registered instruments. They may also decide that recording additional or corrective information by means of a scrivener's affidavit or some other method is sufficient to remedy the problem. If done improperly or inappropriately, rerecording instruments could result in title problems, harm to property interests, and fraud or unethical conduct. Title problems could occur, for example, if a materially altered instrument is recorded without due consideration for priority issues. Unethical or illegal conduct could occur if a materially altered instrument is recorded without the consent of the parties to that instrument. The statutes reflect a policy decision that it is not the register's responsibility to attempt through the verification process to prevent such problematic or wrongful acts.

58. G.S. 47-36.1.

3.2.3.3 Certified Copies

The statutes provide that "[a] duly certified copy of any deed or writing required or allowed to be registered may be registered in any county."[59] The statute also provides that the register "may rely on the record keeper's certification on a presented document that the document is a certified copy and is not required to further verify the proof or acknowledgement . . . or to determine whether the document has been changed or altered after it was certified."[60] Consequently, when a document is submitted for recording as a certified copy of a previously recorded document, the register checks only to see that it is a document with a record keeper's "certified copy" mark. The register is not responsible for looking for alterations that make the document different from what was certified by the record keeper—in other words, not truly a certified copy. Note, however, that if a presenter has used a certified copy of a document as part of an instrument together with pages that were not part of the certified copy, the instrument for verification purposes is the same as any other newly submitted instrument.

A copy is "certified" for recording purposes when it bears evidence that the copy was issued by the keeper of the official record. There is no law or regulation that specifies how this evidence should be placed upon the record, or precisely what the markings must contain. Accordingly, registers should exercise reasonable discretion in examining the record keeper's markings, which should be on reproduced pages of the official record or otherwise logically associated with it, such as with a cover sheet from the record keeper. A notary public cannot "certify" a document to be from an office in this sense, nor can the copy be issued by someone other than the record keeper.

The ability to record a certified copy enables someone to make a record in several counties provided that the instrument is properly registered in any one county. It enables someone to correct a recording made in the wrong county by obtaining a certified copy from that county and recording it in the correct county. The certified copy rule also enables someone to make a record in one county of a previously registered instrument recorded elsewhere without having to locate the original instrument.

These provisions do not restrict acceptable certified copies of previously recorded documents to instruments from a North Carolina register

---

59. G.S. 47-31(a).

60. *Id.*

of deeds office.[61] In addition, nothing prohibits a certified copy from being recorded in the same county in which the original recording occurred. Such a recording may be undertaken, for example, to address concerns about priority based on the sequence or timing of registration. The register should not be concerned with the reason for the rerecording.

The statutes expressly provide that certain kinds of instruments are to be recorded as certified copies. Logically, an uncertified copy of such an instrument cannot be recorded if a statute specifically requires recording a certified copy. This certified copy requirement, therefore, is important for what it excludes—uncertified copies of such instruments. The following are among the documents that the statutes authorize to be registered as certified copies:

- annexation ordinance (G.S. 160A-29);
- governmental unit order or court judgment closing street or road [G.S. 153A-241 (counties); G.S. 160A-299(a) (cities)];
- judgment transferring title to property (G.S. 1-228);
- license to dispose of radioactive materials (G.S. 104E-10.2);
- permit for sanitary landfill or hazardous waste disposal site (G.S. 130A-301); and
- federal government acceptance of title to land by purchase, condemnation, or otherwise [G.S. 104-7(c)].

Registers should consult the statutes for unintentional omissions from this list or for additions or changes to this list as a result of new legislation.

---

61. Prior to 1993, the statutes contained two conflicting provisions. G.S. 8-20 allowed registration of a certified copy "from the office of the register of deeds of any county . . . without further proof." G.S. 47-31 more broadly provided that "[a] duly certified copy of any deed or writing required or allowed to be registered may be registered in any county," which was interpreted as requiring registers to certify the acknowledgment. William A. Campbell, *Recording Certified Copies*, Land Rec. Bull. No. 16 (UNC School of Government, Nov. 1992). In 1993, G.S. 8-20 was repealed, and G.S. 47-31 was amended to say that registration could occur "without further certification." Presumably these correlative changes would not have been made if the legislature intended to limit acceptable certified copies to those from a register's office.

3.2.3.4 Uncertified Copies or Instruments Not Requiring Verification

As described in Section 3.2.3.1 of this chapter, certain kinds of instruments must contain notarial officers' signatures. As described in Section 3.2.3.3 of this chapter, the statutes expressly allow registration of certain kinds of certified copies of documents. By implication, these instruments cannot be recorded as uncertified copies. The statutes also expressly provide that certain kinds of documents must be registered, but the statutes attach no requirement that the documents be verified or that they be certified copies. Documents that must be registered include the following:

- affidavit for removal of manufactured home from vehicle registration files issued by the Division of Motor Vehicles [G.S. 47-20.6(a) (though called an "affidavit" in the statute, this document need not be notarized, and it is therefore not an affidavit in the legal sense of a written statement given under oath with a jurat)]; assessment roll of water and sewer authorities [G.S. 162A-6(a)(14a)];
- commissioners' report of partition proceeding (G.S. 46A-57);
- notice of open dump issued by the Department of Environment and Natural Resources [G.S. 130A-301(f)];
- memorandum of condemnation action or supplemental memorandum issued by the Department of Transportation (G.S. 136-104, -111);
- municipal or county memorandum of condemnation (G.S. 40A-43);
- notice of foreclosure (G.S. 45-38);
- owner memorandum of action for condemnation compensation [G.S. 40A-51(b)];
- petition, decree, or order in bankruptcy (G.S. 47-29);
- statement canceling notice of disposal site issued by the Secretary of Environment and Natural Resources [G.S. 130A-310.8(f)];
- tax waiver or consent to transfer issued by the Secretary of Revenue (G.S. 47-18.2); and
- certificate of corporate merger or consolidation issued by the Secretary of State [G.S. 47-18.1(c)].

There is no prohibition in the statutes against recording copies or unsigned or unacknowledged instruments that are not specifically required to be verified or to be certified copies. As described in Section 3.2.1 of this chapter, the statutes direct a register to register all presented instruments meeting statutory and local prerequisites. Of course, *all* recording prerequisites must be met, including any applicable document specifications and payment of any required fees.

3.2.4 Verification

The statutes direct that "[t]he register of deeds shall not accept for registration any instrument that requires proof or acknowledgement unless the execution of the instrument by one or more signers appears to have been proved or acknowledged before an officer with the apparent authority to take proofs or acknowledgements, and the said proof or acknowledgement includes the officer's signature, commission expiration date, and official seal, if required."[62] Registers therefore must verify the presence of specified basic notarial certificate elements for instruments that require them. If, after reviewing the certificate, the register decides that the instrument cannot be verified and registered, the register should inform the person presenting the instrument of the defect. A presenter who wants to contest the register's determination may apply to the district court of the county for an order directing the register to record the instrument.[63] To issue the order, however, the district court must find that the instrument meets the verification requirements.[64]

A register may wish to consider verification in three analytical steps:

1. Is the instrument one for which a notarial certificate is required? The types of instruments specifically identified in the statutes as requiring such elements are listed in Section 3.2.3.1 of this chapter.
2. If a notarial certificate is required, was it taken before an officer authorized by North Carolina statute?
3. If a notarial certificate is required, what within it must be verified, and does the instrument contain these elements?

As previously noted, the verification statute refers to a required acknowledgment or proof. An *acknowledgment* is a record made by a notary or other official authorized under North Carolina law on a document indicating that the official personally witnessed a properly identified signatory

62. G.S. 47-14(a).
63. G.S. 47-14(b).
64. *Id.*

execute or confirm having executed the document. A *proof,* also known as a verification, occurs when a signatory certifies under oath or affirmation that he or she witnessed someone else execute or acknowledge having executed a record. Although the statute does not also refer to a *jurat* or oath or affirmation, this is an equivalent record that is appropriate for documents that require the signatory's vow of truthfulness before the notary or other official. Accordingly, an acknowledgment, proof, or jurat may be the appropriate form of certificate for verification.

The statute refers specifically to three elements for the register to verify: the officer's signature, commission expiration date, and official seal, if required. The register is not responsible for examining the presenter's choice of a form of certificate, determining the official's compliance with the notary law prescriptions for proper certificate completion, or assessing the instrument's legal enforceability. Although the notarial officer's compliance with these requirements would seem to be a straightforward matter of basic compliance with standard practices, registers sometimes encounter problematic components the sufficiency of which cannot easily be determined. In such circumstances, the register must use reasonable judgment and may wish at least to point out the questionable aspect to the presenter.

Three questionable situations occur with surprising frequency. Occasionally, a register sees a seal, signature, and commission expiration date but no certificate at all. A register who notices the complete absence of a certificate may reasonably conclude that verification cannot be completed because there is no record of the implicitly essential notarial act. However, a register is not expressly required to examine the certificate and likely would not be deemed to have acted irresponsibly by registering such an instrument. Similarly, if there is no party's signature despite a completed certificate for one, a register could reasonably refuse to accept the instrument on the basis that no acknowledgment could have occurred. But a register is not legally obliged to check for the party's signature and should not be deemed to have acted irresponsibly by registering an instrument without one. A third situation of this sort that occasionally arises is when an instrument has a complete acknowledgment for one signature but also another party's signature without one. The register may reasonably register such an instrument. The statute requires verification of "the execution of the instrument by *one or more signers,*"[65] which can reasonably be interpreted as indicating that any one verifiable act is sufficient. There also is good reason to register such an instrument because it likely will have binding legal effect at least with respect to the party whose signature can be properly verified.

Registers also encounter difficulty in verification when instruments are presented with notarial certificates that are in languages other than English for registration purposes. The statutes do not require that documents or certificates be in English, but the register must be able to verify that verification requirements are met. Registers cannot reasonably be expected to be able to interpret all languages and characters from across the globe. Furthermore, presenters should understand that English is the predominant language for official transactions in North Carolina. The presenter must provide the register with enough information on which the register may reasonably rely in performing verification including, if necessary, a translation that the register reasonably deems reliable of unfamiliar foreign language verification components, which may be included with the instrument on the public record if the register so desires.

3.2.4.1 Authorized Officers

Once the register has determined that the instrument offered for registration requires a notarial certificate, the register next must ensure that the certificate was completed before someone with apparent authority under North Carolina law for registration purposes. The register questions whether the officer has "apparent" authority by being among those *identified by North Carolina law* as authorized to complete notarial certificates on instruments presented for registration. This is a different question than asking if the official's jurisdiction authorizes the official to perform the act. The register does not check with the official's jurisdiction to determine if the person actually has the authority indicated and is not expected to research the laws of the official's governing jurisdiction. Rather, the register consults the North Carolina statute regarding authorized officials and, if the official is among those listed, the register may conclude, absent contrary information, that the apparent authority exists.

Sometimes an instrument will have a legally valid acknowledgment but it cannot be registered because the officer, although empowered to take the

---

65. G.S. 47-14(a) (emphasis added).

acknowledgment in his or her jurisdiction, is not one of the officials whose notarial acts the register may accept for registration verification purposes in this state according to the North Carolina statutes. For example, a New Jersey attorney may have notarial powers under New Jersey law, and an instrument notarized by a New Jersey attorney may be legally sufficient both in New Jersey and North Carolina. But those are not issues the register considers. An attorney is not one of the officials the North Carolina statutes authorize for a real estate instrument to be registered in this state. Therefore, a certification completed by a New Jersey attorney, as such, would not be sufficient for verification purposes. The converse is also true. If, for example, an instrument contains an acknowledgment completed by a clerk of court of another state, North Carolina law provides that such an official has the apparent authority in this state to take acknowledgments for real estate instrument verification purposes. A register therefore will verify such an acknowledgment without questioning whether a clerk of court actually has notarial powers under the laws of the clerk's state.

The statutes distinguish between North Carolina officials and out-of-state officials, as the following sections describe.

3.2.4.1.1 NORTH CAROLINA OFFICIALS

The authorized North Carolina officials (listed in G.S. 47-1) are the following:

- notaries public;
- supreme court justices;
- court of appeals judges;
- superior and district court judges;
- magistrates (see certificate requirement described in Section 3.2.4.2 of this chapter); and
- clerks of superior court and their assistants and deputies.

Although registers of deeds are not included in this list, by statute registers are notaries ex officio for acknowledging instruments and may certify their notarial acts under the seal of the office of register of deeds.[66] Assistant and deputy registers of deeds are also ex officio notaries for the

66. G.S. 10B-21(b) provides that a register "may" use the official seal to take the acknowledgment of an instrument, but G.S. 47-5 expressly provides that if the instrument is to be recorded in his or her office, the register need not use the official seal. Use of the seal may avoid arousing the concern of those unfamiliar with G.S. 47-5.

purpose of taking proofs of execution.[67] If they attend a school for notaries, their ex officio status extends to the taking of acknowledgments as well.[68] They are to attest their proofs and acknowledgments under the register's seal. The notarial powers of registers and their deputies and assistants are discussed in more depth in Chapter 1, Sections 1.4.4 and 1.6.2 of this book.

The statutes are inconsistent about the ex officio status of assistant and deputy clerks of superior court. G.S. 10B-21(a) makes the same provisions for them as for assistant and deputy registers; that is, they may take proofs of execution but may take acknowledgments only after attending a school for notaries. However, G.S. 47-1 expressly authorizes them to take the acknowledgments of deeds and other instruments to be recorded. Registers need not determine if a notary school has been attended and may rely on the appearance of capacity on the instrument without concern about actual legal authority.

Any of the officials listed in G.S. 47-1 (as discussed above) may complete a notarial certificate in North Carolina regardless of where in the state the instrument is to be registered or where the person executing the instrument resides. For example, a Guilford County resident could acknowledge execution of a deed before a Mecklenburg County notary for land being conveyed (and for a deed being registered) in Brunswick County. A qualification to this rule is that if a magistrate acknowledges an instrument to be recorded outside the county in which he or she holds office, the acknowledgment must be accompanied by a certificate of the clerk of superior court of the county where the magistrate holds court—in the form required by statute—that at the time of the acknowledgment the magistrate was a serving magistrate of that county.[69]

3.2.4.1.2 FEDERAL AND OUT-OF-STATE OFFICIALS

Out-of-state officials authorized to take acknowledgments are listed in G.S. 47-2. They include the following officials from any state or territory of the United States, as well as other countries, unless otherwise noted:

- notaries public;
- judges of courts of record;

67. G.S. 10B-21(b).
68. *Id.*
69. G.S. 47-44.

- justices of the peace of a state or territory of the United States (see certificate requirement discussed in Section 3.2.4.2 of this chapter);
- clerks of courts of record;
- commissioners of deeds;
- commissioners of oaths;
- mayors or chief magistrates of incorporated municipalities;
- ambassadors;
- ministers;
- commercial agents of the United States;
- officers of the United States Army, Air Force, Navy, Marine Corps, Coast Guard, or Merchant Marine of the rank of warrant officer or higher; and
- consuls, vice-consuls, consuls general, vice-consuls general, associate consuls, and "any other person authorized by federal law to acknowledge documents as consular officers."[70]

Inclusion of the last category, "any other person authorized by federal law to acknowledge documents as consular officers," authorizes certain persons associated with the military to exercise notarial powers in connection with documents executed by military personnel and certain other persons identified in 10 U.S.C. § 1044a. Individuals vested with consular and therefore notarial powers include judge advocates; civilian attorneys serving as legal assistance attorneys; adjutants, assistant adjutants, and personnel adjutants, including reserve members when not in duty status; all other members of the armed forces, including reserve members when not in duty status, who are designated by regulations of the armed forces or by statute to have these powers; and, for the performance of notarial acts outside the United States, all employees of a military department or the Coast Guard authorized by regulations of the relevant secretary or by statute to exercise these powers outside the United States. A register should be able to rely on a statement within the certificate, including a reference to the applicable federal statute, that the officer is authorized to take the acknowledgment, at least absent some apparent reason to conclude otherwise. This approach is supported by 10 U.S.C. § 1044a(d), which provides that "[t]he signature of any such person acting as notary, together with the title of that person's offices, is prima facie evidence that the signature is

---

70. G.S. 47-2.

genuine, that the person holds the designated title, and that the person is authorized to perform a notarial act." Federal law therefore authorizes a register to rely on an appearance of authority based on information provided in the instrument.

The statutes contain a qualification regarding certificates made by justices of the peace of other states or territories. They must be accompanied by a certificate made by the clerk of superior court of the county of the justice's jurisdiction—in the form required by statute—that at the time the notarial act occurred the official was an acting justice of the peace of that county.[71]

3.2.4.2 Required Elements

For most instruments the statute limits the verification inquiry to "the officer's signature, commission expiration date, and official seal, if required."[72] The following subsections address these three components. As a threshold matter, however, a register must determine whether each of these components is required for the officer who signed the certificate.

If a notary public of another state takes the acknowledgment and the document does not show the notary's stamp or seal and the expiration date of his or her commission, the instrument is recordable if certain other information is provided. It is recordable if the instrument is accompanied by a certificate showing that the notary was an acting notary public of that state at the time the notarial act occurred. This certificate can be from the notary's commissioning authority or a state officer authorized to issue certificates regarding notary commission status. Although the statute's wording is imprecise, apparently if *either* the stamp or seal *or* the expiration date information is missing from the instrument, the additional certificate is required. The notary seal requirement for an out-of-state notary can be satisfied in two other ways. No seal is required if the notary states within the proof or acknowledgment area that the notary is not required to use a seal, or a reference appears that purports to be to a statute in the notary's commissioning state that provides that no seal is required together with a statement that no seal is required. The register relies on the statements and does not check the law of other states to confirm their truth or accuracy.[73]

---

71. G.S. 47-44.
72. G.S. 47-14(a).
73. G.S. 47-2.2.

If an out-of-state justice of the peace takes the acknowledgment, it must be accompanied by a certificate of the clerk of a court of record that at the time the justice was in fact a justice of the peace of that county and state.[74] If a North Carolina magistrate acknowledges an instrument to be recorded outside the county in which he or she holds office, the acknowledgment must be accompanied by a certificate of the clerk of superior court of the county where the magistrate holds court—in the form required by statute—that at the time of the acknowledgment the magistrate was a serving magistrate of that county.

If an out-of-state official—other than a justice of the peace or notary—who does not have a seal of office takes an acknowledgment, except as described below in this section, the document must be accompanied by a certificate of a clerk of a court of record that the official was an official of that county and state at the time.[75]

The statute provides that if a military, naval, or merchant-marine officer takes the acknowledgment, no seal is required, but the officer must give his or her name, rank, and ship or military organization and use the form set forth in the statute.[76] Such officers also have consular authority under 10 U.S.C. § 1044a, however, and by virtue of that statute are not required to use any particular certificate form. Whenever such consular authority is exercised by someone affiliated with the military, the certificate should refer to the official's capacity and the authority under which it is being exercised, such as by mention of the statute.

3.2.4.2.1 OFFICER'S SIGNATURE

As described in Chapter 4, Section 4.5, registers check electronic filings for the appearance of a notarial officer's signature, and the submitters are responsible for verifying that it meets the electronic recording rules. No questions arise in the vast majority of cases in which a North Carolina notary complies with notarial law and signs in ink by hand.[77] A register is not required to test signature ink to ensure it is what it appears to be. But there are circumstances in which a register can reasonably conclude that there is insufficient evidence that the officer actually signed the certificate, as when the written name is initialed, indicating that someone signed

---

74. G.S. 47-44.
75. G.S. 47-45.
76. G.S. 47-2.
77. G.S. 10B-35.

someone else's name, or when the script of a name appears in a stamped or imaged form that anyone could have placed on the document. A signature associated with an acknowledgment certificate is sufficient if it appears to be affixed by the officer as indicated in the certificate and any seal. The registration statute does not require that the register be able to match every letter in the written signature to every letter of the official's name as it appears in the seal or certificate. Electronic signatures are discussed in Chapter 4, Section 4.3 of this book.

3.2.4.2.2 COMMISSION EXPIRATION DATE

The statute provides that the register need verify only the presence of a commission expiration date if one is required.[78] The statute does not state that the register must verify that the date that appears on the certificate indicates that the execution occurred before the officer's commission expired. To perform the verification function, sufficient information must be provided for the register to make a reasonable determination about whether an expiration date is required. Some kinds of officials, such as judges and registers, are widely known to have nonexpiring commissions. An expiration date must be provided for a North Carolina notary who is not a notary by means of an indefinite term of office (such as registers or clerks of court). Military and other judicial officials need not provide commission expiration dates. The register may rely on information in the certificate to establish whether an official must provide an expiration date. For an out-of-state notary, the certificate should either provide an expiration date or contain information indicating that the official's commission does not expire. This could include a statement that the commission is indefinite, for life, or for as long as the person holds an office.

3.2.4.2.3 OFFICIAL SEAL

The seal image must appear official. Registers can reasonably expect that the seal of a North Carolina notary contains the essential information about a notary's official capacity as a notary in this state. Therefore, if the seal is for a North Carolina notary, the seal image should appear to include the words "notary public," the notary's name, the words "North Carolina" or its abbreviation, and a North Carolina county name.

If the seal is for an out-of-state or foreign notary, the seal image should contain basic information that indicates the officer's identity and autho-

---

78. G.S. 47-14(a).

rized capacity, including the officer's name, jurisdiction, and capacity as a notary or other officer authorized by North Carolina law. The register cannot reasonably be expected to verify the certificate's actual compliance with another governing jurisdiction's notary laws. As described in Section 3.2.4.2 of this chapter, the statutes authorize substitutes for out-of-state notary seals in some circumstances.

An affixed seal that is not apparently an authorized official seal may not be made compliant by making alterations to it. An affixed seal that is apparently an authorized official seal may become insufficient if marks alter the information relied upon in determining that the seal was an apparently authorized official seal. For example, a seal image would be unacceptable if the name on the image was altered to match the notary's signature.

Nothing in the statutes requires North Carolina magistrates to have seals and, as described above, they are authorized to perform notarial acts within their counties and outside the county with use of a special certificate. Some magistrates nonetheless have and use seals.

The statutes do not require that the seal image be reproducible. But it must be clear and visible enough for the register to perform the verification. The statutes provide that once registered, an instrument is presumed to have a notary's official seal even if the seal's image is not visible when the document appears on the record.[79] This is another reason why a register should ensure that required seals are clear and visible before registering the documents on which they appear.

As described in Chapter 4, Section 4.3 of this book, registers check electronic filings for the appearance of the seal. Electronic submitters are responsible for verifying that the seal meets the electronic recording rules.

Figure 3.1 depicts the verification procedure.

3.2.5 Payment of Recording Fees

All required recording fees must be paid to the register before any instrument is accepted for registration.[80] The applicable recording fees are set out in the uniform fee schedule (see Appendix 1).[81] Deeds and most other instruments have the same charge. A deed of trust or mortgage has a higher charge than other types of real estate instruments to reflect the fact that

79. G.S. 47-14(f).
80. G.S. 161-10(c).
81. G.S. 161-10(b).

no charge is made for the associated satisfaction instrument that is later recorded. In most cases the same fee is charged for an instrument of any length up to a certain number of pages, and an additional per-page fee is added for longer instruments. Plans and Uniform Commercial Code filings have separate fees. There is no fee for recording a satisfaction instrument.[82]

There are three common instances in which an additional fee is charged based on the content of an instrument: nonstandard documents, combined documents, and multiple assignments.

A register charges an additional fee of $25 for registering a *nonstandard document*, as described in Section 3.2.2.1 of this chapter.

If a document presented for recording contains multiple instruments, an additional $10 fee must be paid for each additional instrument.[83] A document contains multiple instruments if it has two or more instruments each of which is separately executed and acknowledged and could be recorded alone. For example, if a document submitted for recording with the title "Deed of Trust and Assignment of Rents" has only one execution and acknowledgment, then it should not be treated as a multiple instrument. On the other hand, if a document submitted for recording with the title "Substitution of Trustee and Request for Notice of Foreclosure" has one execution and acknowledgment for the substitution of trustee and a separate execution and acknowledgment for the request for notice, it should be treated as a multiple instrument and the register should charge the extra fee.

An instrument that assigns more than one deed of trust, mortgage, or other security instrument (such as an assignment of leases and rents) is subject to a charge of $10 extra for a second and each additional indexing reference in the assignment.[84] For example, an additional $10 would be charged for an assignment of two deeds of trust or for an assignment of leases and records recorded separately from a deed of trust. The additional charge reflects the need for the register to make additional cross-references in the index to the original instruments according to the subsequent instrument indexing rule.

---

82. G.S. 45-37.2(a).

83. G.S. 161-10(a)(1).

84. *Id.*

Figure 3.1 Verification Procedure

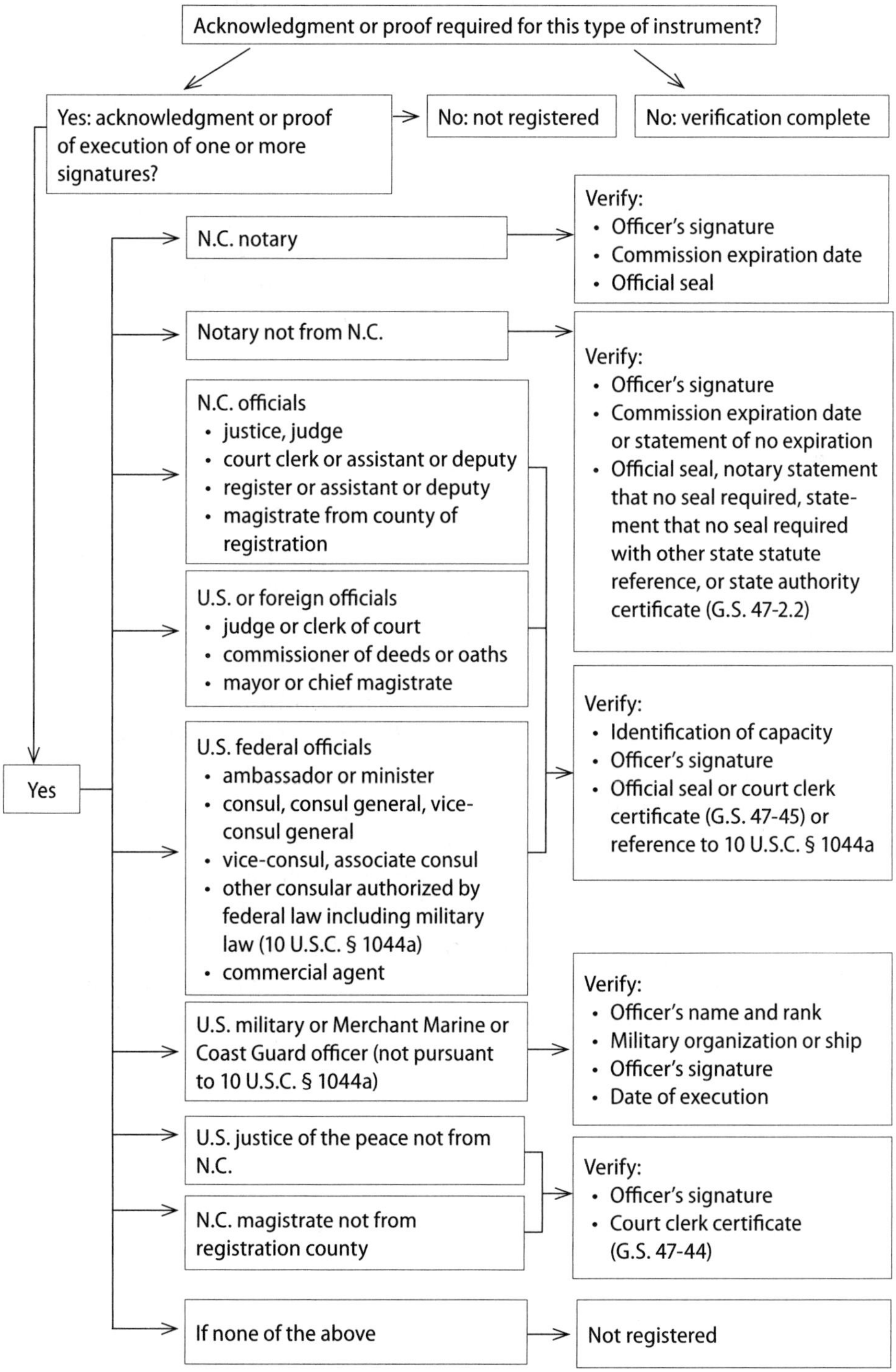

3.2.6 Payment of Excise Taxes

Any applicable state excise tax must be paid before an instrument conveying an interest in real estate may be registered.[85] In some counties, a county excise tax must also be paid. The details of these taxes are discussed in the following sections.

3.2.6.1 Payment of the State Excise Tax

When an instrument conveying real estate is presented, the register must examine it to determine whether an excise tax must be paid. In performing this function, the register relies on information supplied by the presenter, and the presenter is responsible for any misrepresentations. However, as an official sworn to follow the law, the register has inherent authority to refuse to accept an instrument when the presenter does not comply with a patently applicable legal requirement or makes obviously false representations in an attempt to avoid payment of the tax.

3.2.6.1.1 TRANSFERS SUBJECT TO TAX AND EXCEPTIONS

The state excise tax is levied on conveyances of an interest in real estate by all persons and organizations except federal, state, county, and municipal governments and their instrumentalities.[86]

A national bank is not an instrumentality of the federal government; therefore, conveyances of real property by such a bank are subject to the tax.[87] A federal land bank is an instrumentality of the federal government,[88] and conveyances by a federal land bank are therefore exempt. For many years, government-related mortgage lending and guaranty entities, such as the Federal National Mortgage Association or the Government National Mortgage Association, have taken the position that no tax is owed when the entity is a foreclosing secured creditor or grantee of a foreclosure deed. Presenters have relied on a 1971 opinion by the North Carolina Attorney General interpreting the law as not allowing collection of the tax because the government-related entity has "practical ownership" of property and

---

85. G.S. 101-228.30.

86. G.S. 105-228.28.

87. *See* First Agric. Nat'l Bank v. State Tax Comm'n, 392 U.S. 339 (1968), *and* 12 U.S.C. § 548 (2021).

88. *See* 12 U.S.C. § 2011 (2021).

should be treated as a federally tax-exempt grantor.[89] Registers should rely on current legal advice regarding the continued applicability of this claim of exemption.

The state excise tax applies to each instrument by which an interest in real estate is transferred by a non-government grantor except when the transfer is as follows:[90]

- a lease for a term of years;
- pursuant to a will or as a result of intestacy;
- by gift or for no consideration in property or money;
- by merger, conversion, or consolidation, which are entity changes governed by statute;
- a security interest, such as a deed of trust or a mortgage; or
- by operation of law (transfer by operation of law occurs when no instrument of conveyance is necessary—for example, when a joint tenant succeeds after the other joint tenant dies or property passes to another as a consequence of the life tenant's death).[91]

The presenter is responsible for reporting and paying the tax and is therefore responsible for representing that an exception applies.[92] The following sections describe the most common questions that arise about application of the excise tax.

Bankruptcy. When a deed conveys property as part of a plan of reorganization under Chapter 11 of the federal Bankruptcy Code, by federal law no excise tax may be charged.[93] This exclusion does not apply to other transfers by bankrupt debtors, such as those that might occur before the reorganization or that occur in liquidation. The presenter must report that the deed is being registered pursuant to a Chapter 11 plan of reorganization when this exemption is claimed.

Cemetery deed. Cemetery deeds are apparently as taxable as any other transaction unless the cemetery is owned by a unit of government.

Commissioner's deed. When a commissioner is appointed to sell land under judicial order, the commissioner's deed is not a transfer "by

89. Letter from the Attorney General to Austin C. Williams, 41 N.C.A.G. 714 (1972).

90. G.S. 105-228.29.

91. Letter from the Attorney General to Patsy Thomas, 41 N.C.A.G. 204 (1971).

92. G.S. 105-228.32.

93. 11 U.S.C. § 1146(a) (2021).

operation of law," and excise tax therefore appears to be required on such an instrument.[94]

Divorcing spouse deed. A reasonable interpretation of the law governing the excise tax is that the tax is not due when a deed conveys a tenancy by the entireties' interest in a divorce. The nature of equitable distribution of marital property is consistent with an interpretation that a deed dissolving a tenancy by the entireties can be deemed as only re-titling what the grantee spouse already owned. By the parties' agreement or a court determination, spouses are allocated marital property, and its distribution can involve awarding different whole assets to each of the spouses so that the sum of their shares is in the appropriate equitable proportion.[95] Each spouse is treated as already owning awarded assets. Not taxing a deed that dissolves a tenancy by the entireties in an equitable distribution of marital property is consistent with the general rule of not treating such an event as triggering tax consequences for the divorcing spouses. As the Internal Revenue Service said in a ruling, "[a]n approximately equal division of the total value of jointly owned property in a state that is not a community property state, under a divorce settlement agreement that provides for transferring some assets in their entirety to one spouse or the other, is a nontaxable division and does not result in the realization of gain or loss."[96]

If other property is being exchanged in connection with a deed of marital property, there may be consideration on which a tax is due, such as would be the case if one spouse pays the other from separate property or separate financing in exchange for sole ownership.

Entity transfer. Probably the most common question that arises about application of the tax concerns transfers from a holder of an interest in an entity to the entity itself, such as when a shareholder of a closely held corporation transfers real estate to the corporation. The tax applies to any transfer not specifically excepted if the transfer is for consideration and there is no exception for a transfer for consideration by a shareholder or other holder of an interest in an entity to the entity, or vice versa. A transfer of real estate in exchange for a percentage interest in the grantee is a transfer for consideration.[97]

---

94. *Supra* note 90.

95. G.S. 50-20.

96. Rev. Rul. 81-292, 1981-2 C.B. 158.

97. The Attorney General provided an opinion that a transfer from an individual to his wholly owned corporation *without consideration* was not subject to the tax.

Exchange of parcels. The tax applies when there is a conveyance for consideration for money or property in exchange, and a conveyance of one parcel will involve simultaneous taxable exchanges based on the respective values of what is being received.[98] For example, if the owner of Parcel A exchanges it for Parcel B valued at $100,000 and $25,000 cash, the grantor of Parcel A owes the excise tax based on $125,000 received, and the grantor of Parcel B owes an excise tax based on $100,000 consideration for Parcel B.

Foreclosure deed or deed in lieu of foreclosure. Many presenters are confused by a statute that governs payment of taxes in connection with a foreclosure or a deed given to a secured creditor in lieu of foreclosure. G.S. 45-45.2 states that the excise taxes do not "apply to instruments conveying an interest in property as the result of foreclosure or in lieu of foreclosure to the holder of the security interest being foreclosed or subject to being foreclosed," except taxes "levied by Article 8E of Chapter 105 of the General Statutes." Article 8E of Chapter 105 creates the statewide excise tax on real estate conveyances. Thus, the statute makes the separate *county* excise tax that applies in a few counties (as described in Section 3.2.6.2 of this chapter) inapplicable to transfers resulting from foreclosure but leaves the statewide excise tax collectible in all counties. A conveyance to a secured creditor as a result of foreclosure is for consideration paid, and the tax is due on the amount paid or credited for the real estate.[99] Consistent with tax law in general, consideration would include the forgiveness of debt equal to the amount forgiven or discharged, such as occurs when the property is exchanged for the amount of the mortgage loan.

Quitclaim or corrective deed. Frequently a quitclaim deed is used to correct a flaw in a title by confirming the title already thought to be vested in the grantee. Whether the grantor must pay the tax depends on whether any consideration is received for the interest conveyed by the deed. A corrective deed addressing an error or omission in an earlier instrument seldom involves any new consideration on which an excise tax is owed.

Timber deed. Although under North Carolina law timber deeds are sold as personal property rather than real property, the statutes expressly

---

Letter from the Attorney General to Lois C. LeRay, 43 N.C.A.G. 79 (1973). In that same opinion, the Attorney General said that the tax would be due if consideration had been paid for the transfer.

98. *Id.*; letter from the Attorney General to W.C. Massey, 41 N.C.A.G. 480 (1971).

99. Letter from the Attorney General to Julia E. Manning, 41 N.C.A.G. 837 (1972).

provide that "[t]he excise tax on instruments . . . applies to timber deeds and contracts for the sale of standing timber to the same extent as if these deeds and contracts conveyed an interest in real property."[100]

3.2.6.1.2 AMOUNT AND COLLECTION

The state excise tax rate is $1 on each $500 or fractional part thereof of the consideration or value of the interest or property conveyed.[101] An assumed obligation secured by a deed of trust is counted as part of the consideration, and there is no deduction for an assumed loan or other obligation secured by the property.

If the amount paid for the property is not a multiple of $500, the amount of consideration or value is rounded up to the next multiple of $500 before computing the tax. For example, if the amount paid for the property was $27,700, the taxpayer would round the amount up to $28,000, and the tax would be $56. If the amount paid was $32,350, the taxpayer would round the amount up to $32,500, and the tax would be $65.

The transferor (grantor, seller) pays the tax to the register of the county where the land lies.[102] If the land lies in more than one county, the tax must be paid to the county where the most valuable part of the real estate lies.[103]

The statute provides that "[b]efore the instrument may be recorded, the Register of Deeds must collect the tax due and mark the instrument to indicate that the tax has been paid and the amount of the tax paid."[104] This is accomplished with a tax stamp affixed to the registered instrument or with a notation that the excise tax was paid, including its amount.

The person who presents the instrument to the register is responsible for reporting the amount of tax due to the register.[105] The register is therefore not responsible for making determinations about the application of the tax or its amount, nor is it the register's role to challenge a representation that no consideration has been paid for a transfer. This creates an odd dynamic, because although the grantor is responsible for paying the tax to the register, the grantee or the grantee's representative usually presents the instrument, reports the amount of tax due, and delivers payment of

100. G.S. 105-228.30(a).
101. *Id.*
102. *Id.*
103. *Id.*
104. G.S. 105-228.32.
105. *Id.*

the tax amount. The grantee has an interest in ensuring that the tax is paid, because a lien attaches to a taxpayer's real property for unpaid state taxes.[106] The person presenting the instrument is likely to have been authorized by the grantor, according to agreement or as a matter of law, to report the tax due, and the register is not responsible for investigating this apparent authority.

The statute does require that the register "collect the tax due and mark the instrument to indicate that the tax has been paid and the amount of the tax paid."[107] Thus, a register should not accept for registration an instrument for which the presenter reports a tax due unless the tax is paid. If a presenter claims that a tax is not due under questionable circumstances the register deems unclear on the record, the register may make a note in the margin reserved for the register's use about the presenter's representation to clarify why no tax was collected and to provide information that may become useful if the presenter's claim is later scrutinized. The statute provides a mechanism for the county to bring a civil action in superior court for recovery of a tax not paid within thirty days after the register demands payment.[108]

For instruments that have been photocopied or scanned into the records, the amount on the tax stamp on the recorded instrument can be used to calculate the consideration paid for the transfer based on the rate in effect at the time of that transfer. A real estate conveyance tax has been in effect for much of North Carolina's history since the Civil War, initially by the federal government. The amount of the tax has remained generally the same over more than a century even as property values have greatly appreciated. Slight increases in excise tax reflect the government's war financing efforts. On January 1, 1968, the federal tax was repealed, and the state imposed the tax payable to the counties. On August 1, 1991, the tax was doubled, with most of the additional amount paid to the state. Table 3.1 shows the history of the tax rate.

3.2.6.1.3 REFUNDS AND CORRECTIONS

Someone who claims to have paid more excise tax than was due may file a written refund request with the county commissioners within six months

---

106. The lien, which is applied to the excise tax by G.S. 105-228.35, is described in G.S. 105-241(d).

107. G.S. 105-228.32.

108. G.S. 105-228.33.

of payment.[109] The commissioners must hold a hearing within ninety days of the request or at a later date agreed upon by the commissioners and the taxpayer, and the taxpayer may appeal to the North Carolina Secretary of Revenue and the superior court.[110] Before a tax is refunded, the taxpayer must record a new instrument reflecting the correct tax, and if the tax was paid in the wrong county, the taxpayer must record in that county a statement that no tax was due for that reason and include the grantors' and grantees' names and the book and page numbers of the instrument being corrected.[111] The register must be notified that it is a corrected instrument, and the register must notify the finance officer and the Department of Revenue that it has been recorded.[112]

The statute is not entirely clear about refund of the state portion of the excise tax, but it implies that when a refund is due, the county refunds both the county and state portions. The statute provides that after paying the refund with any applicable interest, the county must inform the Department of Revenue, and if the department disagrees with the refund, it "may assess the taxpayer for the amount of the refund."[113]

Someone who has underpaid the tax for a conveyance by an instrument already recorded and wishes to pay additional tax may do so on the public record in two ways. The instrument can be re-recorded, unaltered, with the additional tax. Another method that enables the taxpayer to explain the reason for an additional recording is to use an affidavit that refers to the prior instrument and provides any appropriate explanation, with which the additional tax can be paid and on which the register will mark the payment.

---

109. G.S. 105-228.37(a).

110. G.S. 105-228.37. In Mecklenburg County the county commissioners may delegate approval authority to the county manager. If the manager does not approve, the commissioners must hear the appeal. S.L. 2009-110.

111. G.S. 105-228.37(e).

112. *Id.*

113. G.S. 105-228.37(c).

3.2.6.2 Separate County Excise Tax

The counties of Camden,[114] Chowan,[115] Currituck,[116] Dare,[117] Pasquotank,[118] Perquimans,[119] and Washington[120] are authorized by local acts to levy an excise tax, sometimes referred to as a land-transfer tax, of not more than $1 per $100 of consideration or value on instruments conveying interests in land. This tax must be paid by the transferor before the register may record an instrument of conveyance. Although the same exceptions that apply to the state excise tax generally apply to the county-authorized excise tax, the register of each county in which such a tax is collected should consult the applicable authorizing statute. As described in Section 3.2.6.1.1 of this chapter, G.S. 45-45.2 makes the county excise tax inapplicable to a transfer to the secured creditor as a result of foreclosure, an exception also set forth in the acts authorizing the tax.

3.2.7 Satisfaction Instruments

One of the most common types of instruments that registers handle is a satisfaction instrument. These instruments deserve special attention in this section not only because of their frequency, but also because over the years they have taken so many different forms and have been recorded by so many different procedures. Regardless of form or procedure, satisfaction instruments are important to owners, lenders, and title searchers as a record that a deed of trust or other security instrument no longer binds the real estate. To understand the nature of satisfaction instruments in the records requires a basic knowledge of both their function and the different methods and forms that have been used.

3.2.7.1 Nature and Function

A satisfaction instrument relates to a deed of trust or other security instrument. A security instrument is an agreement between the lender and borrower about property becoming subject to compelled sale if a loan is unpaid. As far as the parties to the transaction are concerned, a deed

114. S.L. 1985-954.
115. S.L. 1985-881.
116. S.L. 1985-670.
117. S.L. 1985-525.
118. S.L. 1989-393.
119. *Id.*
120. *Id.*

Table 3.1 History of Real Estate Excise Taxes in North Carolina

August 1, 1991–current	$1.00 per $500; one-half to county, one-half (county may retain 2% of this one-half) to state[a]
January 1, 1968–July 31, 1991	$0.50 per $500 (all to county)[b]
July 1, 1940–December 31, 1967	$0.55 per $500 when exceeds $100 (federal)[c]
June 21, 1932–June 30, 1940	$0.50 per $500 when exceeds $100 (federal)[d]
March 28, 1926–June 20, 1932	None[e]
December 1, 1917–March 27, 1926	$0.50 per $500 when exceeds $100 (federal)[f]
September 9, 1916–November 30, 1917	None[g]
December 1, 1914–September 8, 1916	$0.50 per $500 when exceeds $100 (federal)[h]
July 1, 1902–November 30, 1914	None[i]
July 1, 1901–June 30, 1902	$.25 for over $2,500 up to $3,000; $0.25 for every additional $500 greater than $3,000 (federal)[j]
July 1, 1898–June 30, 1901	$0.50 for over $100 up to $500; $0.50 for every additional $500 greater than $500 (federal)[k]

a. 1991 N.C. Sess. Laws ch. 689, § 338; 1991 N.C. Sess. Laws ch. 1019.
b. Excise Tax Reduction Act of 1965, Pub. L. No. 89-44, § 401(b), 79 Stat. 136, 148; 1967 N.C. Sess. Laws ch. 1019.
c. Revenue Act of 1940, ch. 419, § 210, 54 Stat. 516, 522–23 (originally to expire July 1, 1945, extended by Revenue Act of 1941, ch. 412, §§ 505, 521(a)(24), 55 Stat. 687, 706–07).
d. Revenue Act of 1932, ch. 209, § 725, 47 Stat. 169, 275 (eff. 15 days after enactment) (originally to expire July 1, 1934, extended to July 1, 1935, by National Industrial Recovery Act, ch. 90, § 212, 48 Stat. 195, 206; July 1, 1937, by Joint Res. 74-36 of June 28, 1935, ch. 333, 49 Stat. 431; July 1, 1939, by Joint Res. 75-48 of June 29, 1937, ch. 402, 50 Stat. 358; July 1, 1941, by Revenue Act of 1939, ch. 247, § 1, 53 Stat. 862.
e. Revenue Act of 1926, ch. 27, § 800, 44 Stat. 9, 99 (conveyance tax omitted) (eff. 30 days after enactment).
f. Revenue Act of 1924, ch. 234, § 800, Schedule A(5), 43 Stat. 253, 331, 333, 335; Revenue Act of 1921, ch. 136, § 1100, Schedule A(6), 42 Stat. 227, 301, 303, 305; Revenue Act of 1918, ch. 18, § 1100, Schedule A(7), 40 Stat. 1057, 1133, 1135, 1137; War Revenue Act of 1917, ch. 63, § 800, Schedule A(7), 40 Stat. 300, 319, 321, 323.
g. Revenue Act of 1916, ch. 463, § 410, 39 Stat. 756, 792.
h. Act of Oct. 22, 1914 (Emergency Internal Revenue Tax Act), ch. 331, § 5, Schedule A, 38 Stat. 745, 753, 759, 762 (originally to expire Dec. 31, 1915, extended to Dec. 31, 1916, by Joint Res. 64-2 of Dec. 17, 1915, ch. 4, 39 Stat. 2).
i. Act of Apr. 12, 1902, ch. 500, § 7, 32 Stat. 96, 97.
j. Act of Mar. 2, 1901, ch. 806, §§ 5, 8, 31 Stat. 938, 940, 942, 946.
k. Act of June 13, 1898, ch. 448, § 6, Schedule A, 30 Stat. 448, 451, 458, 460.

Table 3.1 History of Real Estate Excise Taxes in North Carolina (*continued*)

October 1, 1872–June 30, 1898	None[l]
August 1, 1864–September 30, 1872	$0.50 for up to $500; $1.00 for over $500 up to $1,000; $0.50 for every additional $500 greater than $1,000 (federal)[m]
October 1, 1862–July 31, 1864 (effective March 3, 1863, tax not to exceed $1,000)	$0.50 for over $100 up to $500; $1.00 for over $500 up to $1,000; $2.00 for over $1,000 up to $2,500; $5.00 for over $2,500 up to $5,000; $10.00 for over $5,000 up to $10,000; $20.00 for over $10,000 up to $20,000; $20.00 for every additional $10,000 greater than $20,000 (federal)[n]

l. Act of June 6, 1872, ch. CCCXV (315), § 36, 17 Stat. 230, 256.
m. Act of June 30, 1864, ch. CLXXIII (173), § 151, 13 Stat. 223, 291, 299 (N.C. was in rebellion from the U.S. until July 4, 1868).
n. Act of July 1, 1862, ch. CXIX (119), § 94, Schedule B, 12 Stat. 432, 475, 479, 481–82; Act of Mar. 3, 1863, ch. LXXIV (74), § 6, 12 Stat. 713, 721 (N.C. was in rebellion from the U.S. until July 4, 1868).

of trust becomes inoperative when the obligation it secures is paid. The absence of a public record indicating that a deed of trust has been satisfied does not necessarily mean that the owner continues to have an unpaid loan obligation or that there is an enforceable lien on the property. Nevertheless, a registered deed of trust continues to be an apparent encumbrance on the property, thereby impairing the property's marketability, until some action releasing or canceling the deed of trust is also recorded.

In most cases a single deed of trust for a single parcel is given as security for a single loan, and that security is released when the loan has been paid, either after the completion of all scheduled payments or earlier, through refinancing or payoff upon a sale. However, the lender and borrower can agree to any other arrangement they deem sufficient. This can include multiple deeds of trust or other security instruments for a single loan, or a release of a deed of trust before the loan has been paid. The parties also can change the security arrangement whenever they agree to do so. For instance, some of the real estate subject to the deed of trust can be released while the security interest remains in place against the rest.

No one should simply assume that an instrument that includes the word "satisfaction" in the title means the loan has been paid or all of the real estate subject to a deed of trust has been released. Most satisfaction instruments state that the indebtedness has been fully paid and the entire real estate is released, but some state that the security is released but the indebtedness has not been paid, and others only partially release the real estate while remaining effective against the rest. These are concerns for the parties and title searchers and not for registers, except that registers should not make indexing entries that are plainly inconsistent with the clearly expressed nature of a satisfaction instrument. Thus, an instrument entitled "Partial Satisfaction" or "Partial Release" is best indexed as such or by some other means and not simply as a "Satisfaction," but a register likely should not index an instrument entitled "Satisfaction" as a "Partial Satisfaction" or "Partial Release" based on the register's presumption of what is intended.

Ordinarily, the secured party lender or the trustee attends to making a record of satisfaction by submitting routine documents that can be processed without special attention. Occasionally, however, this normally routine procedure develops hitches and questions can arise. The following sections review the different ways that records of satisfaction can be made for security instruments, which include deeds of trust and mortgages, and discuss possible problems and questions related to this process.

3.2.7.2 Historic Methods of Satisfaction

Over the years, the methods for making a record of satisfaction have changed substantially. In the early years, the sole method for recording evidence that a deed of trust was no longer effective was the use of a deed of release in which the trustee released, or quitclaimed, his or her interest in the secured property to the grantor in the deed of trust.[121] In 1871, the legislature provided for cancellation through a marginal entry on the recorded deed of trust made by the mortgagee or trustee or his or her legal representative, attorney, or agent, which was intended to have the same legal effect as the recording of a deed of release.[122] In 1891, the General Assembly provided for cancellation by the register upon presentation of

121. Richard R. Powell, Real Property 672–73 (Patrick J. Rohan ed., 1975).
122. 1870–71 N.C. Pub. Laws ch. 217.

the note and deed of trust marked paid by the proper parties.[123] In 1917, it added banks to the list of parties that could mark instruments paid and satisfied[124] and also added a special provision for canceling instruments more than ten years old.[125] In 1923, new legislation added a provision creating a presumption of payment fifteen years after the maturity date of the instrument,[126] and in 1935, further legislation added a special provision dealing with obligations made payable to "bearers" without specifying the payee by name and with lost or stolen instruments.[127] In 1987, the General Assembly provided for cancellation by recording a notice of satisfaction executed by the trustee in a deed of trust.[128] In 1995, it provided for cancellation by recording a certificate of satisfaction executed by the note holder.[129]

In 2005, the General Assembly eliminated the process of acknowledgment before the register.[130] In that same year, the statutes were amended to give examples of simplified forms of satisfaction to be generated and recorded by secured parties and trustees. New suggested forms were added in 2011 for showing only a partial release[131] and in 2012 for using the satisfaction to show both the termination of the security interest and the payment of the indebtedness.[132]

Until 2011, a process called *satisfaction by presentation* required registers to review original security instruments and the original instruments they secure for endorsements and other information and, if the presented documents were in order, to make a record of satisfaction for the secured creditor or trustee. The register made a record of satisfaction by rerecording portions of the original instruments that contained the essential information about the original instruments and the satisfaction of the obligations, including pages that showed identification of the security instrument, the original parties to the security instrument, the recording data for the secu-

123. 1891 N.C. Pub. Laws ch. 180.
124. 1917 N.C. Pub. Laws ch. 49.
125. 1917 N.C. Pub. Laws ch. 50.
126. 1923 N.C. Pub. Laws ch. 192.
127. 1935 N.C. Pub. Laws ch. 47.
128. 1987 N.C. Sess. Laws ch. 405.
129. 1995 N.C. Sess. Laws ch. 292.
130. S.L. 2005-123
131. S.L. 2011-312, § 9.
132. S.L. 2012-150

rity instrument as originally recorded, and endorsement of payment. Or the register could make a record of satisfaction with a separate record showing information about the security instrument, language terminating the effectiveness of the security instrument, and the register's signature. When use of this process was terminated,[133] it was still being seen in only a small percentage of satisfaction recordings, frequently for instruments that involved complications in the nature of the security that could not be confirmed as fully satisfied or that entailed other circumstances that are better handled by the parties' attorneys with instruments that they can prepare and record. The methods no longer available included presentation by secured creditors or trustees of original security instruments and notes endorsed by the creditors or trustees; presentation by grantors, mortgagors, or their attorneys or agents of original security instruments and the instruments they secure if the maturity date is more than ten years old; and presentation by bearers or holders of original negotiable instruments and the instruments they secure, signed and marked paid, provided no prior notice was given of a loss or theft of the instruments. The 2011 legislation also ended register responsibility for actions in connection with a notice of loss or theft of a bearer or holder negotiable instrument, a procedure that arose very rarely for many years. The parties are responsible for taking whatever action they deem appropriate in connection with such a circumstance, including the recording of any appropriate instruments.

3.2.7.3 Common Forms of Satisfaction Instruments

Secured creditors must submit a satisfaction record within thirty days after full payment of the secured obligation.[134] The statutes provide several forms for use as satisfaction instruments. They all have some basic information in common: a reference to a security instrument already on record and the parties to it; a statement that the security instrument is satisfied, discharged, or otherwise terminated in whole or in part; a signature in behalf of a secured party or trustee; and an acknowledgment of that signature. Any document that contains this information will be sufficient as a satisfaction instrument; it need not be in any particular form or have any particular title. For example, lenders in other states may submit satisfaction

133. S.L. 2011-246.
134. G.S. 45-36.9(a).

instruments that are in forms common in those states, such as a document entitled "Mortgage Discharge" or "Release of Deed of Trust."

The two most common forms in current use are the statutory forms for *satisfaction of security instrument* and *trustee's satisfaction*. The responsibility for preparing a proper form lies with the secured party or trustee, not the register. The statute requires these parties to identify the type of security instrument the document is, the parties to the original instrument, the original instrument's recording data, and the office in which it was recorded. The satisfaction document also must indicate that the person signing is the secured creditor (or the trustee for a trustee's satisfaction), and it must contain language terminating the effectiveness of the security instrument to which it relates. It must be signed by the secured creditor (in the case of a satisfaction of security instrument) or a trustee (in the case of a trustee's satisfaction) and must be acknowledged.[135] A third type of statutory form, a form of *partial release*, may be provided by a secured creditor or trustee to indicate a satisfaction that releases some but not all of the property.[136] The statutes say that "[n]o particular phrasing is required" for a satisfaction of a security instrument, a trustee's satisfaction of a deed of trust, or a partial release, but they provide forms including the minimum information for the record to be deemed sufficient.[137]

Some presenters still use other forms that were commonly used for many years. A *notice of satisfaction* can be used if signed by the trustee, mortgagee, or other secured creditor and acknowledged.[138] An owner of a note secured by a deed of trust may use a *certificate of satisfaction* to make a record of satisfaction. The certificate must be signed by the note owner or secured creditor and be acknowledged.[139] As described in Section 3.2.7.5 of this book, *deeds of release* also are used, particularly when only a part of the real estate is being released from the security instrument, and they have the same legal effect as a satisfaction but are subject to a recording fee.

Table 3.2 shows the various common forms in use.

---

135. G.S. 45-36.10, .11, .20, .21.
136. G.S. 45-36.22.
137. G.S. 45-36.11(a), .21(a), .22(g).
138. G.S. 47-46.1.
139. G.S. 47-46.2.

Table 3.2 Standard Satisfaction Forms

Type of Instrument	Signatory
Satisfaction of security instrument (no fee) (G.S. 45-36.11)	Secured creditor
Trustee's satisfaction of deed of trust (no fee) (G.S. 45-36.21)	Trustee (secured creditor may also sign that obligation is extinguished)
Notice of satisfaction (no fee) (G.S. 47-46.1)	Secured creditor or trustee
Certificate of satisfaction (no fee) (G.S. 47-46.2)	Owner of note or secured creditor
Affidavit of satisfaction (no fee) (G.S. 45-36.17)	N.C. attorney satisfaction agent
Partial release (fee applies) (G.S. 45-36.22)	Secured creditor or trustee
Deed of release (fee applies) (G.S. 45-41)	Party holding interest

3.2.7.4 Affidavits of Satisfaction

Secured creditors are required by law to submit a satisfaction document for recording or to arrange for a recorded satisfaction by other authorized means within thirty days of full payment or performance of the secured obligation.[140] If the secured creditor fails to provide a satisfaction as required, an attorney licensed to practice law in North Carolina, acting as "satisfaction agent," may record an "affidavit of satisfaction" after completing the steps required by statute.[141]

The borrower's attorney's affidavit of satisfaction must contain information prescribed by statute about the security instrument and about having completed the procedure for demanding a satisfaction instrument from the secured creditor or about the procedure not being necessary under the circumstances, and it must be signed by the borrower's attorney as satisfaction agent and acknowledged or sworn to or affirmed.[142] The regis-

140. G.S. 45-36.9(a).
141. G.S. 45-36.15.
142. G.S. 45-36.13, -36.16.

ter is not responsible for reviewing the affidavit to ensure that it contains the required information. The statute provides that a register may not refuse to accept an affidavit of satisfaction "substantially complying" with the requirements unless it "is submitted by a method or in a medium not authorized for registration by the register of deeds under applicable law" or it is not signed by the satisfaction agent and acknowledged as required by law for a real estate conveyance.[143] The statute expressly states that a register is not "required to verify or make inquiry concerning" "the truth of the matters stated" in the affidavit or "the authority of the person executing" it.[144] An instrument purporting to be an affidavit of satisfaction that is not apparently signed by the borrower's attorney cannot be registered. The register must verify that the instrument is signed by the satisfaction agent, and only the borrower's attorney can be a satisfaction agent. No fee is charged for recording an affidavit of satisfaction as defined in the statute.[145]

3.2.7.5 Deeds of Release

A record that a security instrument has been terminated also may be accomplished by recording a deed of release.[146] To be recorded, a deed of release must be acknowledged in the same manner and is subject to the same register verification and recording fee requirements as any other deed.

As mentioned previously, sometimes a lender wants to release a security instrument from particular real estate even though the underlying obligation has not been paid in full. This occurs, for example, when a deed of trust or mortgage applies to several lots and the lender is releasing only one lot in connection with a partial payment of the obligation secured by the deed of trust. A form of satisfaction called a *partial release* may be used.[147] Practitioners customarily use partial release deeds for this purpose.

Occasionally, an instrument's contents do not clearly reflect whether it is intended to be a satisfaction instrument as that term is used in the statutes or a deed of release. A register may reasonably rely on the title of an instrument submitted for registration unless the register sees that the instrument obviously is misnamed. For example, an instrument entitled

---

143. G.S. 45-36.18(c).
144. G.S. 45-36.18(c)(2).
145. G.S. 45-37.2(b).
146. G.S. 45-41.
147. G.S. 45-36.22.

"satisfaction" can properly be recharacterized as a deed of release if the register notices that the instrument contains granting language; that is, the trustee's or mortgagee's representative grants or conveys the premises back to the grantor or mortgagor. It is not the register's responsibility, however, to review the contents of instruments to ensure that the drafters have not inappropriately characterized the instruments.

3.2.7.6 Documents of Rescission

The statutes authorize anyone who erroneously records a satisfaction instrument to record a document of rescission that identifies the erroneous satisfaction or affidavit and states that the error has been made, that the secured obligation remains unsatisfied, and that the security instrument remains in force.[148] Such statements are required to be acknowledged and therefore must be verified.[149] A statute provides sample forms.[150] The document of rescission does not affect the rights of those who acquired a real estate interest between the time the satisfaction or affidavit and the document of rescission were recorded, and the law subjects anyone who erroneously or wrongfully records such an instrument to liability for actual losses, attorneys' fees, and costs.[151]

3.2.7.7 Register Verification and Registration

A register does not accept a document that states it is intended to be a satisfaction instrument unless it has been signed by a party with apparent authority to make such a record, which will be a beneficiary or other secured party or a trustee of a deed of trust. This signature must be acknowledged. This signature component—verifying that the appropriate authorized party appears to have executed the satisfaction record—is an added check that does not apply to deeds and deeds of trust. The statutes require that the register see enough information to determine that the instrument is signed by the appropriate party, the secured creditor or trustee. The instrument is registered if this can be determined from the instrument contents, as would occur, for example, with a phrase such as "the undersigned is now the secured creditor." In that case the signature

148. G.S. 45-36.6.
149. G.S. 45-36.6(f).
150. G.S. 45-36.6(g), (h).
151. G.S. 45-36.6(c), (d).

line need not contain additional information about the signatory's capacity, such as the individual's title.

The register is not required to verify or make inquiry concerning the truth of the matters stated in any satisfaction document or the authority of the person executing the document. The register also does not verify that names are printed, stamped, or typed beneath signatures. The statutes do not authorize registers to reject documents based on the absence of this information.

No fee may be charged by the register for recording a satisfaction instrument.[152]

3.2.8 Plats

A *plat* generally refers to a type of map showing a subdivision of a tract of land into two or more parts. The term *map* is commonly used to refer to any depiction of a part of the earth's surface. The word *plan* also is used to refer to drawings of real estate parcels and improvements made to them. Often these terms are used interchangeably.

Plats are a part of the records in the register's office related to real estate, but special statutory rules govern their recording. Because of the size of most plats, special procedures and equipment are necessary for maintaining the record copies. Plats may be presented to the register for registration in one of two forms: either freestanding or attached to a deed or other instrument. Different registration rules apply to each form. The register must ask two questions when determining whether a plat may be accepted for registration:

1. Does the plat comply with statutory requirements regarding size and material?
2. Does it require review officer or surveyor certification as a condition to registration?

3.2.8.1 Permissible Plat Size and Material

Plats that are submitted in nonelectronic form are subject to dimensional and material requirements. For such plats, counties may choose among the following required dimensions for freestanding plats: 18 by 24 inches only; a combination of 18 by 24 inches and 21 by 30 inches; a combination of

---

152. G.S. 45-37.2(a).

18 by 24 inches and 24 by 36 inches; or a combination of all three sizes.[153] If a county allows something other than all three sizes, the register must submit the specifications to the North Carolina Association of Registers of Deeds for inclusion on a master list made available to the public.[154] Freestanding plats must have at least a 1½ inch border on the left side in landscape format and on the top side for portrait format, and at least a ½ inch border on the other three sides. Some plats are subject to special requirements, as described in Section 3.2.8.3 of this chapter.[155]

Plats or maps attached to deeds or other instruments must be no larger than 8½ by 14 inches.[156]

The statutes provide that "[e]ach plat presented for recording shall be a reproducible plat, either original ink on polyester film (mylar), or a reproduced drawing, transparent and archival (as defined by the American National Standards Institute)."[157] Plats are thus subject to a reproducibility requirement that is not imposed by statute on other kinds of recorded documents. By enforcing the requirement that plats be drawn in original ink on mylar or be reproductions made on "transparent and archival" material, the register ensures the creation of a permanent and readable record. The statutes also provide, however, as follows: "In those counties in which the register has made a security copy of the plat from which legible copies can be made, the original plat may be submitted in the form of black line on white paper instead of transparent and archival and may be returned to the person indicated on the plat."[158] Accordingly, a register may choose to accept plats on paper as long as they are reproducible.

Registers may choose to accept plats electronically. Only submitters whom the register has approved may do so, and the register may specify the format of the submitted file that will result in a record compatible with the register's plat recording system. The submitter must either be a United States federal or a state governmental unit or instrumentality or a trusted submitter who has entered into a memorandum of understanding regarding electronic recording with the register in the county in which

153. G.S. 47-30(a).
154. *Id.*
155. *Id*
156. G.S. 47-30(n)(1).
157. G.S. 47-30(b).
158. *Id.*

the electronic document is to be submitted.[159] The required certifications must appear on the digitized image on the public record.[160] Plats submitted by trusted submitters must contain the submitter's name in the following completed statement on the first page of the document image:

> Submitted electronically by __________ (submitter's name) in compliance with North Carolina statutes governing recordable documents and the terms of the submitter agreement with the __________ (insert county name) County Register of Deeds.[161]

3.2.8.2 Certification Requirements and Exceptions

The statutes require county boards of commissioners to designate one or more review officers to review plats for compliance with all statutory requirements before the plats are registered. The commissioners' resolution appointing the review officer is to be recorded with the register and indexed with the review officer's name as a grantor.[162] The statutes also specify the types of plats that may be registered without the review officer's certification.[163] The review officer certifies the plat in substantially the following form after determining it is legally sufficient and may be recorded:[164]

> State of North Carolina
>
> County of ________________
>
> I, ________________, Review Officer of ________________ County, certify that the map or plat to which this certification is affixed meets all statutory requirements for recording.
>
> ________________ ________________
>
> Date Review Officer

The register is prohibited from recording a nonexempt plat unless it contains this certification by a review officer.[165] A register who notices a problem with statutory compliance may bring it to the review officer's attention but may not overrule the review officer.

---

159. G.S. 47-30(o).
160. G.S. 47-30(o)(3).
161. G.S. 47-30(o)(4).
162. G.S. 47-30.2(a).
163. G.S. 47-30.2.
164. G.S. 47-30.2(b).
165. *Id.*

Each plat presented for registration must include a certificate made by a surveyor about the survey's preparation. The review officer verifies the presence of this certificate, which must be substantially in the following form:

> I, _________________, certify that this plat was drawn under my supervision from an actual survey made under my supervision (deed description recorded in Book _______, page _______, etc.) (other); that the boundaries not surveyed are clearly indicated as drawn from information bound in Book _______, page _______; that the ratio of precision as calculated is 1: _______; that this plat was prepared in accordance with G.S. 47-30 as amended.
>
> Witness my original signature, registration number and seal this _______ day of _______, A.D., _______.
>
> Seal or Stamp _________________
>
> Surveyor
>
> Registration Number[166]

There are only three exceptions to this certificate requirement. First, some plats have special requirements, as described in Section 3.2.8.3 of this chapter. Second, a plat is acceptable even though it does not comply with the current surveyor certificate requirement if, when it was signed, it complied with the statutory certificate requirement then in effect.[167] The presenter is responsible for proving that the plat was so prepared.[168] The third exception applies to a plat prepared by a registered land surveyor but not registered before the surveyor's death. Such a survey may be filed "for preservation" provided that the review officer first certifies that the plat qualifies for this exception.[169] The statute does not explain the significance of recording *for preservation*, but a reasonable interpretation is that the plat should be filed by some method that indicates to those examining it that it was filed for such a purpose separately from plats ordinarily registered.

The following types of plats may be registered without review by the review officer and without a surveyor certificate:

- maps of municipal boundaries and annexations [G.S. 47-30(j)];
- highway right-of-way plans [G.S. 47-30(l)];

166. G.S. 47-30(d).
167. *Id.*
168. *Id.*
169. G.S. 47-30(h).

- transportation corridor official maps [G.S. 47-30(l)]; and
- condominium plans [G.S. 47C-2-109(a)].

If a plat shows a created subdivision that is subject to land use regulations, which means it is subject to review officer certification of compliance, the surveyor must indicate that on the plat.[170] The following types of plats are exempt from review officer examination and may be recorded without a review officer's certification, but they must include a certificate signed by a surveyor stating that the survey is one of the types exempted:[171]

- a survey located in a portion of a county or municipality unregulated as to an ordinance that regulates parcels of land [G.S. 47-30(f)(11)(b)];
- a survey of an existing parcel or parcels of land or easements that does not create a new street or change an existing street [G.S. 47-30(f)(11)(c)(1)];
- a survey of an existing feature, such as a building or other structure, or natural feature such as a watercourse [G.S. 47-30(f)(11)(c)(2)];
- a control survey [G.S. 47-30(f)(11)(c)(3)]; and
- a proposed easement for a public utility [G.S. 47-30(f)(11)(c)(4)].

The following types of plats are exempt from review officer examination, but the review officer must first certify that the plat meets the exception before it is recorded:[172]

- A category with a specific statutory exception, such as a court-ordered survey; recombination of existing parcels if the total number of lots is not increased and the resultant lots meet or exceed subdivision standards; division in which the resultant lots are greater than ten acres and no street dedication is involved; government acquisition of strips for road widening or opening streets or for public transportation system corridors; or division of a tract no greater than two acres into not more than three lots, if no street right of way dedication is involved and if the resultant lots are equal to or exceed the subdivision standards. [G.S. 47-30(f)(11)(d); G.S. 153A-335; G.S. 160A-376]

---

170. G.S. 47-30(f)(11)(a).
171. G.S. 47-30.2(c).
172. *Id.*

- Information available to the surveyor is such that the surveyor is unable to make a determination to the best of the surveyor's professional ability whether the listed conditions regarding review officer apply [G.S. 47-30(f)(11)(e)]

Finally, the review officer's certification is not required for plats or maps attached for illustration purposes only to deeds or other instruments. These maps and plats must be no larger than 8½ by 14 inches. Three kinds of such attachments are allowed. One is a map that contains the language specified by G.S. 47-30(n), which is as follows:

> THIS MAP MAY NOT BE A CERTIFIED SURVEY AND HAS NOT BEEN REVIEWED BY A LOCAL GOVERNMENT AGENCY FOR COMPLIANCE WITH ANY APPLICABLE LAND DEVELOPMENT REGULATIONS AND HAS NOT BEEN REVIEWED FOR COMPLIANCE WITH RECORDING REQUIREMENTS FOR PLATS.[173]

This notice makes clear that the submitter is using the map only as an illustration of a text description in the instrument and is not intending to show any subdivision or other regulated change in boundaries. The other two kinds of permitted plat attachments are allowed by G.S. 47i-30(m), specifically a plat with the original signature and seal of a registered land surveyor, or a certified copy of a plat with such a signature and seal. These two kinds of plats must comply with the same review officer requirements as apply to freestanding plats.[174] An attached map is presented for recording pursuant to G.S. 47-30(m) or G.S. 47-30(n), and it is recorded as part of the instrument to which it is attached and not in the plat files or books.

Figure 3.2 illustrates the review officer plan presentation requirements.

---

173. *Id.*; G.S. 47-30(n).

174. G.S. 47-30(m). The statute is not clear about whether a plat that qualifies under G.S. 47-30(m) is exempt from review officer certification if it has a surveyor's certificate complying with G.S. 47-30(f)(11)(b) or (c). G.S. 47-30.2(c) does not include subsection (m) plats in its list of exceptions for review officer presentation, and the (m) certificate is a statutory requirement for any attached plat that does not have the (n) legend. Consequently, a register may presumably require any plat submitted under (m) to be presented to the review officer, at least for confirmation of compliance with (m).

Figure 3.2 Plan Presentation Requirements

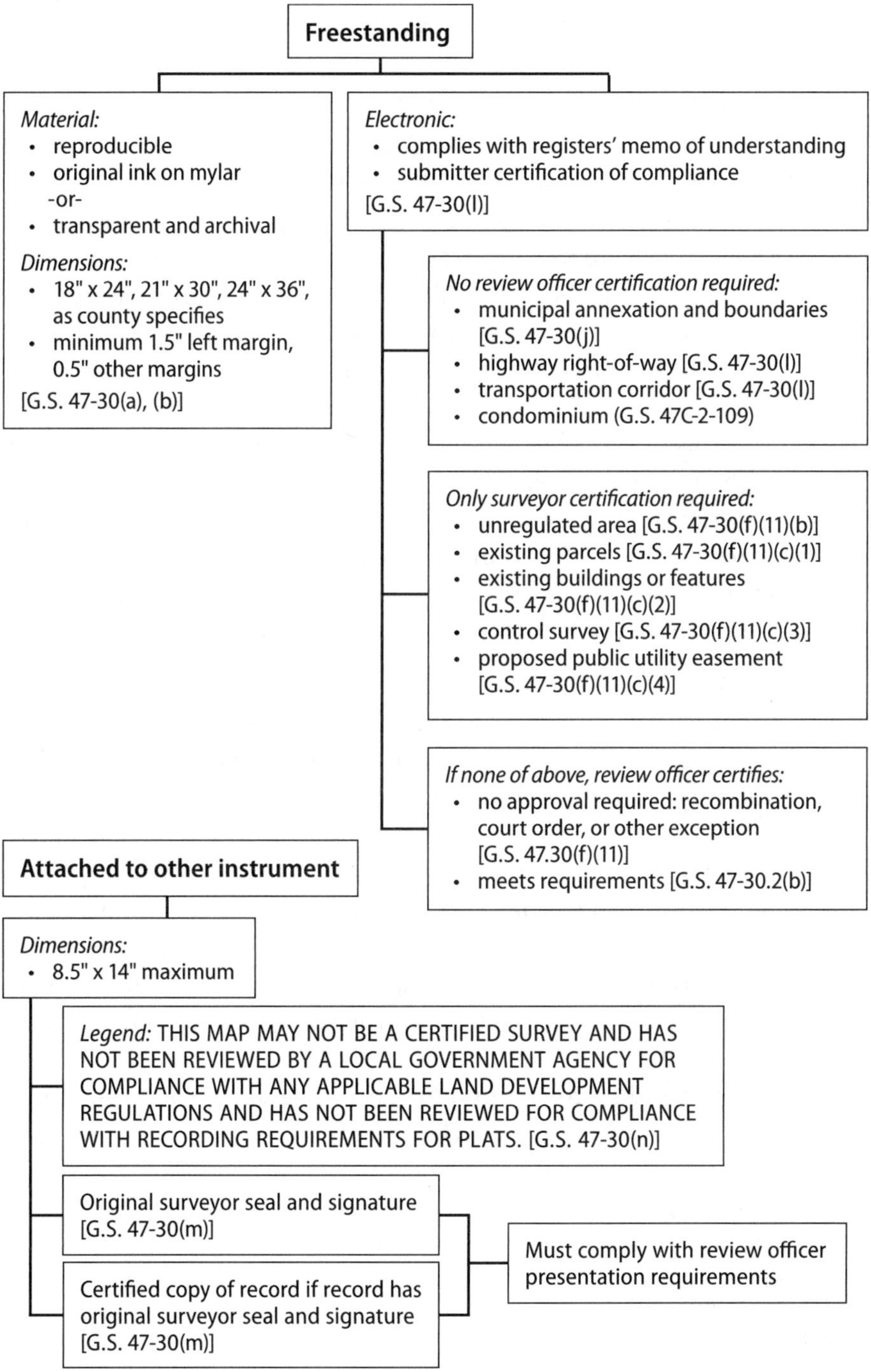

3.2.8.3 Plats Requiring Special Treatment

The four categories of plats discussed in the following sections need not meet the registration requirements discussed in the preceding section. They have their own special requirements.

3.2.8.3.1 HIGHWAY RIGHT-OF-WAY PLANS

The statutes allow plans showing highway right-of-way projects to be recorded in a special file with the register if the Department of Transportation (DOT) certifies a copy of the cover sheet, plan, and profile sheets. The certified copies are to be approximately 17 by 11 inches and are to be recorded in a special book for this purpose. These plans may be filed electronically if the register agrees to accept plans in that medium.[175] The fee is $21 for the first page of each original or amended plan and for each profile sheet recorded and $5 for each additional page.[176] These plans are exempt from the usual plat requirements and from certification by a review officer.[177] There is no requirement for a signature.[178]

Highway right-of-way plans are subject to an unusual provision in the statute allowing the DOT to remove plans from the file when an altered or amended plan is presented to the register.[179] In essence, the right-of-way file is a place for the DOT to make current plans available to the public.

3.2.8.3.2 CONDOMINIUM PLANS

Condominium plans differ in three respects from the typical plat that a register receives for recording. Any particular condominium project will always have several sheets of plans; most of the plans will be of a building or buildings rather than of a land area; and the plans will have been prepared by an architect or engineer, not a registered land surveyor. Although condominium plans are not expressly exempted from the requirements for certification by a review officer, they appear to be exempt and are instead reviewed as part of the local land-use approval of condominium developments and associated requirements for the recording of condominium-related documents.

The fee for recording condominium plans is the same as for plats, and a separate fee is to be charged for each sheet.[180]

---

175. G.S. 136-19.4(c).
176. G.S. 161-10(a)(4).
177. G.S. 47-30(l), -30.2(c).
178. G.S. 136-19.4(c).
179. G.S. 136-19.4(d).
180. G.S. 47C-2-109(f).

3.2.8.3.3 ANNEXATION MAPS

When a municipality extends its corporate limits to annex new territory, a map of the annexed area is required to be recorded in the register's office.[181] These maps do not have to meet any particular requirements, they do not have to be prepared by a registered land surveyor, and they do not have to meet any size requirements. In many cases, the map is a part of the annexation ordinance and will be recorded as part of the ordinance in the real property records. In other cases, the map will meet the county's size requirements for freestanding maps and can be recorded with other maps and plats. Annexation maps are exempt from the requirement of certification by a review officer.[182]

3.2.9 Farmland District Notices

By statute all counties must enable the owner of certain kinds of poultry, swine, or dairy farms to record a notice of the farm's presence.[183] The statute does not specify the nature of the notice to be given. Presumably the county or a landowner directed by a county may record a notice with the register that includes the statutorily required information. The notice should be indexed in a manner similar to other notices concerning real estate.

3.2.10 False Lien Claims and Documents Purporting to Be Records of Birth or Marriage

Registers are public officials who take oaths to maintain the laws of North Carolina. A register may justifiably be concerned about placing on the public record an instrument that is presented for the obvious sole purpose of harassment, fraud, or commission of a crime, or an instrument that appears to have no conceivable legitimate purpose for being in the public real estate records.[184] For example, some wrongdoers file a "nonconsensual lien" against a targeted public official that claims a security interest unless the target responds within a given time, but the official knows nothing about the claim. Although the frivolous nature of these kinds of instru-

181. G.S. 160A-29.

182. G.S. 47-30(j), -30.2(c).

183. G.S. 106-741(a).

184. For an extensive discussion of frivolous liens and the potential methods for combatting them, see Emily Roscoe and Charles Szypszak, *Privacy and Public Real Estate Records: Preserving Legacy System Reliability Against Modern Threats*, 49 Urb. Law. 355 (2017).

ments may be obvious, they still could cause delay or complication while the circumstances are investigated and costs to the target if judicial relief must be sought. Someone who files a fraudulent or frivolous instrument may be prosecuted for a criminal act, such as common law fraud or the statutory felony of filing a false lien or encumbrance.[185] Someone harmed may have a civil remedy, such as for fraud as well as for slander of title.[186]

A statute authorizes registers to reject instruments that seem to be falsely claiming a lien against an owner or beneficial interest holder, and the law requires certain actions if this occurs or if a court declares a lien to be false.[187] The statute provides that "if a register of deeds has a reasonable suspicion that the lien or encumbrance is false, fictitious, or fraudulent . . . , the register of deeds may refuse to record the lien or encumbrance" and that the register will not "be liable for recording or the refusal to record a lien or encumbrance" according to this law.[188] Note that this law is permissive and not mandatory—it does not impose a duty on registers to review documents claiming liens or encumbrances and judge whether they appear to be valid. This legislation is aimed at documents that claim a lien against public officials when the presenters obviously had no financial transaction involving the officials. According to the Federal Bureau of Investigation, such tactics may be indicated by "documents that contain peculiar or out-of-place language," including "references to the Bible, The Constitution of the United States, U.S. Supreme Court decisions, or treaties with foreign governments, personal names spelled in all capital letters or interspersed with colons (e.g., JOHN SMITH or Smith: John), signatures followed by the words 'under duress,' 'Sovereign Living Soul' (SLS), or a copyright symbol (©), personal seals, stamps, or thumb prints in red ink, [and] the words 'accepted for value.'"[189] There have been prosecutions and convictions against those using lien claims as a tactic to intimidate and harass officials.

---

185. G.S. 14-118.6(a); G.S. 44A-12.1.

186. Allen v. Duvall, 63 N.C. App. 342, 345, 304 S.E.2d 789, 791 (1983), *rev'd on other grounds*, 311 N.C. 245, 316 S.E.2d 267 (1984).

187. G.S. 14-118.6.

188. G.S. 14-118.6(b).

189. Federal Bureau of Investigation (FBI) Counterterrorism Analysis Section, *Sovereign Citizens: A Growing Domestic Threat to Law Enforcement*, L. Enforcement Bull. (Sept. 1, 2011), https://leb.fbi.gov/articles/featured-articles/sovereign-citizens-a-growing-domestic-threat-to-law-enforcement.

If a register refuses to record an instrument based on this law, the presenter may record a "Notice of Denied Lien or Encumbrance Filing" on a form that the North Carolina Secretary of State has approved. A recording fee is not necessary for this notice. Any interested person, including the presenter, then has ten business days to file a court action to challenge the rejection. If the court determines that the document was recordable, the order can be filed with the register. If the court finds that there is no basis for the proposed filing, the court will order that the proposed filing is void and that it will not be recorded, a copy of the order is filed with the register, and the party who submitted the instrument must pay the recording fee for this order. If a register receives a court order declaring that a filed lien or encumbrance is false, and therefore void, in addition to filing the order the register is required to conspicuously mark on the first page of the original record previously filed the following statement: "THE CLAIM ASSERTED IN THIS DOCUMENT IS FALSE AND IS NOT PROVIDED FOR BY THE GENERAL LAWS OF THIS STATE."[190]

Owners who are aware of the potential for frivolous liens can lessen their risk of problems with a conveyance or mortgage finance if they periodically check the registry for something unexpectedly indexed in their names. An owner who finds out about a fraudulent filing can report it to law enforcement and at least begin to address it with court action if necessary. Most owners are probably not alert to the possibility of such a filing, nor will they take such steps to check. Owners naturally may be surprised that someone can even file a false lien claim with the register and that the owner would not normally receive notice of its filing.

One method for enabling an owner to be alerted to a potentially frivolous filing is a program by which someone may enroll a name and email address with the register's system to receive an email message when an instrument is recorded that is indexed with the enrolled name. The register's recording and indexing vendor may be able to provide this service. Of course its usefulness depends on the currency of the information provided by someone who wants to receive the notice, as well as the recipient's actions upon receiving such a notice.

Discovery of a frivolous lien should not automatically cause harm to the subject of the filing. Although lenders may have a contractual right to refuse to close before the lien can be resolved, lenders exercising good

190. G.S. 14-118.6(c).

judgment and fair dealing should not give a fraudulent document more weight than it deserves. Responsible lenders who seek to have relationships of trust with their borrowers should be interested in working to close loans despite an apparently frivolous lien claim, including with borrowers who are most likely to be a target—law enforcement, judicial officers, and other public officials. A lender's decision about making a loan to someone upon detection of an apparently frivolous lien should include the same considerations that apply to anyone else—the borrower's ability to repay the secured loan and rights in the property based on market value and non-frivolous matters in the title.

If someone presents a document for recording in the real estate records that is unattached to a real estate document, purports "to impact an official record of birth," and is not a record filed within the state's official system, G.S. 161-14.02 directs the register to mark the first page of that purported birth record as follows: "THIS DOCUMENT IS NOT AN OFFICIAL BIRTH RECORD." If someone presents a document for recording that "(i) purports to impact an official record of marriage meeting the requirements of G.S. 51-16 and (ii) is not a marriage license, a return, or an amendment or correction of a marriage license," G.S. 161-14.03 directs the register to conspicuously mark the first page with "THIS DOCUMENT IS NOT AN OFFICIAL MARRIAGE DOCUMENT." This marriage annotation does not apply to attachments to land records, orders, or judgments issued by a court, or to separation agreements presented for registration.

3.3 Internet Record Redaction

Document preparers sometimes include personal identification information on documents without considering that this information will become a permanent part of the public record. The subject of the information may not be alert to this disclosure when the instrument is recorded and may later regret its appearance. Unfortunately for such individuals, once something has become part of the public record there is no assurance that it has not been disseminated beyond the registers' office—for example, by authorized copying or duplication. They may also be unaware that a register may not simply remove information from a public record. The risks of improper use of this information are exacerbated when the record in which it is contained is available on the register's public Internet website.

A register who sees such information on a presented record may bring this to the presenter's attention. But a register is not authorized to refuse to record an instrument because it contains such information. The statute expressly provides that certain prohibitions against making personal identification information available to the general public do not apply to registers of deeds.[191] If a document that is registered causes unlawful harm, a court may issue an order that declares the document void or otherwise addresses its legal effect, and that order when recorded is linked to the original harmful record with the subsequent instrument indexing method.

The statutes authorize removal of information from a registered real estate record on a website: that is, redaction of personal identification numbers from Internet records.[192] Individuals may request redaction of their Social Security, taxpayer identification, driver's license, state identification, passport, checking account, savings account, credit card, or debit card number or personal identification code or password contained in the public records displayed on the register's Internet website available to the general public. Redaction applies only to the identified personal information—not the entire record—and only to records on the Internet website. A request should be legibly signed by the person to whom the information belongs or by someone with demonstrated legal authority for such a person, such as someone with an applicable power of attorney, and it may be submitted in person or by mail, facsimile, or electronic transmission. It must specify the relevant document and the nature and location within the document of the information to be redacted. Access to inspection of the requests for redaction is restricted to the register of deeds, the clerk of court, their staff members, or to another party by court order.

Registers are authorized but not required to redact such personal identification information from the Internet website without a request.[193] Also, registers should keep in mind that two separate records exist after redaction: the unredacted original record within the office and the Internet record from which information was redacted. Both of these are public records and must be managed as such.

---

191. G.S. 132-1.10(c)(6).
192. G.S. 132-1.10(f).
193. G.S. 132-1.10(f1).

Registers must conspicuously post signs for public viewing stating prescribed information about the redaction right and the procedure for requesting the redaction, as described in Section 132-1.10(g) of the North Carolina General Statutes. A substantially similar notice must be posted on any Internet website containing the records and available to the general public.[194]

3.4 Uniform Commercial Code Filings

Some types of property related to real estate, such as fixtures, can have characteristics that implicate both real estate registration law and the law governing personal property, chiefly the Uniform Commercial Code (UCC). Often this property becomes subject to a deed of trust without need for a separate security instrument, and deeds of trust commonly are written to capture such property. Lenders may use a form of security instrument designed to address UCC requirements that also can be recorded with the register, such as the UCC-1 Financing Statement. Although the register of deeds is the appropriate office for the filing of certain UCC records pertaining to real property interests, the UCC filing system is fundamentally different than the real estate instrument recording system, and there are different filing requirements.

3.4.1 Notice Filing System

With real estate instruments, such as deeds and deeds of trust, a drafter and presenter must be complete and accurate in describing the interest being conveyed to give the constructive notice and associated priority in the race-recording system. By statute, the UCC system does not require the same type of completeness as other real estate instruments recorded with the register. The UCC is a "notice"-recording system, which requires, in essence, that a creditor record sufficient information to alert a purchaser or other potential creditor to inquire further about the nature of a secured financing agreement pertaining to the identified real estate.

---

194. G.S. 132-1.10(g).

Most UCC filings with a register of deeds are made to give notice of a security interest in a fixture. A *fixture* is a movable thing that will be attached to and become part of real estate, such as windows, built-in heating and air-conditioning systems, and permanently installed shelves and appliances. These types of movable property at one point may be considered personal property and subject to personal property security interest rules while unattached to real estate. The UCC aims to give the creditor a security interest aligned with the deed of trust rules when the fixture becomes part of the real estate. In most cases that protection can be achieved with the deed of trust, but creditors may gain additional protection by recording a UCC financing statement. The fixture filing rules also apply to as-extracted collateral or timber to be cut.[195]

By recording an instrument that complies with the UCC, the creditor gives public notice that there is a security interest in the described collateral. The UCC requires minimal information to give this notice. Unlike a deed or deed of trust, the borrower is not even required to sign a UCC financing statement. The statement triggers an obligation to make further inquiry to learn the complete state of affairs about the secured financing and the exact nature of the covered property. Those details will be in a security agreement that is not required to be recorded.

3.4.2 Registration

A deed of trust or mortgage can function as a UCC financing statement if it describes the covered goods and indicates they are or are to become fixtures related to the real estate described in the deed of trust or mortgage.[196] In that case the register records the deed of trust or mortgage the same way as any other deed of trust or mortgage, and the termination of the security interest is accomplished with a satisfaction of the deed of trust or mortgage. Creditors may also meet the UCC recording requirements by filing a separate financing statement. When filing a separate UCC record most creditors use a form that is in the statutes known as a "UCC-1,"[197] and to amend a prior recording they use a "UCC-3."[198] Termination of a security interest shown on a financing statement can be accomplished with

195. G.S. 25-9-501(a).
196. G.S. 25-9-502(c).
197. G.S. 25-9-521(a).
198. G.S. 25-9-521(b).

a termination statement, usually shown on a UCC-3. But the statutes are explicit that these particular statutory forms are not required; a creditor may use another format provided the minimum information is included.[199] The grounds on which a register may refuse to record a UCC filing are specified by statute,[200] as are the actions a register must take if such a filing is refused.[201] The grounds are as follows:

- The record is presented without the filing fee.[202]
- The record is presented by an unauthorized method, such as an electronic filing with a register that has not authorized electronic filing.[203]
- The record is an initial financing statement or amendment adding a secured party but does not provide the secured party's name and mailing address.[204]
- The record is an assignment, reflected in an initial financing statement or an amendment, but does not provide the name and mailing address of the assignee.[205]
- The record is either an initial financing statement or an amendment adding a debtor but does not provide the debtor's mailing address or indicate whether the debtor is an individual or an organization, or if the debtor is an organization.[206]
- The record is a continuation statement filed more than six months before the expiration of the financing statement to which it relates.[207] Most financing statements are effective for five years after the date of filing. This can be extended for successive five year periods measured from the date of expiration if a continuation statement is filed within the period six months before expiration. When a continuation statement has been timely filed, the new expiration date is an additional five years after the date the financing statement would have become ineffective (not five years

199. G.S. 25-9-521.
200. G.S. 25-9-520(a).
201. G.S. 25-9-520(b).
202. G.S. 25-9-516(b)(2).
203. G.S. 25-9-516(b)(1).
204. G.S. 25-9-516(b)(4).
205. G.S. 25-9-516(b)(6).
206. G.S. 25-9-516(b)(5).
207. G.S. 25-9-516(b)(7).

from the date the continuation statement is filed). A financing statement is effective for thirty years for a public finance transaction or manufactured home transaction and indefinitely if a debtor is a transmitting utility and the financing statement so indicates.[208]

Additionally, a register may refuse to accept a UCC record for registration if the register "is unable to index the record" because it is one of the following:

- An initial filing statement that does not include the debtor's name, including a surname for an individual.[209]
- An amendment that provides a different or additional debtor's name but does not include a last name for an individual.[210]
- A filing that does not provide a sufficient description of the real property to which it relates.[211]
- An amendment or information statement identifying an initial financing statement that is no longer effective (expired and not continued).[212]
- An amendment that does not identify the initial filing statement to which it relates or does not include the debtor's name, the secured party's name, a description of the collateral and an indication that it is related to real property, an indication that it is being recorded in the real estate records, and the identity of the real property owner if the debtor is not the owner.[213] By statute, a record is treated as an initial financing statement if it does not connect to a prior filing by indicating that it is an amendment or identifying an initial filing statement to which it relates.[214] If the instrument indicates it is an amendment, it is not recordable unless it refers to the initial filing statement to which it relates.

208. G.S. 25-9-515.
209. G.S. 25-9-516(b)(3)(a)–516(b)(3)(c).
210. G.S. 25-9-516(b)(3)(c).
211. G.S. 25-9-516(b)(3)(d).
212. G.S. 25-9-516(b)(3)(b)(2).
213. G.S. 25-9-502(b), -9-512(a), -9-516(b)(3)(b)(1).
214. G.S. 25-9-516(c)(2).

- An information statement that does not identify the initial filing statement to which it relates and include a statement about the reason for the information statement.[215]

Upon any refusal to register a UCC submission and no later than three business days after the record is received by the register, the register must communicate to the presenter the fact of and the reason for the refusal and the date and time the record would have been filed had it been accepted.[216]

Registers are not required to maintain UCC records filed prior to July 1, 2001, including any indexes of these records as of June 30, 2001.[217]

3.4.3 Indexing

Article 9 of the UCC prescribes specific indexing requirements for UCC financing statements, amendments, and assignments filed with a register of deeds office. Debtors and record owners listed on financing statements are indexed as grantors, and secured parties are indexed as grantees.[218] If an amendment adds or changes a name, that name must also be indexed.[219] If an assignment is reflected in an initial financing statement or in an amendment, the assignor is indexed as a grantor and the assignee is indexed as a grantee.[220] All subsequent UCC statements, including amendments, must reference the file number of the original financing statement.[221] A UCC amendment is a subsequent instrument subject to the indexing requirements discussed in Chapter 5, Section 5.4.2 of this book..

3.4.4 Information Requests

The UCC requires that upon request registers provide an acknowledgment of a filed UCC record.[222] The acknowledgment can be in the form of an image of the record showing the file number (book and page) and the date and time of filing.[223] The register may instead note this information on a copy of the record if one is provided by the person making the request.[224]

---

215. G.S. 25-9-516(b)(3)(b)(1), -9-518(b).
216. G.S. 25-9-520(b).
217. G.S. 25-9-710(e).
218. G.S. 25-9-519(c), (d).
219. G.S. 25-9-519(c)(2).
220. G.S. 25-9-519(e).
221. G.S. 25-9-519(c)(1).
222. G.S. 25-9-523(a).
223. *Id.*
224. *Id.*

3.5 Torrens Law

The register's main role in real estate transactions is to provide a method for the parties to a transaction to make a public record of their conveyance. In this usual role the register does not certify title nor confirm that ownership has been transferred. North Carolina law gives registers responsibility for a rarely used alternative method by which owners can obtain a certificate of title from the register, known as *Torrens registration*. Many counties have no Torrens registrations, few have seen any use of it, and future use is likely to be extremely rare throughout the state. However, some counties, particularly in the east, have existing land registrations and occasionally must register transfers, issue new certificates of title, or register withdrawals of real estate from the registration system. This section provides an overview of the register's role in the Torrens process.

3.5.1 Background and Use

In the early 1900s, a number of states, including North Carolina, enacted new laws to adopt a land registration system first introduced in Australia by Sir Robert Torrens based on a method used for ships. In the Torrens system, an owner can obtain from the register a certificate showing title. Unlike in other countries that use the system, in this country only a court may determine ownership rights and the register may not issue such a new registration certificate without a court order. So, in the American version of the system a Torrens registration necessarily involves a court process.

North Carolina's version of this system was enacted in 1913[225] and remains the law today. The system saw only slight use when it was first enacted, and today it is almost never used for new registrations.[226] Because of the need for court involvement, registration requires time and money for filing fees, attorneys' fees, and compensation for a court-appointed title examiner. The burden of such an investment largely explains why the system has mostly been used only by investors in large tracts of land, such as timber companies, that are making a long-term investment. As a law commentator noted more than eighty years ago: "In the eastern part of North Carolina where the system is most used, large tracts of forest-covered swamp lands have been bought up by large lumber corporations

---

225. 1913 N.C. Pub. Laws ch. 90.

226. *See* Charles Szypszak, *Public Registries and Private Solutions: An Evolving American Real Estate Conveyance Regime*, 24 WHITTIER L. REV. 663 (2003).

(mostly foreign) and the titles thereto registered for the purpose of establishing definitely the boundary lines, thereby obviating once and for all the possibility of boundary disputes and the acquisition of title to these lands by adverse possessors."[227] Most transactional attorneys are unfamiliar with Torrens registration and may be concerned about the possible complications of transfers with registered titles if for no reason than other attorneys' and lenders' unfamiliarity with it.

3.5.2 Title Registration

To register real estate in the Torrens system, the peaceable possessor of land brings a proceeding in the superior court in which the land is situated.[228] The petition must identify "all known liens, interests, equities and claims, adverse or otherwise, vested or contingent, upon such land."[229] The State of North Carolina must be named as a party.[230] Interested parties will be served with notice of the action, and the clerk of court will publish newspaper notice.[231] The N.C. Attorney General's office has issued rules and forms for use in a Torrens proceeding.[232] The court clerk will appoint an examiner of titles, who must be an attorney. The clerk may set a reasonable fee to be paid by the petitioner for the examiner's compensation.[233] The examiner reviews the submitted evidence and searches title independently, if necessary, and files with the clerk a report about title and any encumbrances on it.[234] The superior court considers the report and any objections to it, the judge or jury decide disputed facts, and a decree is entered.[235] The judge's approval of the decree determines exclusive ownership.[236]

---

227. Frederick B. McCall, *The Torrens System—After Thirty-Five Years*, 10 N.C. L. Rev. 329, 337 (1931–32).

228. G.S. 43-6.

229. G.S. 43-8.

230. *Id.*

231. G.S. 43-9, -10.

232. 12 N.C.A.C. 02H, §§ .0101–0201.

233. G.S. 43-4, -5.

234. G.S. 43-11.

235. G.S. 43-11(c), -12.

236. G.S. 43-12.

When the court decree is registered, the register issues an owner's certificate of title, under the seal of the register of deed's office, substantially as follows:

State of North Carolina – County of ___________

The certificate of ____________

I hereby certify that the title is registered in the name of _________ to and situate in said county and State, described as follows: (Here describe land as in decree.)

Estate ______ (here name the estate and any limitation or encumbrance thereon, as fee simple, upon condition, in trust, subject to encumbrance, and the like).

Under decree of the land court of _____ county, entitled _____.

Registered No. ____, Book No. ____, page ____.

Witness my hand and seal, at office at ___ this ___ day of ____, A.D. _____.

(Seal) ___________________________

Register of Deeds[237]

The register indexes the certificate on the grantor index in the name "Registered estate no. ___" and on the grantee index in the name of the registered owner.[238] The fee for recording new certificates and for making entries, including noting deeds of trust, is the fee for recording instruments in general, and the fee for issuing a certificate to the owner is the certified copy fee.[239]

3.5.3 Deeds of Trust and Other Liens and Claims

Registered property may be the subject of deeds of trust, mortgages, and other security interests the same as unregistered property. An instrument granting a security interest is presented to the register with the certificate of title, and the register notes on the owner's certificate and the record of it the name of the trustee or secured party if it is something other than a deed of trust, the amount of the secured obligation, and the date of

237. G.S. 43-15.
238. G.S. 43-13.
239. G.S. 43-5.

maturity.[240] When the security instrument is satisfied, the register notes this upon the owner's certificate and the certificate of title in the records.

If a deed of trust or mortgage is foreclosed, or property is conveyed under execution for taxes, upon receipt of evidence of the sale the register calls in and cancels the outstanding certificate of title and issues a new certificate to the purchaser.[241] If the former owner does not surrender the certificate, the foreclosing party or purchaser may institute an action with the clerk of the superior court to compel it.[242]

If real estate taxes on a registered parcel are delinquent, the tax collector is required to file a memorandum of this with the register, and the register notes the delinquency on the record copy of the certificate of title.[243] When the taxes are paid, the register notes this on the record copy.[244]

If a judgment or notice of lis pendens is entered in superior court, the court clerk, upon request of an interested party, certifies this event to the register.[245] The register enters on the record copy of the certificate of title the date and amount of the judgment, and it becomes a lien on the property.[246] The register may bring an action in superior court for a subpoena to recover the owner's copy of the certificate of title to mark the lien upon it.[247]

3.5.4 Ownership Transfers

The registered owner may convey the property with an instrument attached to the certificate substantially as follows:

> The owners (giving the names of the parties owning land described in the certificate) hereby, in consideration of ________________ dollars, sell and convey to the purchaser (giving name of purchaser) the lot or tract of land, as the case may be, described in the certificate of title hereto attached. The transfer shall be indexed on the grantor and grantee indexes in the same manner as deeds are indexed.[248]

---

240. G.S. 43-36.
241. G.S. 43-36(f).
242. *Id.*
243. G.S. 43-46.
244. *Id.*
245. G.S. 43-45.
246. *Id.*
247. *Id.*
248. G.S. 43-31.

An instrument in this form must be signed and properly acknowledged by the parties and will have the same legal effect as a deed. Before registering the transfer, the register must see proof that all delinquent taxes or liens, if any, have been paid; if there are outstanding liens, the new certificate must note them on the new certificate.[249] The register cancels the old certificate and issues a new certificate to the grantee with the same number.[250]

If a registered owner transfers a part of the land or a partial interest, the instrument must specify what is being transferred and what is being retained. For a transfer of a separate lot or parcel of a registered estate, the instrument must describe the lot transferred either by metes and bounds or by reference to an attached plat, and in every case the instrument must be accompanied by a plat showing the boundaries. The plat does not have to be a new survey. The register cancels the old certificate and issues new certificates for each owner, with new numbers.[251] An owner who subdivides without a conveyance may submit an application together with a plat showing the subdivision, and the register issues new certificates with new numbers for each of the subdivided parts.[252]

The procedure for transferring registered title to property owned by someone who dies is to file a petition with the clerk of the superior court.[253] After service and a hearing, the court will direct that the outstanding registered certificate of title be surrendered to the register for cancellation, and a new certificate is issued in the name of whomever the court determined to have succeeded to ownership as a devisee or heir.[254]

3.5.5 Indemnity

By statute, when property is first registered in the Torrens system, and when someone becomes a new owner of registered land as an heir or devisee, the new owner must pay one tenth of 1 percent of the assessed tax value into an assurance fund. The payment is made to the clerk of court and paid over to the State Treasurer.[255] This fund is to be available if someone suffers loss through fraud or negligence in the issuance of the

---

249. G.S. 43-37.
250. G.S. 43-31.
251. G.S. 43-32.
252. G.S. 43-34.
253. G.S. 43-17.1.
254. G.S. 43-17.1–17.5.
255. G.S. 43-49.

certificate of title or registration, but only after all other remedies have been exhausted.[256] To make a claim, an action must be brought against the State Treasurer and all other persons who may be liable in superior court.[257] By statute, the fund is to include deposits made when tracts were first registered, subject to any claims that may have been paid. Claims on this fund are unlikely today, especially given the rarity of new registrations and the availability of title insurance as indemnity against loss resulting from title problems.

3.5.6 Release from Registration

An owner who wants to withdraw property from the Torrens registration system so that transfers may be made without register certificates in the same manner as unregistered property may do so by presenting the ownership certificate to the register with a statement in the margin substantially to this effect:

> I (or we), ________, being the owner (or owners) of the registered estate evidenced by this certificate of title, do hereby release said estate from the provisions of Chapter 43 of the General Statutes of North Carolina insofar as said Chapter relates to the form of conveyance, so that hereafter the said estate may, and shall be forever until again hereafter registered in accordance with the provisions of said Chapter and acts amendatory thereof, conveyed, either absolutely or upon condition or trust, by any form of conveyance other than the certificate of title prescribed by said Chapter, and in the same manner as if said estate had never been registered.[258]

The register attests to this statement on the owner's certificate with a signature and seal and makes a similar notation in the margin of the recorded certificate.[259] Also, persons claiming an interest in registered real estate may bring an action in superior court for its removal from the Torrens system.[260]

---

256. G.S. 43-50.
257. *Id.*
258. G.S. 43-25.
259. *Id.*
260. G.S. 43-56.

Chapter 4

Electronic Recording

Chapter 4

Electronic Recording

4.1 Electronic Instruments and Transactions

Electronic instruments and their registration in electronic form offer a presenter the efficiency of speedy recording without having to travel to a register of deeds office or wait for mail to be delivered. North Carolina's statutes and regulations aim to establish basic statewide uniformity in electronic filing methods and submission prerequisites. These same statutes and regulations also give individual county registers the authority and responsibility to determine who may submit electronically in their counties and to specify requirements for submissions they will accept. The North Carolina statutes do not require any register to accept electronic submissions, nor do they require registers who decide to accept electronic documents to accept them from anyone other than whom the register authorizes. This gives registers significant discretion to meet citizens' needs within their particular counties. But the goals that led the legislature to authorize electronic recording are best achieved if all registers across the state strive to follow practices that meet submitters' reasonable expectations. Even within a single county, consistency and predictability are important aspects of a reliable and efficient system. Practitioners count on familiarity within their localized recording system, and they value the guidance they can get from local offices staffed by people with whom they can communicate. Consequently, while the public benefits from progress toward statewide uniformity in electronic instrument procedures, for the foreseeable future the system's integrity will continue to rely on knowledgeable, diligent, and helpful local registers of deeds.

As described in the other sections of this chapter, there is a range of methods that can be used to record a real estate instrument electronically. It can be simply a submitter's scanning of an original paper instrument and transfer of the digital file to a register who will enter the image into the county's database of real estate instruments and index it in the consolidated index. The process can also be entirely paperless. The phrase *e-closing* is often used to describe a situation in which the parties use instruments that are "born digital"—such as when a deed of transfer, promissory note, and deed of trust are all prepared, signed, delivered, and recorded only in electronic form from the start, and no tangible documents were scanned into electronic form. For institutional lenders who make many mortgage loans, a fully electronic closing such as this offers the potential for being both a more efficient and more secure method than the traditional paper method. This is possible due to the authentication that can be embedded in the digital records and the closed system in which they can be transmitted and maintained. Instruments can be stored in what is sometimes called an *electronic vault*, with an original record that, when properly managed, offers additional verification, authentication, and auditability possibilities than a paper record. A transaction closed by this method requires a lender who is equipped for handling electronic signatures and documents, an electronic notary who has the means and is authorized by state commissioning authority to acknowledge electronic signatures, and a closing agent who can submit the files through a trusted submitter approved by the register of deeds in the county in which the real estate is situated.

An added advantage of a fully digital transaction for a lender is the ability to transfer the note and deed of trust within a commercial registration system, such as Mortgage Electronic Registration Systems, Inc. (MERS), which can track changes in servicing rights and beneficial ownership interests in mortgage loans. A commercial registration system, which in some ways replicates the public deed registration system, has efficiencies that make loans more valuable to investors than a system that transfers paper notes, which requires more resource-intensive handling. A public benefit of this kind of controlled record keeping is that it can help alleviate a difficulty frequently encountered by property owners who cannot trace a mortgage ownership history through changes in note holders to someone who is willing to provide a recordable satisfaction for a fully paid loan, which may be necessary to close on a sale or new financing.

The introduction of electronic recording has involved a reconfiguration of the register's role in screening submitted instruments to determine if they are recordable. In their verification of submitted instruments, registers have historically insisted that the elements they check be on what they could see as an original signed instrument, unless the instrument is a certified copy of something already recorded. With paper documents received by hand delivery or mail, registers look for hand-applied ink signatures that can be distinguished from the print used to create the instrument before it was signed. With electronic recording, technology offers those who generate the instruments methods of retaining proof of originality, such as the use of digital signatures generated with an encryption process. The digital evidence trail also can be used to reveal alterations made to a record after the digital signature was applied, by use of a function that creates a digital representation of the entire record. Technology can also generate an audit trail that provides a history of actions involving the instrument, including when it was opened and signed, as well as user information about the generation of the instrument and any alterations to it. Although register of deeds offices could be equipped to take advantage of these types of digital security measures to authenticate notary signatures and other aspects of authenticity, such a step would involve substantial investments in technology. It would also be a departure from the basic nature of the American recording system, which principally is a means for those with interests in real property to make a public record of their conveyances, rather than a system that directly involves a government office as a gatekeeper. Accordingly, as the next section explains, North Carolina statutes currently give the submitter substantial responsibility for ensuring that instruments comply with originality requirements.

Electronic recording has now been available to registers for many years. The Uniform Real Property Electronic Recording Act (URPERA), adopted in North Carolina in 2005, authorized presentation and recording of real estate instruments in electronic form in all counties.[1] URPERA overcame the former requirement that documents be paper "originals" when it more broadly defined a "document" to include "information that is . . . [i]nscribed on a tangible medium or that is stored in an electronic or other medium and is retrievable in perceivable form."[2] URPERA was intended nationwide "to remove any doubt about the authority of the recorder to receive and

1. S.L. 2005-391 (codified at Chapter 47, Sections 16.1 to -16.7 of the North Carolina General Statutes (hereinafter G.S.)).

2. G.S. 47-16.2(1), -16.4.

record instruments in electronic form."[3] Still, the drafters of URPERA noted that the proposed uniform law was not intended to answer all the questions about recording in various states, noting that "gaps may have to be filled legislatively and . . . conflicts may have to be resolved. Each legislature will have to review its own existing laws to determine what collateral real property laws need to be modified and how to do it."[4] Foundational issues have been addressed in the statutes and regulations, and they are discussed in this chapter. The reality that technology is always evolving means that the laws and regulations will continue to change as new capabilities and risks emerge, and registers should be closely attuned to such changes and modifications required in recording and indexing practices.

By statute, the North Carolina Secretary of State provides guidance about electronic records and signatures in register offices. The secretary receives advice regarding standards for electronic records and signatures from a state advisory body, the North Carolina Electronic Recording Council (NCERC), a majority of which hold office as registers of deeds.[5] The following other groups interested in real estate transactions each appoint a member: the North Carolina Bar Association, the North Carolina Society of Land Surveyors, the North Carolina Bankers Association, the North Carolina Land Title Association, the North Carolina Association of Assessing Officers, and the North Carolina Department of Natural and Cultural Resources. The secretary has adopted Electronic Recording Standards that the NCERC developed. These standards provide guidance to registers and submitters about the format and procedure for electronic record submissions and for the maintenance of electronic records.[6]

The NCERC also has published recommended best practices for electronic recording.[7] Registers may choose to mandate submitter compliance with aspects of these best practices by including them in the memorandum

---

3. Unif. Real Prop. Elec. Recording Act, Prefatory Note, 7B U.L.A. 264 (Supp. 2005).

4. *Id.* § 3 legis. note, 7B U.L.A. 270 (2006).

5. G.S. 47-16.5.

6. North Carolina Uniform Real Property Electronic Recording Act, Report, N.C. Elec. Recording Council (2011), https://www.sosnc.gov/documents/forms/notary/North_Carolina_Electronic_Record.pdf.

7. Best Practices for Electronic Recording, N.C. Elec. Recording Council (2018), https://sosnc.gov/documents/guides/land_records/Best_Practices_for_Electronic_Recording.pdf.

of understanding between the register and the submitter. These practices include the following:

- Images submitted for recording must be clear and clean without any visual "noise" that will interfere with examination when entered into the public record.
- Notary seals must be sufficiently dark and legible for the register to be able to inspect them to see if they meet verification requirements, as described in Section 4.5 of this chapter.
- Submitters are responsible for ensuring that all local requirements are met prior to submission of any instruments, including the need for prior approvals, as described in Section 4.6 of this chapter.
- Instruments will be processed in due course only while the register's office is open to the public for business. The recording times for electronic recording should be consistent with the recording times for paper recordings. Neither the submitter agreement nor any other agreement or representation by the register should state or imply that electronically submitted instruments will be processed instantaneously upon transmission or that they will take priority over instruments submitted in person or by mail.
- Submitters may only submit specifically allowed types of instruments. Registers may choose to have a short list of common real estate instruments that may be submitted electronically to avoid issues arising about the need for the instrument to have a verifiable image of a notary acknowledgment. When there is such a restriction on instrument types, the NCERC recommends that the county post information about it on the county's website.
- Instruments should be submitted individually unless the submitter intends them to be recorded together with consecutive instrument numbers. This keeps registers from receiving a package that threatens to monopolize office resources with the need to process numerous instruments from a single submission before attending to instruments from other submitters.
- Registers should specify whether there will be confirmation of an electronically submitted instrument's recording and, if so, how that information will be provided. Registers may also wish to specify that any acknowledgment shall be returned to the address on

record for the trusted submitter and not to any different address that may be shown on or accompany a specific instrument. By statute, registers are not required to return electronically submitted instruments according to how a desired recipient is indicated on a submission.[8]

- The register should confirm that authorization to submit electronically extends only to the submitter identified in the memorandum of understanding (MOU). Any new name, transfer, or reorganization such that the submitter would be known by a new name (including but not limited to an acquisition, a merger, or an addition of a new partner to a partnership), requires the register's approval and execution of a new MOU before a submitter with the new name may submit instruments for electronic recording.
- Indexing will be according to the same rules and practices that apply to instruments submitted by other means and not necessarily according to any instructions that may accompany an electronic submission.
- The register should make clear that to rerecord an instrument already in the public record the submitter should obtain a certified copy from the register and submit it, for the reasons explained in Section 4.8 of this chapter.

Registers should regularly review these recommended best practices and consider whether experience or changes in the statutes or regulations require variations or additional specified best practices. These are matters to be included in the training of everyone who works in the register's office. Registers should also periodically review vendors' and submitters' compliance with established agreements and take steps to correct non-adherence.

4.2 Electronic Recording Systems

To enable electronic recording within their counties, registers enter into arrangements that connect trusted submitter systems for receipt of files that will be processed within the register of deeds system. Whatever the submission method, registers are responsible for all aspects of record-

8. G.S. 161-30(a1).

ing, indexing, and maintaining the office's records. Accordingly, although registers must rely to some degree on information technology experts in county departments and with contracted vendors, registers are responsible for managing those arrangements to ensure they meet the requirements of applicable laws and regulations and protect the integrity of the register's records. To fulfill this responsibility, registers need a basic understanding of the features that should be expected of a user-friendly and reliable electronic recording system, including the following principal considerations.

Registers should consider the security of the transmission link between the submitter and the register's system. The register's system is subject to various forms of security risk. Someone may attempt to introduce malware, such as ransomware or a virus, which activates when someone clicks on a link or attachment. Government office networks are popular targets for ransomware attacks, which are commonly started with a link in an innocent-looking email or attachment to an email. *Phishing* attacks trick someone into opening messages and providing information such as credit card or bank account personal identification numbers that provide access to accounts. Malware can also block access to the network until a demand is met, or it can corrupt data or secretly obtain information, some of which is personally sensitive and deemed private.

To protect against attacks on their systems, registers should have rigorous access control over devices that are connected to relevant networks and ensure everyone with access is well trained in identifying the risks and takes protective measures, such as being alert to signs of suspicious messages or traffic. Registers should also work with their county information technology departments and vendors to enable technological tools, such as a virtual private network (VPN) that establishes a point-to-point connection to the registers' devices and protects against someone else gaining control of information.

The need to consider security also applies to submitter payments. As discussed in Chapter 1, Section 1.11.3 and Chapter 3, Sections 3.2.5 and 3.2.6 of this book, the statutes require that registers receive all applicable recording fees and excise taxes before any instrument is recorded. As described in Chapter 1, Section 1.11.4 of this book, acceptable methods of payment include credit cards, debit cards, and electronic fund transfers, all of which can be arranged with electronic submissions. Use of electronic fund transfers through the automated clearing house (ACH) is a common and convenient method for accepting electronic recording charges.

Registers may also arrange to draw funds from prepaid internal escrow accounts established by the submitter for payment of the fees and excise taxes. The statutes do not permit registers to accumulate charges for billing on a periodic basis.

One source of general guidance about register of deeds recording systems is a set of recommendations from the N.C. Electronic Recording Council (NCERC), the role of which is described in Section 4.1 of this chapter. The NCERC makes several recommendations that are aimed at ensuring the integrity of electronic recording with registers, including the arrangements that registers make with vendors who enable the transfer of records from trusted submitters.

An important NCERC recommendation is to maintain a technology-neutral system to receive, store, and archive electronic documents.[9] As the NCERC explains, "[b]y vendor specific, it is meant that a party desiring to electronically record documents must use a specific vendor's product in order to communicate with a recorder's internal processing system."[10] Technology neutrality enables a register to continue to operate the system without interruption if the vendor ceases to support its system for any reason, whether going out of business, failing to perform, or making contractual demands that the county is not prepared to accept.

Another important NCERC recommendation is to maintain reliable backup and restoration procedures for electronic data.[11] Registers should have arrangements for regular backups before any problems might occur and procedures for responding if there are problems with functionality, including threats, such as denials of service attacks.

The NCERC also makes the following recommendations for long-term preservation of electronic records:[12]

- Maintain multiple copies of the record. The different copies should be separate enough so that an alternative is available in case one is corrupted or access to it is denied because of foul play, even if the alternative might not be fully as current as the other.

---

9. *North Carolina Uniform Real Property Electronic Recording Act*, Report, *supra* note 6, at 17-18.

10. *Id.*

11. *Id.* at 18-19.

12. *Id.* at 8-9.

- Maintain the original, unchanged recorded file in the original file format throughout the life of the record. Changes in format can render some of the record inaccessible.
- Perform periodic audits on the records and the system to ensure long-term accessibility to the records. These audits should be part of a scheduled and strictly followed procedure regardless of whether there have been any apparent threats to the system.
- On a continuing basis, develop planning and implementation procedures for conversion and migration of permanent or archival digital records, and the systems that support them, to new formats, storage media, and technologies.
- Assure that digital information can be managed and authenticated by currently acceptable technologies, which may involve maintaining metadata. Metadata are a set of data that give information about other data, such as the table structure for entries made in indexing real estate instruments. This metadata may not be apparent to those who use the records in a computer system, but they can be essential to the system's usefulness.
- The NCERC echoes the recommendation of the N.C. Department of Natural and Cultural Resources about preservation duplicates described in Chapter 2, Section 2.4.4 of this book. When digital technology is used for archival or legal records, the NCERC recommends that the original record should be transferred to microfilm for permanent preservation. This recommendation is based on the archive manager perspective that microfilm can be read physically with magnification and is not subject to unresolvable corruption, as may occur with digital files, as discussed in Chapter 2, Section 2.4.4 of this book.

Registers should make a practice of periodically reviewing these recommendations and keeping abreast of evolving considerations about the security of electronic submissions and digital storage. Given the complex and ever-changing nature of these considerations, registers should have an expert trusted advisor who is unaffiliated with any trusted submitter or current systems vendor who can audit the register's systems and procedures and make recommendations for any needed changes to improve record integrity and security.

4.3 Trusted Submitter Agreements and Responsibilities

Registers may accept electronic documents from two kinds of submitters: the government or a *trusted submitter.* Someone can become a trusted submitter only by first agreeing to the register's requirements in a memorandum of understanding. The *submitter* takes responsibility for complying with the originality requirements that apply to the instruments they submit. Submitters also are responsible for complying with other aspects of the North Carolina statutes and the N.C. Secretary of State's rules about electronic notary certifications.

The trusted submitter's responsibilities are reflected in a statement they are required to include on any instrument submitted electronically. G.S. 47-14(a1)(5) requires that such instruments state the following on the face of the image that will be in the public record:

> Submitted electronically by _______ [submitter's name] in compliance with North Carolina statutes governing recordable documents and the terms of the submitter agreement with the _______ [insert county name] County Register of Deeds.

A key aspect of the trusted submitter's required attestation is confirmation of compliance with originality requirements. Under Chapter 47, Section 14(a1)(3) of the North Carolina General Statutes (hereinafter G.S.), an instrument requiring verification must have a notarial officer's signature with a certificate for a party's signature. G.S. 47-14(a2) provides as follows: "Submission to a register of deeds of an electronic document requiring proof or acknowledgement is a representation by the submitter that, prior to submission, the submitter verified the officer's signature required under subdivision (a1)(3) of this section to be one of the types of signatures listed in this subsection." This subsection also provides that "the register of deeds may rely on this representation for purposes of determining compliance with the signature requirements." In other words, the trusted submitter—not the register—is responsible for ensuring that an instrument requiring verification is submitted only if it (1) meets the same signature requirements as apply to paper instruments or (2) meets the requirements for an electronic signature. The submitter's certificate is an attestation of compliance with these requirements.

As explained in Chapter 3, Section 3.2.3 of this book, if by its nature an instrument requires notarization, the North Carolina statutes only permit its recording with a register of deeds if it has an original notarial officer's signature or is a certified copy of it as it was already recorded. For a paper instrument, this means an original ink signature. Because a notary may only complete a notarial certificate if the notary witnessed a party's signature, verification of the notary signature originality is a step that ensures the instrument being recorded is the instrument that a party actually signed—not a modified version of it. Accordingly, when a trusted submitter gives the attestation required by G.S. 47-14(a1) of compliance with the statutes with respect to an instrument that the submitter initially possesses in paper form, the submitter is attesting that the notary's signature is original in the same way that registers have always done when the instrument is presented at the counter. This originality requirement also means that a photocopy of an instrument requiring verification may not be submitted. Similarly, a submitter could not properly record an altered document that does not conform to the paper document recording requirements.

In addition to a notary's traditional ink signature on a paper instrument, the statute allowing electronic recording through a trusted submitter allows submission of an instrument with "an electronic signature as defined in G.S. 10B-101(7)."[13] Use of the term "electronic signature" is significant. It is sometimes used interchangeably with *digital signature*, but as applied in electronic commerce they are not always the same. An *electronic signature* can be anything that a signer applies intending it to be signature and that is logically associated with or attached to a document. It can be as simple as someone adding a name to the end of a message, as is common with email, or an inserted digital image of a signature, as is common with an electronic document file. A digital signature is a type of electronic signature, but this term is understood within electronic commerce to involve a more secure type of technology with encrypted data that is unique to the signer. North Carolina's statutory definition of acceptable signature invokes the broader type of signature, allowing "those forms of electronic signature which have been approved by the Secretary as authorized in G.S. 10B-125, as an acceptable means for an electronic notary to affix the notary's official signature to an electronic record that is being notarized." G.S. 10B-125, to which the definition refers, provides that the N.C. Secretary of State "shall adopt rules necessary to establish standards, procedures, practices, forms, and records relating to a notary's electronic signature and electronic seal. The notary's electronic seal and electronic signature shall conform to any stan-

13. G.S. 47-14(a2)(2).

dards adopted by the Secretary." The rules that the secretary has adopted pursuant to this statutory empowerment provide that an electronic notary signature "shall be independently verifiable and unique to the electronic notary" and "attached or logically associated with the document, linking the data in such a manner that any subsequent alterations to the underlying document or electronic notary certificate are observable through visual examination."[14] Although this allows a wide range of methods by which the electronic signature can be made, significantly the secretary's rules also require that "an image of the notary's handwritten signature shall appear on any visual or printed representation of an electronic notary certificate regardless of the technology being used to affix the electronic notary's electronic signature."[15]

Due to the requirement that a notary's signature must be "attached or logically associated with the document" in a visual manner, the notary's signature on an electronically submitted instrument must be visually detectable on the instrument being submitted to a register. This ensures that anyone examining the public record will be able to see evidence that the record was apparently signed. The digital evidence trail of the act of an electronic signing is not a required part of what is submitted to the register of deeds or included in the register-maintained public record. However, the rule would not allow, for example, the register to accept an instrument that does not have a visible signature while the submitter keeps evidence of the act of signing in a separate database.

Another important aspect of the required electronic signature within the statutory definition is the provision that says the signature must be attached to or logically associated in a manner that would visually reveal alterations "*to the underlying document*."[16] The term "underlying document" distinguishes the instrument actually signed from any later-generated copy of it. Accordingly, a submitter could not properly submit something the submitter received as a scanned copy of an instrument that requires verification, because examination of the copy would not reveal if there had been any alterations to the original, underlying document, which exists elsewhere.

---

14. Title 18, Chapter 07C, Section .0401(a), (d), of the North Carolina Administrative Code (hereinafter N.C.A.C.).

15. 18 N.C.A.C. 07C, § .0401(e).

16. *Supra* note 14 (emphasis added).

Table 4.1. Basic Statutory Allocation of Authentication Responsibilities for Instruments Requiring Verification

Parties and their agents	Comply with applicable jurisdiction law for enforceability against the parties
Notary official	Complete notary certificate with visible notary signature and seal for party signature that complies with applicable jurisdiction law
Trusted submitter	Submit only an original notarized instrument that complies with North Carolina law requirements and memorandum of understanding with the register
Register of deeds	Verify completion of notary certificate based on submitted image

Table 4.1 depicts the basic statutory allocation of authentication responsibilities for instruments requiring verification.

The allocation of responsibilities for electronic recording means that security of electronic submissions in any particular county rests to a significant degree on the register's decisions about acceptable vendors and the protections included in the submitter agreement and monitored and enforced by the register.[17] Registers must continually assess the reliability of submitters as trustworthy, insist on agreements with them that protect the integrity of the process, and be vigilant for any signs that the process is being abused. At a minimum, the submitter agreement should make clear that the submitter acknowledges and agrees to the following terms and conditions:

- Instruments will be submitted only in compliance with North Carolina statutes and regulations and the terms and conditions of the submitter agreement.
- The register will be relying on the submitter's statutorily required attestation on the first page of any document of compliance with North Carolina statutes and regulations and the terms of the submitter agreement with the register.

---

17. An example of a vendor memorandum of understanding is provided in Addendum K to the North Carolina Electronic Recording Council's 2011 report (*supra* note 6), which is an attachment to the North Carolina Secretary of State's Electronic Recording Standards, available at https://www.sosnc.gov/documents/forms/notary/North_Carolina_Electronic_Record.pdf.

- Instruments will be processed in due course only while the register's office is open to the public for business. Neither the submitter agreement nor any other agreement or representation by the register should state or imply that electronically submitted instruments will be processed instantaneously upon transmission or that they will take priority over instruments submitted in person or by mail.
- Instruments will be registered only after the register has determined that all applicable requirements have been met and the register has accepted, recorded, and indexed the instrument in the public record pursuant to applicable state law.
- The submitter is responsible for any costs charged by any third party in connection with the electronic recording process.
- The register is not responsible for retaining such records as may be required to evidence originality. As described throughout this chapter, the register's role in verifying an electronically submitted instrument is to see that the notary officer certificate elements appear in the image that will be entered into the record. To the extent that an issue arises about whether a party's or notary's signature on the instrument met the requirement of being associated with or logically associated with the instrument such that alterations would be visually observable, the trusted submitter—not the register—bears responsibility for evidence of it.
- Only the submitter that is specifically named in the agreement is authorized to submit instruments to the register. Any successor or assign to that submitter (including but not limited to a successor by merger or other transfer of assets or reorganization) must first separately enter into an agreement with the register. This confinement is necessary not only for the register to make an independent assessment of reliability with respect to anyone who is going to be authorized to submit, but also to have clear responsibility for any failure to adhere to the commitment in the agreement.
- Authorization to submit may be terminated without prior notice for noncompliance with the agreement. There should be no right to warnings or prior notice before termination, because the register may appropriately take steps to ensure that every single submission is made by a trusted submitter who is abiding by the agreement.

- Neither the register nor the county will be liable to the submitter for any special or consequential damages arising from, or as a result of, any delay, omission, or error in the transmission or receipt of electronic documents.

The register should closely monitor the approved trusted submitter's faithful compliance with the agreement. The register should immediately investigate any apparent instances of noncompliance and assess whether corrective actions and assurances of future compliance are sufficient to warrant continued authorization to submit. The term *trusted* is an intentional and important part of the relationship. The register may and should terminate the authority if there is concern about the submitter's commitments.

4.4 Presentation of Electronic Submissions

As described in Chapter 3, Section 3.2.1 of this book, G.S.161-14 requires that "all instruments shall be registered in the precise order in which they were presented for registration." The order of presentation determines the priority of rights among competing claimants to the same property interest. The North Carolina statutes do not provide explicit guidance about when an instrument is deemed to have been presented in one of the four ways this occurs: physical presentation at a register of deeds office, overnight mail, regular mail, or electronic transmission. By whichever method an instrument is presented, the submitter will want to search the records up to the moment of presentation, checking to see if anything has been previously submitted that might take priority. Traditionally, this was done by a combination of searching the consolidated index and checking the temporary index and any instruments at the counter pending the register's processing into the index, together with other public records that are customarily searched, such as the superior court docket of *lis pendens*. With physical delivery of an instrument, the submitter could know priority at the moment of recording. Submitters could use mail when there were no serious concerns about priority due to a lapse between checking the index and having a recording received through the mail and processed. This reasoning applies to instruments such as assignments or satisfactions, which are important title evidence but are unlikely to implicate recording priority issues. With respect to mail submissions, the public and registers follow the long-standing practice, and reasonable submitter expectation, that an instrument sent by mail would not be deemed presented until the register's office has processed it.

The expectations of submitters and registers may not be as neatly aligned with electronic recording. The moment at which presentation is deemed to occur with an electronic submission is not addressed in the North Carolina statutes, and it is not the subject of any long-standing practices or expectations. Someone who sends a message or uploads a file knows that what was sent or uploaded will be almost immediately available to the recipient unless there is a technical problem. The recipient, however, will only see what was sent after opening the file. The Uniform Real Property Electronic Recording Act (URPERA), which was adopted in North Carolina in 2005 to facilitate and encourage electronic recording, did not address the question of when a register is deemed to have received an electronically submitted instrument.[18] The issue has not been explicitly addressed by North Carolina legislation, which in substantial part can be attributed to the reality that important features of real estate transactions are based on custom and established practices, and any legislation attempting to make new rules about priority may threaten to upset established rights based on those customs and established practices. Additionally, as long as recording by physical presentation at a register's office remains available to the public, there is a means of recording with full knowledge of both prior recorded instruments and the timing of the recording. The upshot is that submitters should take into account that no register of deeds office is necessarily monitoring an electronic filing for immediate processing, and registers may wish to be clear in the memoranda of understanding and other information given to submitters that no such expectation should exist.

While submitters should not expect instantaneous processing of an electronic filing, they may reasonably expect that registers will process it in due course together with other submissions during the hours of operation. There is no prescribed amount of time that would be deemed reasonable, as processing depends on many circumstances, such as the volume of filings that need to be processed by all methods of submission, available staff, and the time of day when a submission is received. In many cases, completion of registration processing by the close of business the same day may be

---

18. Unif. Real Prop. Elec. Recording Act § 3 legis. note, 7B U.L.A. 270 (2006).

a reasonable expectation, and by end of the next business day is likely a reasonable expectation for instruments that are submitted too late in the day to be processed the same day they are received.

4.5 Register Verification of Electronic Instruments

G.S. 47-14(a) contains the following requirement, commonly referred to as *register verification*: "The register of deeds shall not accept for registration any instrument that requires proof or acknowledgement unless the execution of the instrument by one or more signers appears to have been proved or acknowledged before an officer with the apparent authority to take proofs or acknowledgements, and the said proof or acknowledgement includes the officer's signature, commission expiration date, and official seal, if required. The register of deeds shall accept an instrument for registration that does not require proof or acknowledgment if the instrument otherwise satisfies the requirements of G.S. 161-14." As described in Section 4.3 of this chapter, the North Carolina statutes authorize trusted submitters to submit instruments requiring verification if the notary has signed it by hand or with an electronic signature allowed by the North Carolina notary laws.[19] The statutes further provide that the trusted submitter's required attestation "is a representation by the submitter that, prior to submission, the submitter verified the officer's signature required under" North Carolina law and that "the register of deeds may rely on this representation for purposes of determining compliance with the signature requirements."[20] In other words, the trusted submitter—not the register—is legally obliged to ensure that an instrument requiring verification either meets the original notary official signature requirements for paper or it has what constitutes a notary's electronic signature under North Carolina law. Because of this notary signature requirement, a trusted submitter should not submit a document for recording if it requires verification and the submitter has it only in the form of a photocopy or digital image.

As described in Chapter 3, Section 3.2.3.1 of this book, notary official signature verification is required for deeds, deeds of trust, satisfactions, and powers of attorney, among other specified instruments. With paper

19. G.S. 47-14(a2).
20. *Id.*

submissions, registers ensure that the document is the version signed by a notary who completed a certificate for a party's signature. The register is not responsible for ensuring that originality requirements are met with instruments that are submitted electronically, nor is the register responsible for ensuring that a party's signature complies with applicable law for the manner in which that party may sign. The notary official is responsible for ensuring that any notarized party's signature complies with the applicable law and regulations. For a paper instrument, the notary official is responsible for seeing a party's hand-applied ink signature. For an electronic instrument, the notary official is responsible for seeing a party's signature that meets the definition of electronic signature under the law of the jurisdiction in which the signing is taking place.

The laws governing electronic notarization vary among the states and countries in which notary officials are commissioned. In some cases, an electronic notarization varies from a traditional paper notarization only in the sense that the party's signature will be an electronic signature as is allowed under the laws in the applicable jurisdiction. Those laws may also have varying requirements about whether notaries must be specially commissioned to perform electronic notarizations and what they must include in the certificate of the notary act. Jurisdictions differ about whether the signer must be physically present with the notary, or whether the two must be in the same jurisdiction. The laws that vary from the traditional requirements for physical presence often include enhanced requirements for identifying the signer and keeping a record of the notary act, which in some respects make the notarization more secure than traditional paper notarization. The notary is responsible for knowing the particular jurisdiction's requirements and for complying with them. The register is not responsible for researching or policing these matters, which would be an unreasonable expectation.

Because the register's verification of an electronic submission is limited to inspection of the appearance of the required notarization verification elements, the trusted submitter will be the depository of any evidence that any originality requirements were satisfied, both with respect to ink signatures and electronic signatures. There is no express statutory requirement that the trusted submitter maintain this evidence in a publicly accessible record. This is no different than paper submissions made directly to registers, for which there is no such proof maintenance requirement. Registers typically have scanned images of the original instruments, returning the originals to those who recorded them, in which case the public relies on the register to follow proper verification practices to protect the integrity of the public record. Trusted submitters fill this role with electronic submissions. Registers should consider the importance of this trusted submitter role when they authorize someone to be one and as they consider if someone who is a trusted submitter should continue to be one.

4.6 Prerequisite Approvals and Other Information Subsequent to Instrument Execution

Except as noted in this section, electronic submissions are subject to the same requirements as paper submissions for prerequisite approvals from other offices. The statute authorizing registers of deeds to choose to accept electronic submissions requires that "evidence of other required governmental certification or annotation appears on the digitized image of the document as it will appear on the public record."[21] These requirements are discussed in Chapter 3, Section 3.2.2 of this book. Depending on a particular county, this may be the inclusion of a parcel identifier number (PIN) on the face of the instrument[22] or a tax collector's certification on a deed that no real estate taxes are owed on the property being conveyed,[23] among other things. The submitter is responsible for ensuring that this information is shown, and compliance is part of the required trusted submitter's certification of compliance with the applicable statutes.[24] The register should reject an instrument that is missing any of the required information.

The statute does not specify a procedure for how the trusted submitter is to obtain evidence of government approvals that must be shown on an instrument. A register may require in the memorandum of understanding simply that such certifications must appear on an instrument before it is submitted, which a trusted submitter can accomplish, for example, by obtaining a required certification on an original paper record before scanning it and submitting it to a register electronically. Alternatively, a county may establish a mechanism for submitters to obtain required certifications

21. G.S. 47-14(a1)(4).
22. G.S. 161-30(b).
23. G.S. 161-31.
24. G.S. 47-14(a1).

electronically from a responsible office, with visible certification becoming part of the record before it is submitted to the register of deeds.

As discussed in Chapter 3, Section 3.2.2.3 of this book, counties may choose to require that the register not accept for registration any instrument affecting real property unless the face of the instrument shows the name and address of the person to whom the instrument is to be returned and the grantee's or owner's permanent mailing address. This requirement does not apply to electronic submissions, which registers are not likely to routinely return to a physical mailing address. The statutes expressly provide that a register "shall not be required to return a recorded map or instrument that was submitted electronically but may return to the submitting party a recorded map or instrument that was submitted electronically in accordance with an authorizing agreement."[25] The NCERC encourages registers to provide notification and recording information similar to what is provided in the traditional paper recording process.[26] This information can be provided by return mail, as is common with paper submissions, but is more likely to be sent by electronic transmission through the same channel as was used for the submission.

The drafter name requirement discussed in Chapter 3, Section 3.2.2.2 of this book fully applies the same as for paper format. The submitter must ensure that a required drafter name appears on the first page before transmitting the instrument electronically to the register.

4.7 Electronically Submitted Plats

The recording of plats with a register has always involved special considerations for several reasons, including the need to have images that are sufficiently clear to show the fine details and special handling considerations of plats due to their sizes. Plats that are recorded with North Carolina registers of deeds also involve regulatory approval considerations, as described in Chapter 3, Section 3.2.8 of this book. The contents of electronically recorded plats are subject to the same requirements as plats submitted on other media. They involve special handling considerations.

---

25. G.S. 161-30(a1)

26. *North Carolina Uniform Real Property Electronic Recording Act, Report, supra* note 6, at 17.

For the presenter, plats typically involve greater expense in their preparation than other kinds of submissions, a cost that can be exacerbated by unpredictable or inconsistent recording requirements. In some ways, a digital format can lessen these burdens. Digitally generated plats can incorporate information in existing databases, eliminating some duplication of effort that is necessary when drawing on physical media. They also enable automated boundary drawing and labeling. With respect to the recording process, digital plats recorded electronically afford both the presenter and the register a means of streamlining the preparation and recording process. Their use can eliminate some of the more troublesome steps involved in going from plat preparation to a stored image in the register's system.

As with the electronic recording of instruments, registers control who may submit plats electronically, and the requirements for their submissions, through a trusted submitter memorandum of understanding.[27] Similar to an electronically recorded deed or other instrument, the digital image of the plat that will appear on the public record must contain the submitter's name in the following completed statement on the first page of the plat image the following statement:

> Submitted electronically by __________ (submitter's name) in compliance with North Carolina statutes governing recordable documents and the terms of the submitter agreement with the __________ (insert county name) County Register of Deeds.[28]

This required statement clearly assigns responsibility for compliance with any governmental approval or originality requirements. There is no requirement that the register of deeds confirm originality of any signatures on the plat, nor is there any notarization requirement as a condition to recording.

Evidence of any review officer certification, if required as described in Chapter 3, Sections 3.2.8.2 and 3.2.8.3 of this book, must appear on the digital image of the plat as it will appear on the public record.[29] The submitter is responsible for getting any required review officer signature before submitting the instrument to the register for recording. The North Carolina statutes do not specify how this process is to occur. As with other office certifications, as discussed in Section 4.6 of this chapter, the submitter can

27. G.S. 47-30(o)(1), (2).
28. G.S. 47-30(o)(4).
29. G.S. 47-30(o)(3).

obtain the signature before scanning the plat for submission to the register, or the county may have arrangements for digital submission to the review officer with subsequent submission to the register. The register may specify the acceptable method in the memorandum of understanding.[30]

4.8 Previously Recorded Electronic Instruments and Corrections to Them

The verification responsibilities with electronic recording require submitters to attend to special considerations if they want to record an instrument that has already been recorded electronically. As described in Chapter 3, Section 3.2.3.2 of this book, the requirement that transactional instruments contain an acknowledgment of a party's signature means that someone cannot simply make additions or changes to a recorded, notarized instrument and record it without having it re-signed and re-acknowledged. There is no reason to believe that a submitter can do this when submitting electronically.

With a paper recording, a register can usually see that something has been changed or added to a previously recorded instrument. Because with an electronic submission registers only look for the appearance of the verification elements, as described in Section 4.5 of this chapter, there is greater likelihood that an instrument would be submitted with changes that were made after the instrument was signed and acknowledged. However, with an electronic submission, the trusted submitter must attest that all statutory requirements have been met, and these requirements include the same originality verifications to which a paper submission would be subject. A trusted submitter would be making a false statement of compliance by knowingly submitting an instrument for recording that required verification and was not newly signed and acknowledged after it had been altered. Prohibited alterations without new signatures and acknowledgment include the same prohibited matters as for paper instruments, including additions, substitutions, corrections, or interlineations.

Electronic recording entails special considerations if a trusted submitter wishes to record an instrument that was previously recorded but that has not been altered after it was signed and acknowledged. As described in

30. G.S. 47-30(o)(1), (2).

Chapter 3, Section 3.2.3.2 of this book, nothing prohibits the same unaltered instrument from being recorded more than once. Unlike an already recorded paper instrument, however, the version of the record that was the original when submitted for electronic recording the first time is not the same as what appears after being processed into the register's system with recording data shown thereon. A submitter should obtain a certified copy of the already recorded instrument from the register, which can be recorded electronically or by physical delivery or mail.

Chapter 5

Real Estate Instrument Indexing

Chapter 5

Real Estate Instrument Indexing

5.1 Purpose and Effect of Indexing

Registers of deeds maintain indexes so that records can be found. The principal method for accomplishing this goal is to index the names of the parties to the instruments with a reference to the book and page at which an image of the record can be seen. The following sections describe the real estate instrument indexing requirements and procedures.

Registers have thousands of documents in their real estate records and add thousands more every year. Within this multitude, the public needs to be able to find every record that pertains to any name. This can happen only if a reference can be found in the index that leads to every such record.

Many years ago, a register's records were few enough that an index could be kept with handwritten entries on alphabetically separated pages. Now there are so many records that searchers rely on computer functions to match their queries with indexing information that was created by the registers when instruments were accepted and scanned into databases. Unless the indexing information was correctly input in a predictable format, a pertinent record may never be found.

By statute, registers must provide an index with entries that link every name for a party whose name appears in a recorded instrument to where that instrument can be seen in the records.[1] The creation and maintenance of a complete index is an important responsibility that requires both expertise and diligence. Unlike many government filings, there are no legal restrictions on the types of instruments that may be recorded with registers or how the parties are to be identified within the instruments.

---

1. Chapter 161, Section 22(a) of the North Carolina General Statutes (hereinafter G.S.).

Names of parties often appear in conspicuous and predictable places within customary documents, but drafters also use unconventional forms and put names in obscure or surprising places within documents. Also, often names appear in unusual forms and their components are not easily discernible. This leaves registers to examine each presented instrument to extract the indexing information according to their best understanding of what the instrument seems to be and how the indexing laws and rules apply to it.

Entry of the parties' names into the index is an essential step in the creation of the public record. A recorded instrument can give notice to others only from the time it becomes available to those examining the records, which occurs only when the document is indexed. Thus, indexing is an essential part of registration. By statute, "[n]o instrument shall be deemed registered until it has been indexed in a manner to put a reasonably careful and prudent examiner on notice upon inquiry, and, if upon inquiry, the instrument would have been found."[2] This statute is consistent with how the courts have approached questions about when a document is deemed sufficiently indexed for the public to be held accountable for finding it. In a 1930 case, the North Carolina Supreme Court rejected a strict interpretation that "the [indexing] statute should be complied with to the exact letter," noting that "the underlying philosophy of all registration is to give notice, and that hence the ultimate purpose and pervading object of the statute is to produce and supply such notice."[3] The court said "that the indexing and cross-indexing of the deed of trust in the case at bar is not a strict compliance with the statute," but if "there was sufficient information upon the index and cross-index to create the duty of making inquiry," the indexing created a lien on the property.[4] The North Carolina Court of Appeals applied this rule to hold that a judgment docketed with a clerk of court under the name "Philips" instead of "Phillips" provided sufficient notice of a judgment lien. The court of appeals described the rule as follows: "'The primary purpose of the law requiring the registration and indexing

---

2. G.S. 161-22(h).

3. West v. Jackson, 198 N.C. 693, 694, 153 S.E. 257, 258 (1930).

4. *Id.* at 694–95, 153 S.E. at 258; *see also* Cuthrell v. Camden Cnty., 254 N.C. 181, 185–86, 118 S.E.2d 601, 604 (1961) (creditors deemed to have knowledge of a lien despite absence of some name information, applying the rule that charges a creditor "with a knowledge of all facts which an ordinarily careful examiner of the records would have made him cognizant of").

of conveyances is to give notice, and . . . an index will hold a subsequent purchaser or encumbrancer to notice if enough is disclosed by the index to put a careful and prudent examiner upon inquiry, and if upon such inquiry the instrument would be found.' "[5] Therefore, according to both the statutes and court analysis of responsibilities, a register is expected to be accurate enough that a reasonably diligent searcher will be able to find a recorded instrument in the index.

A register's duty of care in indexing instruments must be viewed in relation to the difficulties of identifying parties' names in instruments and entering them in a way that reasonably diligent searchers can expect to find them. With basic instruments in customary forms, this is likely to be a straightforward matter of entering information into indexing systems without oversight or error, and registers have proofreading and double-checking practices to make sure this does not happen. The Minimum Standards for Indexing Real Property Instruments (hereinafter the Minimum Standards), developed by the North Carolina Association of Registers of Deeds and approved by the bar and promulgated by the North Carolina Secretary of State, address the common possibilities with guidance about how names should be indexed. But when there is no restriction on how documents can be composed, no set of rules can possibly address all name variations, and registers sometimes do not have any clear guidance for a particular instrument. They must rely on judgment to index the instrument in a manner that can reasonably be expected to enable a title examiner to find it with ordinary care. Title examiners similarly must rely on their reasonable understanding of how any particular instrument would be indexed. As Rule 1.01 of the Minimum Standards states, the "rules are intended to promote predictability in the appearance and sorting of names in alphabetical indexes. Reliance on the [alphabetizing and sorting] procedures in these rules is not intended to define the standard of care for a reasonably careful and prudent user of a register's index. Users may be expected to search for names according to variations in appearance that should reasonably be anticipated."[6]

---

5. Hinnant v. Philips, 184 N.C. App. 241, 248, 645 S.E.2d 867, 872 (2007) (quoting *Cuthrell*, 254 N.C. at 184, 118 S.E.2d at 603).

6. North Carolina Association of Registers of Deeds (NCARD), Land Records Committee, *Minimum Standards for Indexing Real Property Instruments* (2012),

5.2 Prompt Indexing

The register is required to index and cross-index every instrument "immediately" after it is filed.[7] At the latest, each instrument must be indexed on the permanent or a temporary index within twenty-four hours of registration.[8] Typically, registers enter indexing information in their permanent electronic system very shortly after registration. If index entries are not made directly into the permanent system and a separate temporary index is used, the indexing information for an instrument may remain on the temporary index for a maximum of thirty days,[9] and by the end of thirty days from the filing date it must be in the permanent index.[10]

5.3 Structure, Contents, and Order of Index

The statutes direct that "the register of deeds shall follow the rules specifying minimum standards and procedures in land records management adopted by the Department of Secretary of State,"[11] and the basic rule for indexing set forth in the statute directs that "[t]he full names of parties shall be entered in the indexes in accordance with the [Minimum Standards]."[12] The effect of these statutes is to make the Minimum Standards an integral part of the indexing law applicable to the register of deeds office.

The statutes authorize registers to adopt local rules for their offices governing the indexing of various types of instruments and names.[13] Local indexing rules must conform to the indexing standards and all indexing statutes. After adopting local rules, the register must post the rules in two prominent places in the office and place copies near the index books or in user manuals. When the index is available on the Internet, a good practice is to post or link the local rules and Minimum Standards with the index. The local rules must include a list of the register's document type

---

https://www.sosnc.gov/documents/forms/land_records/Minimum_Standards_Indexing.pdf (hereinafter Minimum Standards).

7. G.S. 161-14(a).

8. G.S. 161-22(a).

9. G.S. 161-14(a).

10. *Id.*

11. G.S. 161-22.3.

12. G.S. 161-22(a).

13. G.S. 161-22(g).

abbreviations; a description of the location of the records and indexes; and "[i]dentification of previously applicable indexing rules, the dates during which such rules were used, and the location at which a copy of the rules can be reviewed."[14] The information about old rules is important to help examiners understand how searches for names entered into the indexes over the years may appropriately include looking for names as they may have been formatted under prior versions of the rules. The search functions now available make it more likely that names entered in various formats will be found, but the needs and interests of some users may require knowledge of prior indexing peculiarities or conventions.

The register maintains a single index of all documents related to real property in the "Consolidated Real Property Index."[15] It must be subdivided into an index for grantors and an index for grantees. Rules and guidelines for determining whether a party is a grantor or grantee are discussed in Section 5.4 of this chapter. The index must also allow separate searches for human and nonhuman names.[16] For indexing purposes, human names are names apparently of individual human beings. Rules and guidelines for determining the human name components are described in Section 5.5.2 of this chapter. Nonhuman names are names apparently of entities or organizations, such as corporations, partnerships, government agencies, churches, schools, and charitable organizations. Names identified as trade names for sole proprietorships and other businesses or organizations are considered nonhuman names. Registered instruments must be indexed so that they can be identified by reference to the parties and located by reference to the book and page numbers of the record. The Minimum Standards require that the system "shall enable public users to enter queries for names and view document-specific identification information for all documents for which matching names have been indexed as parties."[17] Users must be able to "narrow their search results from the required sortable fields to within a range of registration dates. The system may, but is not required to,

14. NCARD, Land Records Committee, *supra* note 6, at 4 (Minimum Standards Rule 1.02).

15. *Id.* (Minimum Standards Rule 2.01).

16. *Id.*

17. *Id.* at 13 (Minimum Standards Rule 7.03).

enable index users to further narrow their searches based on other fields and criteria."[18]

A few counties have replaced the traditional grantor-grantee indexes with a parcel identifier number (PIN) index. In this system, each parcel of land is assigned a unique identifier number, and all instruments affecting that parcel are indexed under that number. This type of index shows the chain of title of a particular parcel and is an essential part of an integrated land-records system. Such an index is authorized by statute if approved by the N.C. Secretary of State.[19]

For each entry pertaining to a party and a related instrument, the examiner must be able to see the following categories of information, in any order:

- Indexed party with a status abbreviation if applicable, such as trustee. This is the main access point for searching the index.
- Date registered in this numerical format: 01/15/2010.
- At least one name of a reverse party if there is one, which could be a grantee if the indexed party is a grantor or a grantor if the indexed party is a grantee. If the reverse party has a designated status it is shown.
- Document type. Only one type need be listed. Registers may use a list of suggested types from the Minimum Standards or their own types if they are posted and included in local rules. When too many types are used, or more than one type is used for what is really a single type of document, the use of the document type abbreviations loses much of its usefulness.
- Reference to the book and page location in the records.
- A brief property description that is an abbreviation and approximation of information that appears in the document, which can be descriptive or reference information. Indexers do not supply or verify the provided information.
- The land parcel identification number (PIN) if used by the county.[20]

The rules prescribe the order in which names appear in a paper index or in an electronically produced list. Nonhuman names are treated as a single

18. *Id.* (Minimum Standards Rule 7.04).

19. G.S. 161-22.2(d).

20. NCARD, Land Records Committee, *supra* note 6, at 11 (Minimum Standards Rule 5.03).

string of alphabetical characters. Human names are sorted first by surname and among the same surnames according to given names. If all of these are the same, the third level of sorting is according to date registered. The following is an example of this sort order for human names:

Surname	Given names	Date registered
Adams	James	01/17/2012
Adams	John	02/06/2007
Adams	John	05/01/2009
Adert	Robert	11/12/2004

In most cases alphabetical order is obvious and intuitive, following customary order of letters in the alphabet. John obviously follows James, and Adert follows Adams. The presence of spaces, symbols, or punctuation marks requires special considerations. The Minimum Standards prescribes what characters are recognized and their order, which is based on the common computer programming order known as American Standard Code for Information Interchange, or ASCII.[21] This is the order:

! " # $ % & ' () * + , - ./
0 1 2 3 4 5 6 7 8 9
:;< = >? @
A B C D E F G H I J K L M N O P Q R S T U V W X Y Z
[\] ^ _ ` {|} ~

Thus, these names would appear in this order:

!Let's Go LLC
12 Donuts, Inc.
Brown Industries

When the name has only letters and no spaces, character order is the only consideration. If the name has spaces, as with many nonhuman names, the "nothing before something" rule applies. This means that in effect a shorter word comes earlier in order than a longer word beginning with the same letters. For example, Ad Video comes before Adam Instruments because Ad followed by a space (nothing) comes before any combination of Ad followed by a letter (something).

21. *Id.* at 8, 14 (Minimum Standards Rules 3.06, 7.07).

5.4 Identifying Parties

North Carolina statutes require every registered real estate instrument to be indexed in "the names of all parties" to the instrument being registered.[22] The provision that requires indexing in the names of all parties concludes by giving examples of who is to be considered a party: it lists "grantors, grantees, vendors, vendees, obligors, or obligees."[23] What all of these legal actors have in common is that they are transferring or receiving an interest in property or are undertaking or receiving the benefit of a legally enforceable obligation in connection with the conveyance described in the instrument being registered.

A *party* for indexing purposes is someone who appears in the instrument to be giving or receiving an interest in real estate *by means of the instrument being indexed*. A person can be a party to an instrument without signing it—as with, for example, a grantee in a deed. A person named as a grantor or grantee in an instrument should still be indexed as a party to it even if that person did not sign. The register also should index the name of each party identified in an instrument even though the individual was not a subject of a verified acknowledgment.

Just because someone is mentioned in an instrument does not necessarily mean that the individual is a party to the instrument being indexed. Names often appear in an instrument for individuals who are not parties *to that instrument*: names of prior or abutting owners in the property description, or other parties to loan transactions for which a deed of trust is being given, to name a few. For example, if a deed of trust securing a guaranty describes the parties to a loan instrument for which the guaranty was given, the parties to that loan instrument, who are neither grantors nor beneficiaries of the deed of trust, need not be indexed. Deeds of trust secure obligations that usually are expressed in another instrument that is not recorded, such as a promissory note or a guaranty. In this example, the deed of trust is the instrument being indexed, not the guaranty or the loan instrument.

Deeds of trust commonly include a named party as a *nominee* of a lender. If a deed of trust identifies a nominee as the beneficiary of the deed of trust, the grantor and the nominee must be indexed. The further

22. G.S. 161-22(a).
23. *Id.*

identification of the lender who nominates does not oblige the register to index the lender as well.

Registers also must determine whether to include a party name in the grantor or grantee index, or both. A *grantor* is someone who already owns real estate and is conveying some interest in it, such as a seller giving a deed or a borrower giving a deed of trust. A *grantee* is someone acquiring an interest in real property, such as a buyer receiving a deed or a lender becoming the beneficiary of a deed of trust. A party can be both a grantor and grantee in the same instrument, such as the parties to a real estate contract who are both making and receiving promises.

A register must be concerned with indexing the names of parties that the law requires to be indexed. Those who use the index will expect that a name can be found according to what the law requires the register to do. A register wants to avoid claims of legal responsibility based on indexing errors or omissions. But regardless of whether any claims of legal responsibility can be made, the register wants the document to be found because this is the inherent function of the office. Consequently, a register thinks about more than just what is required. The register also keeps in mind some basic considerations.

What other entries would make the instrument easier to find? The statutes and rules set *minimum* requirements for indexing; they do not restrict registers from making additional indexing entries for names that appear in instruments. Registers do not want to fill indexes with every conceivable entry just to avoid any possible complaints. This would unnecessarily burden indexers making entries and searchers trying to pinpoint relevant instruments in the index. But under unusual circumstances in which a name appears in a capacity or form that seems like it is more likely to be found if indexed in some way other than what is required, an additional entry may be appropriate.

On what custom do examiners rely? The statutes and rules are intended to create a statewide indexing system with which a searcher can expect to find records of interest according to basic indexing information entered the same way in every county. The statutes and rules also allow and anticipate that a register may adopt and follow indexing approaches that supplement these uniform requirements to meet the customs and expectations of those who regularly use that county's indexes. This may include continuing to make indexing entries in a way that is no longer required but also not inconsistent with the Minimum Standards. Registers are responsible for deciding whether continuation of local indexing approaches is a reasonable method of enhancing findability or merely perpetuation of an obsolete practice to suit those who are unwilling to adapt to improvements.

Make the additional entry if unsure. No one has a better sense than registers of the index or how searchers will find the necessary information. If a register is wondering whether another entry would be useful, there is probably good enough reason to go ahead and add it even if technically it is not required.

The register's task is made more difficult when drafters do not follow simple steps to identify the parties to be indexed. The frequency with which this occurs is surprising given the fact that the drafter's best interest is to make the register's task easy so that the instrument will be found by later searchers. When the indexing information is unclear or hard to find in the instrument and the document is not indexed as the drafter wishes, any harm that results may be traced back to the drafter. Table 5.1 lists some steps drafters can take to protect their interests.

5.4.1 Representatives

Sometimes someone with legal authority conveys the property of another. The most common examples of such a situation are when a trustee conveys after a foreclosure sale, or a commissioner or sheriff sells the property of a debtor. The statutes provide as follows: "Whenever, any deed or other instrument conveying real property by a trustee, mortgagee, commissioner, or other officer appointed by the court, or by the sheriff under execution, is filed with the register of deeds for the purpose of being recorded, it shall be the duty of the register of deeds to index and cross-index as grantors the names of all persons recited in said instrument to be the persons whose interest in such real estate is being conveyed or from whom the title of such real estate was acquired by the grantor in such instrument."[24] The index entry for the person whose interest is being conveyed is important to the title searcher because this is the name in the preceding chain of title. The searcher likely will not be looking for the name of the individual making the conveyance, such as the trustee, commissioner, or sheriff.

By the same principle, conveyances executed by an attorney-in-fact must be indexed in the grantor index in the names of both the attorney and the principal—that is, the person who executed the power of attorney and

24. G.S. 161-22.1.

Table 5.1 Drafting Techniques for Indexing Considerations

- *Clearly indicate the names of the parties and their capacities as grantor or grantee.* This can be done with forms that clearly depict this information or by use of the words "grantor" or "grantee" in parentheses after the name.
- *Put all names of the parties to the document in the forefront of the instrument,* not in the middle or in attachments. Although registers will look throughout the instrument while indexing, a register should not be expected to find buried names.
- *Clearly distinguish parties' names* from additional information about them and referential names from other documents or agreements. Confusion is common with complex financial structures such as securitized trusts—it can be difficult or impossible to distinguish between a party's name and descriptive information about the investment structure.
- *Avoid adopting names for real estate title with symbols or unusual spacing or punctuation that will result in unfamiliar alphabetizing.* Public recording of real estate instruments is essential to ownership; the public's ability to find them in the record is a primary consideration.
- *Ensure that names appear consistently throughout the document and in signatures.* This means both drafting carefully and paying close attention to names when the documents are completed at closing.
- *Clearly set out a brief description of the property for indexing reference.* Too often this information is added at the last minute and without considering how it will be picked up by the indexer and seen by the searcher of the index.
- *When the document is related to a prior recorded instrument, clearly show the prior document's recording information and the names of the parties to that prior instrument and their original capacities as grantors or grantees.* For example, a satisfaction should clearly identify the parties to the deed of trust or mortgage and the deed of trust's or mortgage's recording data.

the person whose property is being conveyed.[25] Similarly, when property is conveyed for an insolvent in state receivership proceedings or a federal bankruptcy debtor, both the debtor and the receiver or trustee are indexed as grantors. When a conveyance is executed by an executor or administrator of an estate conveying property of a decedent, it should be indexed in the name of the decedent as the real party in interest as well as in the name of the executor or administrator.

25. G.S. 47-115.

5.4.2 Subsequent Instruments

A *subsequent instrument* is any instrument that purports to modify, amend, supplement, assign, satisfy, terminate, revoke, or cancel any previously recorded instrument.[26] A register is not required to examine any page of an instrument beyond the title and the second page to determine whether it is a subsequent instrument,[27] and the register should not be expected to discover the true nature of an instrument by following hidden internal references. If information in the first two pages refers to information elsewhere in the document that the register believes could be helpful in determining the nature of the instrument, it may be appropriate for the register to locate and examine that additional information.

The statute includes the following in its list of examples of subsequent instruments:

- record of satisfaction or other instrument purporting to satisfy a security instrument, which would include a satisfaction of security instrument, a trustee's satisfaction of a deed of trust, a notice of satisfaction, a certificate of satisfaction, or an affidavit of satisfaction;
- appointment or designation of a substitute trustee for a deed of trust;
- affidavit extending the life of a deed of trust;
- cancellation of a notice of hazardous substance or waste disposal site;
- notice of foreclosure;
- assignment of a security instrument or lease;
- modification agreement;
- release or partial release of property from the lien of a security instrument;
- assumption agreement;
- subordination agreement;
- instrument terminating or extending future optional advances; and
- revocation of a power of attorney.

Registers must index the parties to the subsequent instrument as well as the parties to the original instrument if they are named in the subsequent

26. G.S. 161-14.1(a)(3).
27. G.S. 161-14.1(c).

instrument.[28] If the subsequent instrument includes recording data for the original instrument, each index entry must include the recording data as provided in the subsequent instrument.[29] The register is not responsible for verifying the accuracy of the information provided in subsequent instruments.

The first step is to index the original parties to the previously recorded instrument *as they are named in the subsequent instrument.* The original grantors should be indexed as grantors, and the original grantees should be indexed as grantees on the subsequent instrument. Each index entry should contain a reference to the recording data of the previously recorded instrument if the data are provided in the subsequent instrument. When indexing the original parties of a subsequent instrument, the original parties' names are indexed in their original capacities—original grantors as grantors and original grantees as grantees. When the subsequent instrument names original parties but fails to identify their original capacities, the register may index such parties as grantors only or as both grantors and grantees.

The second step is to index the parties to the subsequent instrument. Each index entry should contain a reference to the recording data of the previously recorded instrument if the data are provided in the subsequent instrument. The signatory of the subsequent instrument is indexed as a grantor.

5.4.3 Spelling Discrepancies

Whenever names appear in instruments that seem similar but are composed or spelled in various ways, registers should not assume only one of them is the real name and other variations are misspellings. There are a number of reasons why variations might appear for the same person—a marriage or divorce, use of a nickname, or use of a full middle name rather than an initial. However, unless some obvious information clarifies variations in a name, registers should treat them as if they are for different parties and index each as it appears. By statute, when each word of a signature is legible and it gives the complete name of the party, the signature is the required entry. However, if the printed name is more complete, it is the required entry. If the names are inconsistent—for example, if an apparent

28. G.S. 161-14.1(b).
29. *Id.*

nickname is used in one place and the formal name in another—by statute, both names are to be indexed.[30] By indexing all variations in every case, the register avoids any questions about completeness.

5.4.4 Other Names for Same Party

Sometimes a document includes another name by which a party may be known. One reason this may be included is to make a connection in the chain of title for someone whose name has changed, such as when someone has recently been married or divorced. By rule, when the printed or typed portion of the signature block makes reference to an additional name through terms or acronyms such as "also known as (AKA)," "formerly known as (FKA)," "now known as (NKA)," or "doing business as (DBA)," only the name and the additional name are indexed, not the referential words or acronyms. For example, the name "Jane Smith (FKA Jane Simpson)" is indexed in the names of "Jane Smith" and "Jane Simpson," without the FKA.[31]

5.4.5 Parties to Common Instruments

Although registers must examine every instrument to identify the parties to it, many instruments appear in common form. The following sections describe the likely parties and their capacities in such instruments. Presenters sometimes use familiar titles for instruments with an essential nature not typically found in instruments of that type, and there may be different or additional parties or capacities for indexing, notwithstanding use of the familiar title.

5.4.5.1 Affixing Manufactured Home Notice

A document entitled "affidavit" for removal of a manufactured home from vehicle registration is filed to indicate that a manufactured home has become a part of real estate, though the document usually is not given under oath and therefore actually is not an affidavit in the legal sense. The form is issued by the North Carolina Division of Motor Vehicles to the owner or secured party. It is indexed in the grantor index in the name of the manufactured homeowner and in the grantee index in the name of the

30. G.S. 161-14.2.

31. NCARD, Land Records Committee, *supra* note 6, at 5, 9 (Minimum Standards Rules 3.02, 4.05).

secured party or lien holder if one is indicated.[32] An owner may file a different kind of form, known as a declaration of intent to affix manufactured home, if the manufactured home has not been titled by the Division of Motor Vehicles or the title has already been surrendered. This declaration does not have a division affidavit attached. It is indexed in the same way, with the owner as a grantor and any secured party as a grantee.[33]

5.4.5.2 Assignment of Leases and Rents

An assignment of leases and rents instrument is a security instrument by which an owner, as a grantor, grants an interest to a lender, as a grantee, to collect rents from tenants upon the owner's default in a secured obligation.

5.4.5.3 Assignment of Security Instrument

Deeds of trust and other security instruments are commonly transferred from one lender to another. The record of this transfer is an assignment of security instrument. An assignment relates directly to the deed of trust or other security instrument being assigned and is indexed as a subsequent instrument. The assignor is indexed as a grantor, and the receiving assignee is indexed as a grantee. Also, the original security instrument grantor as named in the assignment is indexed as a grantor, and the original beneficiary as named in the assignment is indexed as a grantee. A cross-reference to recording data for the original security instrument is indexed as it appears in the assignment.

5.4.5.4 Assumed Business Name

A business name certificate, amendment, or withdrawal is indexed in the consolidated index with the person or entity engaging in the business, and the assumed business name, as grantors.

5.4.5.5 Bankruptcy Notice

Someone files a notice of bankruptcy to alert creditors about an owner having filed a federal bankruptcy petition. By federal law, no creditor may foreclose on property owned by a debtor in bankruptcy without the court's permission, known as *relief from the stay*, and no litigation may be com-

32. G.S. 20-109.2; G.S. 47-20.6(a).
33. G.S. 47-20.7.

menced or continued against the debtor without such relief. The name of the debtor in the bankruptcy as shown on the notice is indexed as a grantor.

5.4.5.6 Deed

A *deed* is an instrument that conveys an interest in real estate. An instrument that is a deed usually contains the word "deed" within its title, such as "warranty deed," "quitclaim deed," or "easement deed." Although a deed of trust is a form of deed, it has its own indexing considerations, which are described in Section 5.4.5.7 of this chapter. Customarily, only sellers or persons conveying property sign a deed, and they are indexed as grantors. The buyers or persons receiving a property interest are indexed as grantees. Occasionally, something more than a simple conveyance is happening with a deed, usually indicated by signatures for both parties. This may occur, for example, if two owners are signing one deed to exchange a portion of land along a boundary. When it appears that someone is releasing or conveying something back to a grantor in exchange, both parties should be cross-indexed in grantor and grantee capacities.

5.4.5.7 Deed of Trust

A *deed of trust* is a security instrument by which owners convey an interest in property to a trustee for a lender's benefit. The owners are indexed as grantors, and the lenders, also known as beneficiaries, are indexed as grantees. Customarily, only the owners sign the deed of trust, although sometimes a lender also signs. The trustee usually is an attorney or institution. Those who search indexes look for deeds of trust in the name of the owner and beneficiary, and by statute the name of the trustee is not a required entry.[34]

5.4.5.8 Foreclosure Deed

After a foreclosure, the trustee or mortgagee will record an instrument that will be in the form of a foreclosure deed or notice of conveyance. With it the trustee or lender is transferring the property to the buyer at foreclosure. The trustee or mortgagee who transfers is indexed as a grantor, and the purchaser at foreclosure is indexed as a grantee. The name of the owner whose property is being conveyed also is indexed as a grantor.[35] The origi-

34. G.S. 161-22(d).
35. G.S. 161-22.1.

nal beneficiary also will be indexed as a grantee if and as identified in the notice of foreclosure.

5.4.5.9 Plat

The Minimum Standards require plats to be indexed in the consolidated real property indexes.[36] Each plat is to be indexed in the grantor index in the name of the property owner and in the name of the plat title, as shown in the property designation portion of the plat.[37]

Right-of-way plans recorded by the North Carolina Department of Transportation must be cross-indexed "by number of road affected, if any, and by identification number."[38]

Although no longer recorded, transportation corridor maps were "cross-indexed by number of road, street name, or other appropriate description."[39] The government agencies or units adopting such maps should be indexed as grantors, and the proposed road numbers, street names, or rail lines should be indexed as grantees; this apparently will meet the statutory requirements for cross-indexing. These maps were not recorded in the regular map books or files and should be indexed in the general real property indexes.[40]

Condominium plats are indexed in the deed indexes, with the property owner and condominium as grantors. The index entry should also refer to the book and page and date of recording of the declaration of condominium as shown on the plan.[41]

5.4.5.10 Power of Attorney

With a power of attorney, someone identified as a principal gives an attorney-in-fact the power to sign an instrument or perform other acts in the principal's name. The principal giving the power is indexed as a grantor and the designated attorney-in-fact is indexed as a grantee. When the power of attorney instrument gives more than one person a power, such as when

---

36. NCARD, Land Records Committee, *supra* note 6, at 12 (Minimum Standards Rule 6.01).

37. *Id.* (Minimum Standards Rules 6.02, 6.03).

38. G.S. 136-19.4(c).

39. G.S. 136-44.50(b)(3) (repealed eff. June 21, 2019).

40. G.S. 136-44.50(a)(3), -44.50(b)(4) (repealed eff. June 21, 2019).

41. G.S. 47C-2-109(a); NCARD, Land Records Committee, *supra* note 6, at 12 (Minimum Standards Rule 6.04).

alternate attorneys-in-fact are named, those recipients also are indexed as grantees.

Identifying the parties to a power of attorney instrument can be problematic when the instrument involves securitized trusts. Lenders sometimes use indecipherable references that do not appear to be actual names and whose relationship to the recorded instrument is unclear. For example, the instrument may refer to an appointment being made to an institution in connection with "Securitized Trust ABC, Mortgage Pass-Through Certificates, Series 20015-05." This is not a name of a lender from whom the borrower got the mortgage loan or of anyone else who appears to be in the chain of title for the premises. Some instruments contain long lists of securitized trusts for which the attorney-in-fact is authorized to execute instruments, without respect to whether these trusts in fact hold any mortgages in the jurisdiction. Financial institutions may be including every possible loan arrangement into a single instrument and recording it in every jurisdiction in which it does business, without considering registry indexing or title searches. Even though no one will ever look for such names in the index, and the relevant instruments can reasonably be found with the actual parties involved, if a name appears to be granting a power or receiving it, the register may deem it to be for a party to the instrument being recorded and therefore appropriately indexed. But this may be unclear, and the register cannot reasonably be faulted for not indexing the names in circumstances involving such confusing drafting. For example, the following language in a power of attorney instrument would not require indexing of the names on a schedule:

> ABC Bank ("the Bank") appoints Acme Servicing LLC ("the Servicer") to be the Bank's attorney-in-fact in connection with the Pooling and Servicing Agreements in Schedule A hereto . . .

That the bank is giving powers to the servicer as well as information in the schedule about underlying agreements or loans does not make the names listed in the schedule parties to the power of attorney instrument. On the other hand, a register would index the names on the schedule when language similar to the following is used:

> The trusts identified in the attached Schedule A ("the Trusts"), by and through ABC Bank as Trustee ("the Trustee"), appoint

> Acme Servicing LLC ("the Servicer") to be their attorney-in-fact in connection with . . .

In this example the trusts are named as principals appointing a servicer for them, so they all appear to be parties to the attorney-in-fact instrument. When an instrument ambiguously identifies the relationship of names the presenter should not be surprised by varied interpretations of the indexing requirements and excessive name recording fees.

5.4.5.11 *Request for Notice of Foreclosure*

A lender who makes a loan secured by a deed of trust that is subordinate to a prior recorded deed of trust or mortgage, as well as any other person, may file an instrument requesting notice if the beneficiary of the prior-recorded deed of trust or mortgage exercises the power of foreclosure sale. By statute, the register is to index as grantors the owner who gave the prior recorded deed of trust or mortgage and the person requesting the notice. The register also must include a reference to the recording information for the prior recorded security instrument to which the request refers.[42] The original beneficiary as named in the request also should be indexed as a grantee.

5.4.5.12 *Satisfaction of Security Instrument*

In any form and by any title, satisfaction instruments—commonly in the form of a satisfaction of security instrument, trustee's satisfaction, notice of satisfaction, certification of satisfaction, or deed of release—are records showing that the security instruments, including, but not limited to, deeds of trust, are no longer in effect. Beneficiaries or trustees who give the satisfaction instruments are indexed as grantors. Searchers want to be able to find a satisfaction instrument when they see on the record the deed of trust or other security instrument to which it applies, and this will occur when the satisfaction instrument is properly indexed as a subsequent instrument. Accordingly, owners who were grantors of security instruments as named in the satisfactions are indexed as grantors, and original beneficiaries are indexed as grantees if and as they are named in satisfaction instruments. A cross-reference to recording data for the original security instrument is provided if and as it appears in the satisfaction instrument.

---

42. G.S. 45-21.17A(b).

5.4.5.13 Substitution of Trustee

With a substitution of trustee instrument the beneficiary of a deed of trust is removing someone previously named as a trustee and appointing someone else to that capacity. The beneficiary making the substitution is indexed as a grantor, and the new trustee is indexed as a grantee. A substitution is a subsequent instrument to the instrument that previously named a trustee. Accordingly, owners who were grantors of security instruments as named in the substitution are indexed as grantors, and reference is made to the security instrument recording data as provided in the substitution. Although the original trustee may not be a required index entry, registers commonly do index them as grantees.

5.4.5.14 Uniform Commercial Code Filing

Article 9 of the Uniform Commercial Code (UCC) prescribes specific indexing requirements for UCC financing statements, amendments, and assignments filed with a register of deeds office. Debtors and record owners listed on financing statements are indexed as grantors, and secured parties are indexed as grantees.[43] If an amendment adds or changes a name, that name must also be indexed.[44] If an assignment is reflected in an initial financing statement or in an amendment, the assignor is indexed as a grantor and the assignee is indexed as a grantee.[45] All subsequent UCC statements, including amendments, must reference the file number of the original financing statement.[46] A UCC amendment is a subsequent instrument subject to the indexing requirements discussed in Section 5.4.2 of this chapter.

5.5 Format of Index Name Entries

The basic approach for indexing the names of parties to an instrument is to enter them in all capitals exactly as they appear on the document—that is, as they were expressed by the drafter. In most cases this is simply a matter of entering all characters in the same sequence.

---

43. G.S. 25-9-519(c), (d).
44. G.S. 25-9-519(c)(2).
45. G.S. 25-9-519(e).
46. G.S. 25-9-519(c)(1).

Registers must separately index nonhuman and human names. A name should be recognizable as nonhuman by a word, acronym, or abbreviation in the name indicating an entity (such as "Corporation" or "Inc." or "LLC") or with additional information that follows the name (such as "a North Carolina corporation"). Nonhuman names are not treated any differently if they contain a human name. "James A. O'Neil Products, Inc.," will be entered exactly as it appears. Nonhuman names are entered as one name as the characters appear.[47] Human names are entered into two fields: surname and given names.[48] Section 5.5.2 of this chapter discusses some of the complications that can arise in determining the surname and given name components.

The index entry will contain all of the recognized characters within a name as they appear and without any abbreviations made by the indexer. The system must allow a minimum of seventy characters in each of the fields for nonhuman name, human surname, and human given name. A register may set up the system to allow more in a field.[49] In the very unlikely case that a name has more characters than can fit in the field, the indexer will enter as many characters, including punctuation and spaces, as will fit. The searcher will find it by entering those same characters.

The vast majority of names can be indexed by following these simple procedures. The following sections describe the Minimum Standards for entering names with unusual characters or structures.

5.5.1 Recognized Characters

Names sometimes have letters, symbols, numbers, or other characters that are not common in American names. Indexers will recognize and enter almost every character they see, but practicality requires some reasonable limit. This limit is based on what is on the standard keyboard. Index entries for names include only the following characters, numerals, and

---

47. NCARD, Land Records Committee, *supra* note 6, at 7 (Minimum Standards Rule 3.05(d)).

48. *Id.* (Minimum Standards Rule 3.05(c)).

49. *Id.* at 6 (Minimum Standards Rule 3.04(b)).

symbols, which shall be alphabetized according to the ASCII sequence shown again here:

> ! ” # $ % & ‘ () * + , - ./
> 0 1 2 3 4 5 6 7 8 9
> :;< = >? @
> A B C D E F G H I J K L M N O P Q R S T U V W X Y Z
> [\] ^ _ ` {|} ~

Marks applied to letters, most of which are considered diacritical marks, are ignored. For example, the name “Peña” is indexed as “Pena.”[50]

5.5.2 Components of Human Names

Sometimes the composition of a human name—which part is a family or surname, and which is a given name—can be difficult to determine because the name is unconventionally composed or originates from a culture unfamiliar to North Carolinians. Names may also include such things as suffixes, titles, hyphens, and parentheticals. Registers should use their experience and reasonable judgment to identify what seem to be the components of unusually structured names. The following sections describe Minimum Standards rules that enable registers and index users to anticipate the appearance of human names in the index.

5.5.2.1 Language Convention

Human names typically have two parts: a surname and at least one given name. The surname is generally inherited from a parent or parents. The Minimum Standards provide that “[t]he register of deeds shall assume that all names on a document are in the United States name convention of given name(s) followed by surname.”[51] This means, for example, that if three separate words are given, the register assumes that the last is the surname. Thus, for indexing purposes, the name “Maria Hernandez Sanchez” is indexed with “Sanchez” as the surname and “Maria Hernandez” as given names. Accordingly, neither indexers nor those who use indexes need know or conjecture whether a name is of a culture that uses a word order differently than given name followed by surname. Even if this convention

---

50. *Id.* at 8 (Minimum Standards Rule 3.06).
51. *Id.* at 6 (Minimum Standards Rule 3.03).

does not reflect the intent of the person whose name is being indexed, it is a workable and predictable approach for indexers and searchers.

In rare instances, someone goes by a single word as the complete human name. In this case, the single word is indexed as both the given name and the surname.[52]

5.5.2.2 Hyphenated Surname

Hyphenated surnames most often are created when someone gets married. Part of the hyphenated surname may be the same as the name in which someone previously acquired title to the real estate. To enable connections to be made as names are changed, a special rule applies to how the indexing system will display a hyphenated surname. The register's indexing system is to create a multiple entry when a surname is entered with two or more words separated by a hyphen. The name will appear as it was entered with the hyphen, as both words without the hyphen, and as only the last word as the surname.[53] For example, the name "Jane Smith-Simpson" will be entered with "Smith-Simpson" as the surname and "Jane" as the given name. By computer function the hyphenation in the surname field will result in three appearances in the index: "Smith-Simpson" as surname and "Jane" as given name; "Smith Simpson" as surname and "Jane" as given name; and "Simpson" as surname and "Jane Smith" as given names. The three appearances account for the various ways hyphenated surnames have been entered into indexes over the years, and users will find any of them with searches for any of the variations. Note that this rule only applies to a hyphenated *surname*; that is, when the last two words in a name are connected with a dash or hyphen. *Given* names with two or more words separated by a hyphen are keyed into the index just as they appear on the document. For example, in the case of "Ann Mary-Margaret Hendon," "Hendon" is the surname and "Ann Mary-Margaret" are given names.

5.5.2.3 Surnames in Parentheses

Names in parentheses often reflect newly adopted married names. The Minimum Standards have a special rule for such names. The indexer has an additional entry to make when what clearly appears to be an additional surname is in parentheses before or after the surname, as in "Jane Anne

52. *Id.* at 10 (Minimum Standards Rule 4.07).
53. *Id.* at 8, 15 (Minimum Standards Rules 4.01, 7.10).

(Smith) Simpson." The name is keyed into the index by the surname not in parentheses and also by the surname in parentheses.[54] For the entry with the surname in parentheses, the surname not in parentheses is indexed as the last given name. When indexing the surname not in parentheses, the surname in parentheses is treated as the last given name. Accordingly, "Jane Anne (Smith) Simpson" would be indexed with the surname "Simpson" and the given names "Jane Anne Smith" and with the surname "Smith" and the given names "Jane Anne Simpson."

5.5.2.4 Suffixes

A suffix is a designation given to distinguish someone from someone else in the family with the same given and surname. This includes designations such as Junior, Jr., Sr., II, and III. These suffixes are indexed after the last given name with no comma between the last given name and the suffix. For example, the name "William John Smith, III" is indexed with the given name "William John III."[55]

5.5.2.5 Titles and Degrees

A title such as Reverend, Bishop, Dr., Major, Mr., Ms., and Mrs. is not indexed as part of the human name unless it is with a surname and no other given name or with only what appears on the face of the document to be the spouse's name.[56] In these instances, the title is necessary to distinguish the name. For example, if the parties' names are "Mr. and Mrs. Smith," two names would be indexed, with "Mr." and "Mrs." as the given names. Professional certifications or degrees such as CPA, DDS, and MD are not included in the index entry.[57]

5.5.3 Status Field

Signatories on real estate instruments are sometimes signing in behalf of someone else. A common example is an attorney-in-fact, who signs for a principal pursuant to a power of attorney. Another common example is a

54. *Id.* at 9 (Minimum Standards Rule 4.05).
55. *Id.* (Minimum Standards Rule 4.04).
56. *Id.* (Minimum Standards Rule 4.03).
57. *Id.* at 10 (Minimum Standards Rule 4.06).

trustee for a trust. The following types of status are to be included in an index entry for the person for whom it is associated if it is clearly indicated:

Trustee
Attorney-in-fact
Administrator or administratrix
Executor or executrix[58]

Registers may, but are not required to, include other types of status, such as beneficiary. The status designation is to be shown in the index in a separate field from the name. It is not part of the alphabetizing order for sorting purposes.

5.5.4 Estate Names

An estate is named in a real estate instrument to indicate a transfer as a result of someone's death. Title searchers are therefore most likely to be looking at the deceased person's ownership interests under that person's name. Accordingly, the required entry for an estate name is the human name in it.[59] Reference to the estate is optional, and, if included, should be in a field that does not affect the alphabetical order of the human name being indexed. One option to a register is to enter a reference to the estate in the status field. For example, the required entry for the "John Smith Estate" would be as a human name with "Smith" as the surname and "John" as the given name, with the option of entering estate in the status field. The register has the option of also indexing "John Smith Estate" as a nonhuman name.

5.5.5 Trust Names

A trust can be created during someone's lifetime or with a will at death. If the trust name includes a human name, the person named in the trust is most likely to have been a prior owner of the property. Therefore, the indexing rule requires that when a trust name contains what clearly appears to be a human name, the trust name and the human name are indexed.[60] For example, the "John Smith and Mary Brown Revocable Trust" would be indexed with the full trust name as a nonhuman name and the human

58. *Id.* at 11 (Minimum Standards Rule 5.02).
59. *Id.* at 10 (Minimum Standards Rule 4.08).
60. *Id.* (Minimum Standards Rule 4.09).

names "John Smith" and "Mary Brown." When indexing the human name for a trust, references to the trust are optional; if included, they should be entered in the status field and would not affect the sort order of the human name being indexed.

5.6 Search Aids

Computer-assisted search aids are familiar tools to anyone who uses the Internet. Google, Yahoo, Bing, and other search engines use a number of functions to help searchers find records of interest. The aids suggest to the user variations that may be relevant to the entered search. Lawyers have been using computer search aids in their legal research for decades. The rules require that systems provide searchers with the choice to use several technical search aids.

5.6.1 Equivalencies

The rules require each system to include a number of equivalencies that will automatically associate an entered word with an abbreviation or an entered abbreviation with its full word.[61] Users are likely familiar with Internet search engines that automatically look for equivalencies. For example, if USA is entered as a search, the results will include USA, US, United States, and United States of America.

The rules require index searches to include more than two dozen sets of equivalencies for such common things as corp for corporation and NC for North Carolina. Registers can add other equivalencies to their systems. They may wish to do so for abbreviations that are commonly used within their counties, especially if an abbreviation and its full name seem to be used interchangeably, as may be the case with a bank name that is also an acronym. Registers should keep in mind, however, that additional equivalencies mean additional results on the search return screen and therefore more information for the searcher to consider.

---

61. *Id.* at 16 (Minimum Standards Rule 7.13).

5.6.2 Auto Completion

Auto completion is a feature that suggests matching responses. After several characters are entered (the minimum number is set by the system), a drop-down menu provides a list of possible matches from which the searcher can choose with a click. For the register of deeds system this list will be from names in the database of index entries.[62] For example, someone searching for "Mark Twain" in a library database will immediately be given that option after typing the letters *Twa*.

Auto completion has at least three potential advantages for a register's index. It can speed up a search when there are only a few possible entries that match the query. A name such as "Ptolemy" may be easily found as soon as the first few letters are entered, because there are likely to be very few names beginning with the letters *Pto*. Obviously, auto completion is not so useful in this respect if the name is common, because there will be many possible matching results and additional information will be necessary to find the desired match. Second, with an unusual name, auto completion may reveal a spelling error in the search entry by showing no matches, and the user can correct the spelling until a match is found. Third, the drop-down list may suggest other variations that the searcher may wish to consider. For example, if the person who is the subject of the search sometimes used a shortened version of a given name, or sometimes used a middle initial, the auto completion may serve as a reminder to the searcher to consider the alternatives.

5.6.3 Soundex

Even common names can be spelled in different and unexpected ways, especially with unfamiliar ethnic variations. Someone with an uncommon spelling of a common sounding name also may frequently encounter misspellings—for example, someone named Smyth, who always must note the difference from Smith. Genealogists are familiar with the need to consider spelling variations. One source of spelling discrepancies is immigration officers' having recorded variations of unfamiliar sounding names. To associate names that sound alike but are spelled differently, a soundex system was developed to code names based on how they sound.[63] The soundex code employed by the National Archives and Records Admin-

---

62. *Id.* at 13 (Minimum Standards Rule 7.05).
63. *Id. (Minimum Standards* Rule 7.06).

istration, which is widely used, contains a letter for the first letter of the surname and numbers for the remaining letters of the surname according to a formula.[64] Additional letters are disregarded. For example, Smith is coded S-530. By giving the same value to letters or letter groups that sound alike, names can be compared to see if they are in fact for the same person or family. The Smith code is the same as codes for names such as Smyth and Smythe. By another rule, if a surname has a prefix, such as Van, Con, De, Di, La, or Le, it is coded both with and without the prefix. Therefore, a search for "Van Hoesen" would also find the name "Hoesen." This kind of association can be helpful, because searchers may be unfamiliar with how prefixes are treated in indexing.

Each register is required to provide a soundex system option for indexers' use. The details can vary, and programmers may be able to provide formulas that make more comparisons than are common in the basic approach.

5.6.4 Political Divisions

To assist searchers with finding names, the system will return results for queries that identify a political division and proper name without regard to the order in which the political division and proper name appear or the presence of the word *of*. Political divisions include district, village, town, township, municipality, city, county, and state.[65] For example, if the index includes "Village of Pinehurst," the searcher can also find this by entering "Pinehurst Village."

5.6.5 Words Beginning with *The, A, An*

The system's functionality will return entries both with and without regard to the presence of the articles *the*, *a*, or *an* at the beginning of the indexed name or query.[66] For example, the name "The Farm Incorporated" can also be found with a search for "Farm Incorporated."

---

64. United States National Archives and Records Administration, The Soundex Indexing System, www.archives.gov/research/census/soundex.html.

65. NCARD, Land Records Committee, *supra* note 6, at 16 (Minimum Standards Rule 7.12).

66. *Id.* at 15 (Minimum Standards Rule 7.11).

5.6.6 Results and Punctuation, Symbols, and Spaces

Names that include punctuation, symbols, and spaces within them pose a challenge for both indexers and searchers. These elements make it more difficult to match a query to the search and make it more difficult to anticipate where a name will fall in sort order. As noted previously in the discussion on sort order, the "nothing before something" rule affects the order among words with the same letters but different spacing. The "as it appears" approach cannot eliminate all challenges in finding names with punctuation, symbols, and spaces. Under the rules, names usually will be indexed with such elements. Because the indexing rules have changed over the years, a searcher who is interested in documents indexed for the same person should consider looking for it as it would be indexed both ways. To assist the searcher in this endeavor, the Minimum Standards require that the system enable a searcher to match names both with and without the punctuation, symbols, and spaces within them. In other words, during the search process the system will strip out these elements from names in the database and the name in the query and provide a list of matches of what remains.[67] The search may return matches that would be missed without this function because of slight variations in indexing or searching. In an unusual case this may give more results than the searcher wants, but that is for the searcher to determine. For example, if the searcher is looking for "Auto Parts! Inc." and enters this name as it appears, the return will provide "Auto Parts Inc." as a possible match, and this might be a different name. The searcher needs to determine what variations there may be for the party of interest. The register may have configured the system to give the searcher the option of seeing only exact matches.

5.7 Corrections to Index

If an indexing error or omission is discovered by the register or brought to the register's attention, the register should correct the error in such a way that someone who thereafter uses the index will see the correct information. In addition, someone searching the record should be alerted to the fact that for some prior period the index provided incorrect information, in order to protect persons who may have relied on the erroneous record or

67. *Id.* at 14 (Minimum Standards Rule 7.09).

index entry and whose rights may have been affected by that reliance. The note of correction should state the nature of the error and the time period during which it existed in the index.

The register has no authority to correct an error appearing in an original instrument, such as a misspelled name, a defective property description, or an incorrect loan amount. The register records the instrument as it is and under no circumstances alters the text of a recorded instrument.

A person discovering an error in the registration of an instrument may petition the clerk of superior court for correction.[68]

68. G.S. 47-36.

Chapter 6

Marriage Licenses

Chapter 6

Marriage Licenses

6.1 Registers' Role

Registers of deeds issue marriage licenses to couples who can show that they meet minimum age and other North Carolina law requirements. The license authorizes civil and religious officials to perform a ceremony within the state at which the bride and groom declare their marriage. The officiant and two witnesses of the ceremony sign the license, and the officiant returns the license to the register of deeds, where it becomes a permanent public record of the marriage.

In this procedure, registers do not "marry" people—they perform a function in behalf of the state to check that the couple meets the legal requirements before giving their marriage vows. In most cases, issuing the license is a simple matter without legal complications, allowing the register to be part of a joyous event. However, as this chapter describes, sometimes a register must refuse a license application, and sometimes those who seek it are left with an unsettled legal situation.

Issuing marriage licenses is one of the register's basic functions, along with recording real estate instruments (see Chapter 3 of this book) and maintaining copies of vital records (see Chapter 7 of this book). However, registers' role in marriage law did not begin until after the Civil War. Traditionally, couples who wanted to get married made a public announcement, or banns, of their intent in church so that anyone who had an objection—for example, someone to whom the bride or groom was already married—could intervene. North Carolina law gave a couple an alternative to the banns if they appeared before the county clerk for a license and posted a bond to guarantee their qualification to get married. After the war, the license process shifted to the registers of deeds, and everyone was required to get a license.[1] Over the years registers have been required to check for various qualifications and have been responsible for such things as enforcing prohibitions on interracial marriages and confirming that medical test requirements have been met. The qualifications have changed over time, but North Carolina law still requires couples to get a marriage license from a register of deeds.

What constitutes a marriage is a question of the law of the jurisdiction in which the marriage occurs. In North Carolina, there are penalties for performing a marriage ceremony without a license, but not for getting married without a license. Unlike in some states, in North Carolina couples can create a legally recognized marriage as a result of a ceremony without a license. A couple cannot become married in what some states recognize as a "common law marriage" based on how long a couple lived together and whether they acted as husband and wife.[2] In this state the couple must "celebrate" their marriage in a ceremony, intending in good faith for it to be a marriage.[3]

Becoming married at a ceremony without a license can cause difficult legal problems for the couple. Among other things, without a recorded license no one can determine whether they are in fact married until a court has decreed it. Registers of deeds maintain permanent records of the marriages that have been performed according to required procedure in North Carolina. Of course, many people who live in North Carolina were married outside this state. Whether their marriages are legal is a question of the law in the state or country in which the marriage occurred. Those who ask registers about such legality should be redirected to seek legal advice from an attorney admitted to practice in the state or country in which the ceremony occurred.

---

1. 1871–72 N.C. Sess. Laws ch. 193.

2. State v. Alford, 298 N.C. 465, 259 S.E.2d 242 (1979), *and* State v. Wilson, 121 N.C. 650, 28 S.E. 41 6 (1897).

3. State v. Lynch, 301 N.C. 479, 272 S.E.2d 349 (1980); *Alford*, 298 N.C. 465, 259 S.E.2d 242; *Wilson*, 121 N.C. 650, 28 S.E. 416.

6.2 Capacity to Marry

When a couple applies for a marriage license, the law requires that the register of deeds make a reasonable inquiry to determine that both parties have the legal capacity to marry under North Carolina law. Although the license process is intended to prevent illegal marriages from occurring, getting a license does not make legal what is otherwise illegal. If someone who may not lawfully get married obtains a license, the marriage may be invalid or subject to invalidation in a court action.[4] The licensing requirements are intended to prevent this from occurring. The circumstances about which the register inquires before issuing a license include the couple's marital status, age, and kinship. A register also may refuse to provide a license based on a reasonable determination that the couple otherwise do not meet the capacity to make the representations required of them for a license.

6.2.1 Marital Status

No one with a living spouse may legally marry any other person. Someone who marries while already married or who aids and abets such an act is guilty of a Class I felony.[5] A person once married becomes eligible for remarriage only after the spouse's death or after a divorce from the prior marriage is final. A marriage is not terminated merely by separation or the confinement of one spouse in a prison, mental hospital, or other similar institution. A spouse continuously absent and unheard from by friends or relatives for seven years may legally be presumed dead, but this is a rebuttable presumption, and a register cannot determine that the marriage has been terminated under these circumstances without a court decree.[6]

To determine the couple's unmarried status, the register asks about prior marriages, but he or she does not have the means or responsibility to independently investigate the facts. Registers should stress to the couple the importance of the truthfulness and completeness of the couple's representations under oath. When the information presented is unclear

---

4. For a discussion of marriage laws in North Carolina and many of the practical issues they raise, see Janet Mason, *Marriage in North Carolina*, Popular. Gov. (Winter 2006), at 26, https://www.sog.unc.edu/sites/www.sog.unc.edu/files/articles/article3_21.pdf.

5. Chapter 14, Section 183 of the North Carolina General Statutes (hereinafter G.S.).

6. Stewart v. Rogers, 260 N.C. 475, 133 S.E.2d 155 (1963); Ward v. Bailey, 118 N.C. 55, 23 S.E. 926 (1896); State *ex rel.* Spencer v. Moore, 33 N.C. 160 (1850).

about whether a divorce has become final, a register may appropriately ask for a certified copy of the divorce decree and may attach a copy of it to the file copy of the application. If either party is uncertain about the status of a prior marriage, or if the couple contests the register's refusal to issue a marriage license to them, the register should recommend that the couple consult an attorney.

Occasionally, based on a misunderstanding, a couple may represent to a register that they are unmarried and obtain a marriage license, when, in fact, one of them has not yet obtained a final divorce decree. Under North Carolina law, a marriage that takes place while one of the parties is still married to another is void.[7] A void marriage is a nullity, as if it did not occur. Consequently, if a couple appears before the register having already obtained a license for a ceremony while one of them had not yet received a final divorce decree, the couple may, based on North Carolina law, apply for a license after the divorce from the prior marriage is final and represent that they are unmarried, because their prematurely obtained license and ceremony were nullities. However, this is a representation for the couple to make based on their individual circumstances and the advice of their attorney, not a conclusion about which registers should attempt to give advice.

6.2.2 Age Requirements

Any person at least eighteen years old, if not otherwise incapacitated, may lawfully marry.[8] Younger persons may be issued marriage licenses in the following two circumstances.

Sixteen to eighteen years old with consent. When either party to the proposed marriage is between sixteen and eighteen, the register of deeds may issue a license only if the couple's age difference is no more than four years. In addition, the applicant between sixteen and eighteen must file either a certified copy of a North Carolina district court order authorizing the marriage or a written consent to the marriage signed by the appropriate person, agency, or institution, which could be

- a parent having full or joint legal custody of the underage marriage applicant; or

7. G.S. 51-3; Ivery v. Ivery, 258 N.C. 721, 726, 129 S.E.2d 457, 461 (1963).
8. G.S. 51-2.

- a person, agency, or institution having legal custody or serving as guardian of the underage marriage applicant.[9]

The consenting custodian's or guardian's status may be established with documentary evidence of the appointment. A parent who is divorced, separated, or unmarried may have a court order or a separation agreement establishing that he or she has sole or joint legal custody of a couple's child. Most parents, however, are never involved in a court action or contractual agreement regarding custody of their children. They have equal rights to custody of their children that are not reflected in any formal document. A register should be able to rely on a parent's affidavit that sets forth sufficient facts on which the register may reasonably determine that the parent has the required custodial rights.

Sixteen to eighteen years old and emancipated. A license also may be issued to persons between sixteen and eighteen whom the court has emancipated from parental authority. A certified copy of the emancipation decree or certificate of emancipation must be filed with the register of deeds before the license can be issued under this exception.[10]

6.2.3 Kinship

No two persons of kinship nearer than first cousins may lawfully marry, and the law specifically prohibits marriages between double first cousins.[11] Double first cousins are involved when brothers of one family marry sisters of another, or when a brother and sister of one family marry a sister and brother of another. The children (double cousins) of these marriages cannot marry each other. In computing the degree of kinship, half-blood must be counted as whole-blood, except for existing marriages that would be made subject to question by that method of computation.[12] The statute says that a marriage between two people of prohibited kinship "shall be void" but then provides a number of circumstances under which such a marriage may not be declared void. The North Carolina Supreme Court has interpreted the statute as making such marriages voidable consistent with the common law.[13]

---

9. G.S. 51-2(a1).
10. *Id.*
11. G.S. 51-3.
12. *Id.*
13. *Ivery*, 258 N.C. 721, 129 S.E.2d 457.

6.2.4 Gender

In June 2015 the United States Supreme Court held that the United States Constitution forbids a state from denying a license for marriage between two people of the same sex.[14] This rendered unenforceable the marriage license gender restrictions in this state's constitution and statutes. Accordingly, there now are no gender requirements for a marriage license.

6.2.5 Competency

A marriage is void if at the time of the marriage a party was "incapable of contracting for want of understanding."[15] A register does not have a duty to make inquiry of all applicants to assess their mental capacity. But a register should not issue a license to an applicant who is obviously intoxicated or otherwise incapable of understanding what is occurring. Those who are intoxicated may return when they are sober and apparently capable of understanding what they are doing.

6.3 Issuance of Marriage Licenses

Marriage licenses may be issued to a qualified couple by the register of deeds personally or by the register's assistants and deputies. An assistant or deputy should issue and sign the license in the register's name as assistant or deputy.[16] The following sections describe the required procedure for issuing marriage licenses.

6.3.1 Marriage License

The marriage application, license, and certificate are elements of a three-part form supplied pre-numbered to each register of deeds by North Carolina Vital Records. The register completes the top portion of the form and retains the last page (the application) for the records. The applicants are given the two remaining pages of the form, which constitute the marriage license. These are presented to the person performing the marriage ceremony, who must complete both copies of the certificate and return them

---

14. Obergefell v. Hodges, 135 S. Ct. 2584 (2015).
15. G.S. 51-3.
16. G.S. 51-8.

to the issuing register within ten days after the ceremony.[17] Failure to meet these responsibilities is a criminal misdemeanor offense and also makes the person performing the marriage liable in the amount of $200 to anyone proving in court that the person failed to act as the law requires.[18]

If a person applying for a license submits a current and valid Address Confidentiality Program authorization card issued pursuant to Chapter 15C of the North Carolina General Statutes (hereinafter G.S.), the register must use the substitute address designated by the program.[19]

6.3.2 Application Form and Identity

To apply for a marriage license, a couple must complete the N.C. Vital Records form by providing information necessary for the register to determine eligibility. The statutes do not prescribe what form of identification is sufficient to show that the person making the representations is who he or she claims to be. The register should require both applicants to identify themselves with evidence that a reasonable person would find reliable, which would include but not be limited to government-issued photo identification, such as a driver's license or passport. There is no requirement that applicants for a marriage license have North Carolina or United States identification or proof of residency or citizenship status. However, a North Carolina statute, G.S. 15A-311, prohibits a government official from using a "matricula consular or other similar document" for purposes of determining a person's identity or residence. Couples who meet the specified legal requirements have a constitutional right to marry. Introducing additional requirements could be a denial of constitutional rights of due process, equal protection, and privileges and immunities.[20]

6.3.3 Personal Appearance

Both parties to the marriage should personally appear before the register when the application is submitted. The statutes allow issuance of a license in the absence of one applicant who is over eighteen years of age if the other party appears in person and submits a sworn and notarized affidavit

---

17. G.S. 51-16.

18. G.S. 51-7.

19. G.S. 51-16.1.

20. Loving v. Virginia, 388 U.S. 1 (1967) ("Marriage is one of the 'basic civil rights of man,' fundamental to our very existence and survival.").

from the absent party, with documentation about age and divorce status if required by the county. This procedure is available only when one of the parties is "unable to appear in person,"[21] which would include but is not necessarily limited to a party's incarceration, hospitalization, or deployment in the military. The statute provides the following form of affidavit; it or its equivalent is sufficient if fully completed:

> ___________________, [applicant] appearing before the undersigned notary and being duly sworn, says that:
>
> (1) I, ___________________, [applicant's name] am applying for a license in ___________________ County, North Carolina, to marry ___________________ [name of other applicant] in North Carolina within the next 60 days and I am authorized under G.S. 51-8.2 to complete this Affidavit in Lieu of Personal Appearance for Marriage License Application.
>
> I attach: (1) documentation that I am over 18 years of age as required in county of issuance; and (2) documentation of divorce as required by county of issuance.
>
> (2) I submit the following information in applying for a marriage license:
>
> Name: ____
> *First* *Middle* *Last*
>
> Residence: ____
> *State* *County* *City or Town*
>
> ____
> *Street and Number*
>
> Inside City Limits (Yes or No): _______________________
>
> Birthplace: ____
> *County & State or Country*
>
> Birth Date: ____________________ Age: _______________
>
> Father: ____
> *Name* *State of Birth*
>
> ____
> *Address (if living) or Deceased*
>
> Mother: ____
> *Name* *State of Birth*
>
> ____
> *Address (if living) or Deceased*
>
> Race (optional): _____________________________________
>
> Number of this marriage: 1st, 2nd, etc. _________________
>
> Last Marriage Ended by: ______________________________
> *Death, Divorce, Annulment*

21. G.S. 51-8.2.

Date Marriage Ended: ______________________________________
Specify Highest Grade Completed in School (optional): ____________
Social Security # ____
(If applicant does not have Social Security number, attach affidavit of ineligibility)

I hereby make application to the Register of Deeds for a Marriage License and solemnly swear that all of the statements contained in the above application are true and I further make oath that there is no legal impediment to such marriage.

____
Signature of Applicant

Sworn to (or affirmed) and subscribed before me this ______ day of ___________, ________.

____

[Seal] Notary Public
My commission expires: __________

____
[Notary's typed or printed name][22]

6.3.4 Age

If either applicant for a marriage license is under eighteen years old, a written consent to the marriage or a court decree or order must be submitted, as discussed in Section 6.2.2 of this chapter. The register may require a certified copy of a birth certificate as proof of age.[23]

6.3.5 Social Security Numbers

Each applicant for a license must either furnish a Social Security number or, if an applicant does not have a Social Security number and is ineligible to obtain one, he or she must present a sworn or affirmed statement to that effect to the register of deeds as provided by G.S. 51.8.[24] A statement from a person who is ineligible for a Social Security number in substantially this form would suffice: "I swear (or affirm) that I have not been issued a Social Security number by the United States Government, and I am ineligible to obtain a Social Security number." Nothing needs to be said about why the

22. *Id.*
23. G.S. 51-8.
24. *Id.*

applicant does not have a Social Security number, why the applicant is in the United States, or the country of which the applicant is a citizen. The register of deeds is to retain this statement with the register's copy of the marriage license; it is not forwarded to N.C. Vital Records.

6.3.6 Fees

The fee for a marriage license is set by statute.[25] By statute, portions of this fee are forwarded to the state treasurer for deposit in funds for children's and domestic violence programs.[26] Registers are required to inform the applicants about the portion of the fee to be used for domestic violence programs.[27]

6.3.7 Responsibility of the Register

The statute requires the register to make a "reasonable inquiry" into the couple's eligibility.[28] In many respects, the register must rely on the couple's representations. The register should be deemed to have acted reasonably when there is no good reason to doubt the trustworthiness of a representation.[29] There is no rule to test the reasonableness of inquiries under all circumstances. The statutes expressly provide that requiring the presentation of a copy of the applicant's birth certificate or birth registration card constitutes reasonable inquiry about age.[30] The statutes also provide that the register may require the applicants to furnish whatever evidence the register deems necessary to show that they are authorized to be married.[31]

The law provides that any register of deeds who knowingly or without reasonable inquiry, personally or by deputy, issues a marriage license when there is any lawful impediment or when either applicant is under age without the parental consent required by law may have to forfeit $200 to "any parent, guardian, or other person standing in loco parentis, who sues for the same."[32]

---

25. G.S. 161-10(a)(2).
26. G.S. 161-11.1, -11.2.
27. G.S. 161-11.2.
28. G.S. 51-17.
29. Bowles v. Cochran, 93 N.C. 398 (1885).
30. G.S. 51-17.
31. *Id.*
32. *Id.*

6.4 Marriage Ceremony and Record

After the register of deeds issues a marriage license, the couple appears before someone authorized by North Carolina law to perform a ceremony, known as an *officiant*. The license is returned to the register after the ceremony and the register keeps a record of it. The following sections describe these requirements.

6.4.1 Marriage Ceremony

As provided in G.S. 51-1, an essential requirement for a valid marriage in this state is "the consent of a male and female person who may lawfully marry, presently to take each other as husband and wife, freely, seriously and plainly expressed by each in the presence of the other . . . [i]n the presence of" an authorized officiant. Although the marriage ceremony required in connection with a North Carolina marriage license must be *performed* within the state, whoever performs the ceremony need not be a resident of the state. As noted above, a marriage performed in this state may be valid even if the parties have not obtained a license or the license is invalid, but the person performing the ceremony without requiring a license is subject to both criminal penalties and civil liability.[33] The ceremony must be witnessed by at least two persons. The person performing the ceremony and the two witnesses must sign both copies of the certificate.

In this state there is no requirement or procedure for someone to be licensed or listed on an official register to be an officiant of a marriage. The statute gives the couple a wide range of choice about individuals who may perform the ceremony and complete the license, including the following:

- *Ordained minister of any religious denomination.*[34] Whether someone is ordained is a matter of the religion's practice. There is no governmental license, registration, or approval of ordination for this purpose.
- *Minister authorized by a church.*[35] This could be someone who is not an ordained minister but to whom a church has given the authority to conduct marriage ceremonies.

---

33. G.S. 51-7.
34. G.S. 51-1(1).
35. *Id.*

- *In accordance with any mode of solemnization recognized by any religious denomination.*[36] This could include someone who follows a ceremonial procedure of a religious denomination that does not ordain ministers or that authorizes particular individuals to perform ceremonies.
- *In accordance with any mode of solemnization recognized by any federally or State recognized Indian Nation or Tribe.*[37] The statute defers to the Indian Nation or Tribe to determine the appropriate ceremony.
- *Magistrate.*[38] Although the statute does not expressly state that this is limited to a North Carolina state magistrate, a reasonable interpretation is that the General Assembly had in mind this particular judicial official within this state. Other magistrates can have very different capacities and would only have judicial authority given to them by the laws establishing their offices.

Occasionally, the General Assembly authorizes by special act particular categories of individuals to perform ceremonies, such as superior court judges or mayors.

Registers often are asked whether someone who obtains an ordination credential from an Internet service is authorized to perform a North Carolina marriage ceremony. Registers cannot give an opinion about whether any particular individual or practice meets the statutory requirements, and there is no clear answer in the law. The U.S. Supreme Court said the following many years ago: "Freedom of thought, which includes freedom of religious belief, is basic in a society . . . . It embraces the right to maintain theories of life and of death and of the hereafter which are rank heresy to followers of the orthodox faiths."[39] The legislature and courts traditionally have not wanted to try to be specific about what constitutes "religious" or a "religion" out of respect for religious freedoms and because there is no widely accepted way of going about doing so. At times, however, the courts have needed to determine whether something is to be considered religious for legal purposes, such as for tax exemption or conscientious objection to military service. In this regard, the courts look to apparent

36. G.S. 51-1(2).
37. *Id.*
38. *Id.*
39. United States v. Ballard, 322 U.S. 78 (1944).

"sincerity of beliefs" and familiar models of religious practices broadly conceived.[40] Signing up for an "ordination" for the sole purpose of performing a marriage ceremony, without any consideration of religious practices or beliefs within a social group, possibly could be deemed as not having any relationship to a religious denomination, church, or religious practice as is contemplated under North Carolina's statute identifying legal marriage officiants. The statute plainly contemplates a choice of either a civil or faith-based ceremony, and magistrates are the only authorized purely civil authorities. The references to religious practices and church authority must mean more than simply wanting to perform a ceremony, regardless of faith. The North Carolina Supreme Court's bigamy cases suggest that more than a mere claim of ordination is required. In *State v. Lynch,*[41] the court held invalid a marriage ceremony performed by a bride's father with a mail order certificate. The court said a ceremony performed by a layman with a credential from "the Universal Life Church, Inc.—whatever that is—is not a ceremony of marriage to be recognized for purposes of a bigamy prosecution in the State of North Carolina."[42] In another, more recent bigamy case, the N.C. Supreme Court sustained a trial court's finding that a marriage could not be legally consummated before someone whose occupation was in construction and who did not have any ministerial capacity.[43] These decisions do not necessarily mean that any particular type of ordination will be invalid. These cases involve unusual circumstances and a bigamy prosecution, in which the State had the burden of proving beyond a reasonable doubt that the first marriage was valid to establish the second marriage was bigamous. A court might look at the issue differently if bigamy were not involved and the couple whose rights are in issue both chose the officiant, as is likely in a divorce or probate proceeding. Furthermore, when there is evidence that a ceremony took place, a court presumes "that it was legally performed and resulted in a valid marriage."[44] Someone who wants to have the marriage declared void would have the burden of proving that the mar-

40. United States v. Seeger, 380 U.S. 163 (1965).

41. 301 N.C. 479, 272 S.E.2d 349 (1980).

42. *Id.* at 488, 272 S.E.2d at 354.

43. Mussa v. Palmer-Mussa, 366 N.C. 185, 731 S.E.2d 404 (2012).

44. Kearney v. Thomas, 225 N.C. 156, 163, 33 S.E.2d 871, 876 (1945).

riage was invalid.[45] Nonetheless, there is no clear legal authority on which a couple can rely when choosing an officiant whose ordination is from an organization without a clear religious orientation.

6.4.2 Marriage Records

The officiant is required to return the completed license to the register within ten days after the marriage, "under penalty of forfeiting two hundred dollars ($200.00) to the use of any person who shall sue for the same."[46] The modest amount of the penalty makes it unlikely that someone would sue for it for a single instance of noncompliance. In any event, although a penalty may be imposed, the license does not become invalid merely because the officiant did not return it within ten days. The register should process a license despite its lateness.

Registers also are sometimes faced with a situation in which a license is returned and it is obvious that the ceremony was performed after the license had expired. Thus, the license was invalid at the time the marriage was solemnized. Even though the license was invalid, the marriage is still valid, and the couple is legally married. In such a case, the register should process the license.

By the fifteenth of each month, the register must file with N.C. Vital Records the other copy of all certificates returned to the office during the preceding month.[47] The register keeps a copy of the returned license for the permanent record. The register indexes the marriage certificates by the last name of each applicant for the marriage license. Each index entry must show at least the following information: the full names of the intended husband and wife, the date of the ceremony, and a reference to where the license can be found in the register's records.[48]

---

45. *Mussa*, 366 N.C. at 194, 731 S.E.2d at 410. *See also* Duncan v. Duncan, 232 N.C. App. 369, 754 S.E.2d 451 (2014) (Parties had two ceremonies, the first officiated with Universal Life Church credentials. They stipulated that the first ceremony was essentially the same as the ceremony in *Lynch* that was invalidated. However, the court held that the husband was equitably estopped from arguing that the first was voidable because he was equally negligent in relying on the officiant's credentials.).

46. G.S. 51-16.

47. G.S. 130A-110(a).

48. G.S. 51-18.

The register's record copies of marriage licenses are public records and must be open to inspection during regular business hours.[49] An uncertified copy of a license must be provided to anyone upon payment of the prescribed fee, but a certified copy may be provided only to the following:

- A person seeking a copy of his or her own license.
- The subject's spouse, parent, direct ancestor or descendant, stepparent or stepchild, brother or sister.
- A person seeking legal determination of personal or real property rights. The statute does not further explain who meets this description. A reasonable interpretation is that it includes an attorney of record in litigation, such as a probate proceeding, in which the information on the certificate is pertinent. A register may rely on an attorney's reasonable representation in this regard.
- An authorized agent, attorney, or legal representative of a person described above.[50]

The register's record of marriage licenses is only for returns of licenses that the register has issued. Occasionally, someone who is married in another state or country asks about registering a marriage license in North Carolina. Neither registers nor any other public office in this state keeps records of marriages that occurred in other states or countries. Whether someone is married elsewhere is a matter of the laws in that jurisdiction, and its records establish the legal status.

The license is authorization to an official to perform a marriage "at any place within the State [of North Carolina]."[51] A license returned showing that the ceremony occurred in another state or country is not a record of a North Carolina marriage. Whether the couple is legally married would be determined according to the laws of the jurisdiction in which the ceremony occurred. The statutes do not expressly state whether a returned license showing such a marriage ceremony should be filed with returned licenses for North Carolina marriages. There is a sound reason not to accept such a return: refusal of the return will alert the couple to the issue so that they can take whatever steps may be necessary to clarify or correct the situation.

---

49. G.S. 130A-93(c), -110(d).
50. G.S. 130A-93(c), -110(c).
51. G.S. 51-16.

6.5 Delayed Marriage Certificates

Occasionally, the officiant does not return the marriage license to the register of deeds after the ceremony, perhaps because it is lost. When a license was issued and a ceremony occurred but the license is not returned, the register may issue a "delayed marriage certificate" based on review of evidence of a type specified by statute that attests to the ceremony. The statute provides three types of evidence recently married couples may furnish:

- affidavits of two witnesses to the ceremony,
- an affidavit of one party to the marriage plus an affidavit of one witness to the ceremony, or
- an affidavit of one party to the marriage plus the affidavit of the person who performed the marriage.[52]

In the rare event that a license was issued and a marriage performed before 1935 and none of these listed proofs is available, the register of deeds may issue the certificate based on the affidavit of one of the persons named above and such other written evidence as the register deems sufficient to establish the fact that the marriage ceremony occurred.[53]

If the couple cannot produce the specified evidence, they may bring a special proceeding before the clerk of superior court of the county where the marriage allegedly took place. If, after a hearing and presentation of evidence, the clerk finds that the marriage did take place as claimed, the clerk certifies this finding to the register, who must then issue a delayed marriage certificate.[54]

The delayed certificate must contain the date it was issued and the date the marriage took place. The register should retain a copy of the certificate and file it and the supporting proofs with the other marriage licenses.

This statute applies only when the person who performed the marriage failed to return the license. A register cannot issue the delayed certificate unless the records indicate that the register's office issued the license.

The fee for a delayed marriage certificate with a certified copy is set by statute and is shown in Appendix 1.[55]

---

52. G.S. 51-21(1)–(3).
53. G.S. 51-21(4).
54. *Id.*
55. G.S. 161-10(a)(2).

6.6 Changes in Applications and Licenses

The statutes prescribe the procedures for the register of deeds' correction of errors on an application or license and for changing names. The register may correct any information "incorrectly stated" on the application or license if one party to the marriage presents evidence to the register that the information is incorrect. The evidence required is an affidavit from one or both applicants giving the correct information together with affidavits from two persons who know the correct information. The register should correct the records if the information on the license appears incorrect based on this evidence. The register should also make a new index entry if necessary when a correction affects a name.[56]

A new spouse—husband or wife—may assume the other spouse's name without need for any court procedure.[57] The spouse may then apply to various government agencies to have identification and records show the assumed name. The register does not amend a marriage license to show the adoption of a married name. The names shown on the license will be the names at the time of application. Registers do make amendments for those who change their names with a proceeding in superior court.[58] For such an amendment, a party to a marriage must present an affidavit to the register stating that his or her name has been changed by court order and requesting that the marriage records be amended to show this change.[59] If the other party to the marriage consents to this request (and the register should obtain a signed and acknowledged consent), then the register changes the name on the application for the license, on the marriage license itself, and on the certificate of the officiating officer. The register should also make a new index entry in the changed name. Copies of licenses corrected or changed should be forwarded to N.C. Vital Records so that the changes can be reflected in the state registry.

The fee for a corrected license and certified copy of it is set by statute and is shown in Appendix 1.[60]

---

56. G.S. 51-18.1(a).
57. *In re* Mohlman, 26 N.C. App. 220, 216 S.E.2d 147 (1975).
58. G.S. 101-2.
59. G.S. 51-18.1(b).
60. G.S. 161-10(a)(2).

Chapter 7

Vital Records, Military Discharges, Notary Commissions, and Grave Removals

Chapter 7

Vital Records, Military Discharges, Notary Commissions, and Grave Removals

7.1 Birth Certificates

A birth certificate contains information that is important for many purposes, and a certified copy of it is used as authentic proof of this information. Birth certificates are evidence of name, age, parentage, and citizenship. Certified copies of birth certificates are used to obtain the most prevalent forms of identification: a driver's license and passport. The use of birth certificates to obtain identification is the main reason the law restricts access to them. Birth certificates also are used for many other important evidentiary purposes, including to show a child's birthdate for enrollment in school, to enroll in the Social Security system, to register for voting, to join the military, to prove citizenship for employment, and to establish a right of inheritance.

Local health directors serve as local vital statistics registrars and provide the forms for birth certificates as directed by the North Carolina State Registrar.[1] The State Registrar's North Carolina Vital Records office maintains original vital records, including birth and death certificates, and supervises the recordation of certificates that other officials are authorized to prepare.[2] When a birth occurs in a hospital, the person in charge of the facility collects the data and prepares the certificate and files it with the local registrar

1. Chapter 130A, Section 97(2) of the North Carolina General Statutes (hereinafter G.S.).

2. G.S. 130A-90 to -92.

in the county in which the birth occurred.[3] When the birth occurs outside a hospital, this responsibility rests with the attending physician or other person in attendance, or with a parent or person in charge.[4] Registers of deeds are required to file, index, and preserve copies of birth and death certificates that are furnished by local registrars for their counties.[5]

Registers once were required to restrict certain information on copies of vital records in their offices. By statute, medical or health information on birth certificates may be provided only to the subject, to someone authorized by the subject, or to someone who will use the information for medical research purposes.[6] This restriction was enacted when such information commonly appeared on the forms in the register's office. This information should no longer be present.

N.C. Vital Records handles new birth certificates in the case of adoption and may direct that the county remove the adopted child's prior certificate.[7] A statute directs that the register not provide any copy of a vital record to someone seeking his or her own record but who is known to be deceased, in which case attempted fraud is obvious.[8] By regulation of the North Carolina Department of Health and Human Services, a register must add the word "DECEASED" to a copy of a birth certificate issued for someone known to be deceased.[9]

Subject to the exceptions mentioned previously, any person may obtain an uncertified copy of a birth certificate.

Only the following persons may obtain certified copies of these records:

- The subject of the record (unless the person claiming to be the subject is deceased according to the records).
- The subject's spouse, parent, direct ancestor or descendant, stepparent or stepchild, brother or sister.
- A person seeking legal determination of personal or real property rights. The statute does not further explain who meets this

3. G.S. 130A-101(b).
4. G.S. 130A-101(c).
5. G.S. 130A-99.
6. G.S. 130A-93(e).
7. G.S. 48-9-107; G.S. 130A-93(d).
8. G.S. 130A-93(g).
9. Title 10A, Chapter 41H, Section .0601(e) of the North Carolina Administrative Code (hereinafter N.C.A.C.).

description. A reasonable interpretation is that it includes an attorney of record in litigation, such as a probate proceeding, in which the information on the certificate is pertinent. A register may rely on an attorney's reasonable representation in this regard.
- An authorized agent, attorney, or legal representative of any of the above.[10] A likely source of this type of authority is a power of attorney that includes broad powers such as to manage and conduct all of the principal's affairs or to exercise all of the principal's legal rights and powers. Registers should examine the language in a power of attorney to see that it is broad enough, rather than so narrowly tailored as to exclude obtaining a certified copy of a vital record in someone's behalf. The authority could also be specifically granted in another document, and the register has reasonable discretion to assess the document's scope and apparent authenticity.

A uniform fee is set for a certified copy of a birth certificate, which the register can waive for a copy provided to someone over the age of sixty-two.[11]

The register's birth certificate records are only for births filed through this state's vital records system. They are not for birth records that someone in the public may wish to record, though nothing prohibits recording birth certificates in the real estate records provided the appropriate fees are paid. If someone presents a document for recording in the real estate records that is unattached to a real estate document, purports "to impact an official record of birth," and is not a record filed within the state's official system, G.S. 161-14.02 directs the register to mark the first page of that purported birth record as follows: "THIS DOCUMENT IS NOT AN OFFICIAL BIRTH RECORD."

10. G.S. 130A-93(c), -93(g), -99.
11. G.S. 161-10(a)(8).

7.2 Death Certificates

Death certificates are important evidence for handling the affairs of a deceased person, including for making funeral and burial arrangements. They are important for filing a probate action to handle the deceased's property, for showing the passage of real estate held jointly or in common, for access to bank accounts, for claims on life insurance, and to establish other legal rights. The government uses death certificates to track those who were responsible for child or spousal support. The information in death certificates also is used for collecting data on causes of death and other health trends.

The data for a death certificate is provided by a funeral director or other person who first assumes custody of a body, with medical information provided by a physician or other authorized medical practitioner or officer.[12] A death certificate must be filed with the local vital records registrar within five days after the death, and the registrar must transmit the certificate to the register within seven days of receipt.[13]

Anyone may obtain an uncertified copy of a death certificate. Only the following persons may obtain certified copies of these records:

- The subject of the record (unless the person claiming to be the subject is deceased according to the records).
- The subject's spouse, parent, direct ancestor or descendant, stepparent or stepchild, brother or sister.
- A person seeking legal determination of personal or real property rights. The statute does not further explain who meets this description. A reasonable interpretation is that it includes an attorney of record in litigation, such as a probate case, in which the information on the certificate is relevant. A register may rely on an attorney's reasonable representation in this regard.
- An authorized agent, attorney, or legal representative of any of the above.[14] A likely source of this type of authority is a power of attorney that includes broad powers such as to manage and conduct all of the principal's affairs or to exercise all of the principal's legal rights and powers. Registers should examine the

---

12. G.S. 130A-112, -115.
13. G.S. 130A-97(5), -115.
14. G.S. 130A-93(c), -93(g), -99.

language in a power of attorney to see that it is broad enough, rather than so narrowly tailored as to exclude obtaining a certified copy of a vital record in someone's behalf. The authority could also be specifically granted in another document, and the register has reasonable discretion to assess the document's scope and apparent authenticity.

- A funeral director or funeral service licensee.[15]

.Fees for certified copies of death certificates are set by statute.[16] Also by statute, the North Carolina Department of Administration is entitled to "the requested number of certified copies" of local public records without charge when needed to assist veterans or their beneficiaries in obtaining benefits.[17] The department's Division of Veteran's Affairs normally makes these requests, but they also are sometimes made on behalf of the division by a local veteran's affairs representative.

7.3 Military Discharges

Military discharge records commemorate service to the country and provide documentary evidence of qualification for veterans' benefits. These records are kept by the National Archives and Records Administration (NARA), which is the official repository for records of military personnel who have been discharged from the United States Marine Corps, Navy, Air Force, Army, and Coast Guard. The form most commonly used for veterans' purposes is the *DD Form 214, Report of Separation*. This form includes information about such things as dates of service, last duty assignment and rank, military specialty, and medals and awards. Veterans and their next of kin can quickly obtain this form from NARA without charge.[18] The option of filing a copy with the service member's county register of deeds office is offered as a convenience.

---

15. G.S. 130A-93(c), (c1).
16. G.S. 161-10(a)(8).
17. G.S. 143B-1215(a).
18. Instructions and forms for obtaining military discharge records from the National Archives and Records Administration (NARA) are available at www.archives.gov/veterans/military-service-records/about-service-records.html.

There is no restriction on public access to copies of military discharge records that have been on file for more than eighty years. By statute, access also need not be restricted to discharges that were commingled with real estate records prior to January 1, 2004, which is not normally the case. Otherwise, access to military discharge records is restricted to individuals with an authorized capacity listed in the statute. Access is authorized to the following persons:

- the service member who is the subject of the document, and
- the service member's widow or widower.

Documents also may be recorded and copies of them may be obtained by the following:

- representatives of the North Carolina Division of Veterans Affairs, United States Department of Veterans Affairs, and United States Department of Defense;
- representatives of the North Carolina State Archives; and
- "[a] court official with an interest in assisting the subject or the deceased subject's beneficiaries to obtain a benefit."[19] The statute does not define "court official." A reasonable interpretation is that a court official can be a judge or court clerk as well as someone appointed by a judge or court clerk in connection with a matter involving the subject or the subject's benefit rights.

Additionally, someone may be given access to a document if authorized in writing by one of the following:

- the subject of the document in a notarized writing,
- the subject's widow or widower in a notarized writing,
- a court to represent the subject, or
- the subject's executor acting in behalf of a deceased subject.[20]

Note that a widow or widower is an authorized person but a living subject's current or former spouse is not among those authorized.

The same individuals who are authorized access to a military discharge document are authorized to file one. The statute implies that registers may refuse to accept such documents through the mail. It provides: "A mili-

---

19. G.S. 47-113.2(b)(1)c.
20. G.S. 47-113.2.

tary discharge document shall be accepted for filing upon presentation in person."[21]

Registers must retain completed military discharge copy request forms for one year from the date of the request. Access to completed request forms is limited to the same parties who are authorized to file and obtain copies of the records. The information contained in the index for restricted records should be given the same privacy protections as the records themselves.

No fee may be charged for filing military discharge documents or for providing certified copies of them to authorized recipients. The usual uncertified copy fee applies to a copy that has become unrestricted after being on file for more than eighty years.[22]

7.4 State Vital Records Processing

Registers assist individuals who seek to make corrections to the official state vital records in Raleigh. Registers do not make these changes themselves. By statute, the authority to make additions and corrections rests with the State Registrar, with the functions performed by N.C. Vital Records. Registers collect and forward required documentation to N.C. Vital Records for its review and implementation. This is increasingly done through electronic systems. To fulfill their role, registers must adhere to the state office's current regulations and guidelines. The following sections summarize these requirements.

7.4.1 Delayed Birth Registration

In the usual case, a birth certificate is filed in the vital records registration system within a few days of birth, and the local vital records registrar transmits a copy of the certificate to the register.[23] The statutes authorize late filings for up to one year after a birth.[24] This is a "delayed certificate." Someone can apply for a delayed certificate by submitting an application

21. G.S. 47-113.2(c).
22. G.S. 47-113.2(n).
23. G.S. 130A-97(5); -101.
24. G.S. 130A-103.

through the register with minimum documentation required by N.C. Vital Records.

The elements to be proved for registration of a delayed birth certificate include the person's full birth name, date of birth, place of birth, father's name (except when the law requires a procedure to add a father's name when the mother was unmarried at the time of birth), and the mother's full birth name.[25] N.C. Vital Records requires at least three documents that show the name and date of birth, two that show the place of birth, and one that shows parentage. No more than one of the required documents may be in the form of an affidavit.[26] Such documents may include hospital birth records and admission notes taken at the time of birth by the hospital, kindergarten or first grade records, an attendant doctor's or midwife's record, or another type of evidence that N.C. Vital Records has approved. The state office provides specific guidance about records that may be used. Usually, they must either be originals or certified copies, not photocopies. In collecting documents, registers should be alert to evidence of alterations in the presented proof and to conflicting information that suggests an impropriety.

The register submits to N.C Vital Records the collected information along with a delayed certificate of birth and a description of accompanying proof. The applicant signs the application under oath, or if the applicant is not yet eighteen years old, the application must be signed under oath by the applicant's parent or guardian. The register also signs the completed application and applies the seal of the register's office. If N.C. Vital Records approves the application, a copy of the delayed certificate is returned to the register for recording.[27]

The alternative for someone who cannot meet the requirements of N.C. Vital Records for a delayed birth certificate is to seek a superior court order based on evidence deemed sufficient by the court.[28] The register would play no role in the process except for filing the copy of the certificate forwarded by N.C. Vital Records after that office issues it based on a court order.

---

25. 10A N.C.A.C. 41H, § .0402(a).
26. *Id.* at § .0402(c).
27. G.S. 130A-104.
28. G.S. 130A-106.

7.4.2 Amendments to Birth and Death Records

Amendments to birth and death records are made by application to N.C. Vital Records.[29] The state office has rules for the form of requests. Amendments to birth certificates must be requested by the subject of the certificate or, if the subject is not yet eighteen years old, by the child's parent or guardian. Documentation satisfying N.C. Vital Records requirements must be submitted to show the requestor's identity as well as to prove the facts of the requested change.[30] The regulation gives the following examples of supportive documentary evidence: "early school records, census records, marriage certificates, birth certificates of family members, rolls of federal or state recognized Indian tribes, [and] baptismal records."[31] The time it takes for the request for an amendment to be processed at the state office depends on a number of factors, including workload. In ordinary circumstances, it may take about one month. Expedited service to shorten the process may be available through the mail for an extra fee, and expedited service also may be available through an appointment with walk-in service in Raleigh for an extra fee. Expedited service is maintained for those who have an unexpected emergency. Use of the system when routine service is sufficient burdens the system and creates unnecessary delays.

Minor changes to correct obvious spelling or clerical errors may be requested on N.C. Vital Records forms.[32] The regulations identify the following as minor changes: any obvious clerical error, addresses, occupation, birth order, spelling of informant's name, and spelling of given names of child within four years of birth.[33] The more substantial changes for which supporting evidence is necessary include changes to state of birth (deaths), birthplace of parents (births), county of birth, spelling of given names of child (births) after four years of birth, spelling of father's or mother's name, age of parents, sex of child if incorrectly recorded, date of birth, and hour of birth.[34] A change in the subject's surname or in parentage will be made

29. G.S. 130A-118.
30. 10A N.C.A.C. 41H, § .0910.
31. *Id.*
32. *Id.* at § .0902.
33. *Id.*
34. *Id.* at § .0903.

only with a court order, except as allowed for legitimation, as described in the next section.[35]

A change in the identification of the subject's gender can be made because of sex reassignment surgery, as documented in a written request to N.C. Vital Records. The request must be accompanied by a notarized statement from the physician who performed the sex reassignment surgery or from a physician licensed to practice medicine who examined the subject and can certify that sex reassignment surgery occurred.[36]

When N.C. Vital Records issues a new birth certificate, the register will receive a copy and must within five days forward the certificate being replaced to the state office. N.C. Vital Records keeps the replaced certificate under confidential seal to be released only by court order.[37]

Changes to death records also are made only by N.C. Vital Records according to its rules and procedures. The physician or medical examiner who signed the certificate may make changes regarding the cause of death using N.C. Vital Records forms.[38] The office may allow other corrections upon completion of a form by a family member with supporting information.

7.4.3 Legitimations

If a child is born while the mother is unmarried and the mother later marries the reputed father of the child, the child acquires the legal rights as a child of the reputed father.[39] *Reputed* means generally supposed or accepted by public opinion. This procedure is known as *legitimation by subsequent marriage*. To add the name of the father to the child's birth certificate under these circumstances, the parents complete an N.C. Vital Records form of affidavit with information about the parents and child and provide a certified copy of the marriage record.[40] If the parties marry after the child reaches the age of six, N.C. Vital Records requires additional proof of parentage to show that the father was a part of the child's life at an early age and acknowledged the child even though he and the mother

---

35. *Id.* at § .0909.
36. G.S. 130A-118(b)(4).
37. G.S. 130A-118(e).
38. 10A N.C.A.C. 41H, § .0906.
39. G.S. 49-12.
40. 10A N.C.A.C. 41H, § .1102.

were not married.[41] A combination of school, medical, hospital, and child support records and affidavits of the father's relatives may be sufficient to establish the facts. The register may collect these forms and documents and submit them to N.C. Vital Records for review, approval, and issuance of a new birth certificate showing the father's name.

A man may bring a proceeding in superior court for a determination that a child is his, known as *legitimation*.[42] Upon legitimation, the child acquires legal rights, including inheritance.[43] A man may seek to claim a child born to a mother who is married to another man by providing proof in a superior court proceeding to overcome the presumption that the child was born of the mother's husband.[44] In these circumstances, N.C. Vital Records amends the child's birth certificate upon receipt of a certified copy of a court order of legitimation.[45]

7.4.4 Verification

N.C. Vital Records provides a service to registers of deeds to ensure that the information on local copies of vital records agrees with the state's originals. The request is submitted through an Internet-based system or other means approved by the state office and must contain specified information for birth, death, and marriage records. This service is useful when someone questions the accuracy of the vital record on file with the register.

7.4.5 North Carolina Vital Records Automation System

There were more than 120,000 births in North Carolina in a recent year, 95 percent of which occurred in a hospital. There are about 95,000 deaths each year, which occur in hospitals, nursing homes, at home, and other locations. Keeping records of this many births and deaths depends on careful collection of information and reporting by health officials and other responsible individuals, and the compilation and maintenance of these records by the State Registrar of Vital Statistics and N.C. Vital Records. The state also is part of a nationwide verification system that enables collection and

---

41. *Id.* at § .1102(g).
42. G.S. 49-10.
43. G.S. 49-11.
44. G.S. 49-12.1.
45. G.S. 49-12.1, -13; G.S. 130A-119.

exchange of certificate information, which is important for understanding public health and demographics and preventing fraud.

N.C. Vital Records is part of a nationwide transition from paper to electronic format for vital records. Those who report births and deaths can enter the information into an electronic system that eliminates some of the steps and risks of error of the traditional paper system. While there is likely to continue to be paper copies issued by registers of deeds and N.C. Vital Records for public use, registers will increasingly be accessing the data for these copies through a system that is managed by the state and follows national standards. The North Carolina system is known as the Electronic Records Automation System (ERAS).

The Electronic Birth Registration System (EBRS) is a web-based system that allows hospitals and birthing centers to enter all the information required on the birth certificate and makes data available for reporting and analysis of vital statistics and other public health and administrative needs. Registers who are enrolled in the system may identify and issue certified copies of birth records for applicants born in the State of North Carolina after the date for which EBRS records have been made available.

N.C. Vital Records is also implementing the Electronic Death Registration System (EDRS), which is a statewide online system used to electronically register death certificates.

The system will enable those who provide decedent fact-of-death and cause-of-death information—funeral homes, medical certifiers, and medical examiners—to file death records electronically. Registers will also have statewide access to death certificates through this system. Registers who are enrolled in the system may identify and issue certified copies of death records for subjects who died in North Carolina after the date for which EDRS records have been made available.

By statute, the register charges a fee for a record search in the ERAS and forwards it to the State Registrar, and there is an additional fee that the register retains when a copy is issued.[46] The copy fee may be waived if the subject is over the age of sixty-two years.[47]

---

46. G.S. 130A-93.1(a)(1).
47. *Id.*

7.5 Notary Commissions

Notaries public play an important role in commercial affairs. Their participation in authentication of signatures on important documents helps prevent fraud and provides a means of validating party signatures on certain records and agreements. The two most common functions performed by notaries are completion of a certificate of acknowledgment that someone who provided identification was witnessed signing a document and completion of a jurat that includes a certification that the person signing gave an oath or affirmation that the statements in the document are true to the best of the person's knowledge. As described in Chapter 3, most real estate instruments must be acknowledged or proved before an authorized official, and notaries are the officials who most often perform this function. Registers of deeds give oaths of office to newly commissioned notaries in their counties and keep a record of their commission status. This record enables the public to confirm the capacity of someone whose certification appears on an instrument or who proposes to perform this function.

To become a notary, a qualified person must apply to the North Carolina Department of the Secretary of State and satisfy applicable educational and testing requirements. The N.C. Department of the Secretary of State sends a newly appointed notary's commission, along with an oath notification letter, to the register of the county where the oaths are to be administered.[48] The appointee must then appear before the register within forty-five days of the commission's effective date, which is shown on the oath notification letter.[49] Notaries take the following oath prescribed for all public officials:

> I, __________, do solemnly and sincerely swear that I will support the Constitution of the United States; that I will be faithful and bear true allegiance to the State of North Carolina, and to the constitutional powers and authorities which are or may be established for the government thereof; and that I will endeavor to support, maintain and defend the Constitution of said State, not inconsistent with the Constitution of the United States, to the best of my knowledge and ability, so help me God.[50]

---

48. G.S. 10B-10(a).
49. G.S. 10B-10(b).
50. G.S. 11-7.

Persons with conscientious scruples against taking an oath in the manner described above may substitute the word "affirm" for the word "swear" and may delete the words "so help me God."[51]

Notaries also take the following oath of office:

> I, _________, do swear (or affirm) that I will well and truly execute the duties of the office of notary public according to the best of my skill and ability, according to law; so help me, God.[52]

The oaths should be taken promptly and may be administered any time after the commission is issued until forty-five days after the commission's effective date, after which the register must return the commission to the Department of the Secretary of State. If this happens, the applicant must then reapply to the department.[53]

The notary must pay a fee set by statute to the register who administered the oaths.[54]

After the commission is completed and the oath taken, the register delivers the commission to the notary and notifies the Department of the Secretary of State with the appropriate return form. The register keeps the record of the notary's commission either in the consolidated real estate records, with the notary's name entered as a grantor in the index, or in a separate book. The record may be kept in electronic format as long as the notary's signatures may be viewed and printed.[55] By statute, the following information about the notary applicant required for an application is considered confidential:

- date of birth,
- residence mailing and street address,
- residence telephone number,
- last four digits of Social Security number, and
- personal and business email addresses.[56]

---

51. G.S. 11-4.
52. G.S. 11-11.
53. G.S. 10B-10(e).
54. G.S. 161-10(a)(17).
55. G.S. 10B-10(c).
56. G.S. 10B-7(b).

Consequently, the register's public records should not display this information.

If the Department of the Secretary of State restricts, suspends, or revokes a notary commission, or the notary resigns it, upon receipt of notice the register enters this event and its effective date in the record book.[57]

7.6 Grave Removals

When a body that has been interred is moved from a grave, state statutes and N.C. Department of Health and Human Services regulations require the party removing or causing the removal to record a "certificate of the removal facts" with the register within thirty days after completion of the reinterment. The notice must contain the name of the deceased if known, a description of the removal site and the place at which the remains have been reinterred, the name of the party who removed it, a brief description of the basis upon which the move was effected, and a map showing the old and new locations.[58] By statute, the recording charge is the fee for instruments in general.[59] If the remains are being removed from one county to another, the certificate should be recorded in both counties.[60]

N.C. Vital Records prescribes a form for the certificate and has regulations for registering and indexing. Regulations require the register to keep the certificates and any attachments permanently and to cross-index them at least by name of cemetery of disinterment and reinterment.[61] The consolidated real property records should be deemed an appropriate medium for these records.

57. G.S. 10B-10(c).
58. G.S. 65-106(c); 10A N.C.A.C. 41H, § .1201.
59. G.S. 65-106(c).
60. *Id.*
61. 10A N.C.A.C. 41H, § .1201.

Chapter 8

Assumed Business Name Certificates

Chapter 8

Assumed Business Name Certificates

8.1 Assumed Business Name Filing System

A North Carolina register of deeds office is the point of entry for individuals and entities to comply with North Carolina law requiring public notice of names used in business that are not their own. The requirement applies to humans using artificial names, such as if Pat Adams does business as "Adams Flower Shop," and to business entities using names other than what is shown on their organizational filing, such as if First Time, Inc., a North Carolina corporation, does business as "First-T." Initial filings for assumed business names, and amendments and withdrawals of them, are presented at a register of deeds office, which transmits the data and images to a central database that the North Carolina Secretary of State maintains and that can be searched publicly on the Internet. Registers also maintain indexes of the filings made in their counties. The purpose and function of the requirement to have an assumed business name certificate on file within the state can best be understood within the context of its history.

The North Carolina requirement to record public notice of using a fictitious business name first became law during the Progressive Era, in 1913.[1] At the time, someone selling products using a brand name had to register the name at the federal level. As the North Carolina Supreme Court explained in 1875, the federal name registration had two purposes: to protect the public from "a spurious or inferior article, as an imitation or counterfeit almost always is," and to give some assurance to an inventor of "the exclusive benefit of the reputation which his skill has given to the article made by him."[2] Later enactment of a requirement to file an assumed

1. 1913 N.C. Pub. Laws ch. 77.

2. Blackwell v. Wright, 73 N.C. 310, 313 (1875).

business name certificate in the State of North Carolina was aimed only at fulfilling the first purpose—to protect consumers against deception. Federal law continued to fulfill the second purpose of giving exclusive rights to a name.

Early North Carolina court decisions interpreted the state's business name statute broadly. These cases held that failing to comply with the name registration requirement could bar someone from enforcing a contract. Soon after the requirement was enacted in the state, the North Carolina Supreme Court held that someone refusing to pay a supplier who used a business name without having filed a certificate for it could use this failure to bar a suit for breach of contract.[3] The court reached a different conclusion, however, when a business used a fictitious name that included the individuals' human names. Two brothers with the last name of Aboud were doing business as "Aboud Bros.," and two individuals with the last names of Befarah and Nassif were doing business as the "Raleigh Bargain House, Nassif & Befarah, Proprietors."[4] The court said that the presence of the human last names within the business name was sufficient to prevent the kind of deception that the assumed name statute was intended to prevent. The North Carolina General Assembly reacted quickly to the courts' interpretations of the statute and revised the law to make clear that the statute is violated when there has been no registration of the name even if it has a human last name within it. However, the General Assembly also changed the law to prevent the courts from invalidating contracts based on noncompliance with the assumed name registration requirement. In the second act of all legislation passed in 1919, the General Assembly added a provision to the statute providing "that the failure of any person or persons owning, carrying on, conducting or transacting business as aforesaid, to comply with the provisions of this act shall *not* prevent a recovery by said person or persons on any civil action brought in any of the courts of the State of North Carolina."[5] Consequently, the General Assembly made clear that the intent of the registration requirement is to compel a filing at the risk of a fine, but not to affect the rights of the parties doing business. This has remained the basics of the law in North Carolina.

3. Courtney v. Parker, 173 N.C. 479, 92 S.E. 324 (1917).
4. Befarah v. Spell, 176 N.C. 193, 96 S.E. 949 (1918).
5. S.L. 1919-2 (emphasis added).

In 1967, the manner of registering assumed names was changed. The General Assembly shifted responsibility for maintaining the public record of assumed business name certificates from the clerk of court to the register of deeds.[6] Between 1967 and 2017, individuals and companies complied with the registration requirement by filing a certificate with the register in each county in which business was to be conducted.[7] The register's office also was the place to file a record when the assumed name was being transferred to another person and to file a withdrawal when the name's use was being discontinued.[8] Since December 1, 2017,[9] all assumed business name filings are made according to the procedure described in this chapter, with a filing that is made initially with a register of deeds for entry into a statewide registration database that the N.C. Secretary of State maintains.

As has always been the case in North Carolina, although someone using an assumed name in the state must file a certificate, this filing does not by itself give rights to the name. The North Carolina statutes governing assumed business name certificate requirements state that compliance "does not confer any exclusive rights to the use of an assumed business name in this State."[10] No government agency screens or examines assumed business name filings to determine if the filer has rights to the name shown on a certificate. In the modern business environment, with most goods and services crossing state lines, a state filing gives little actual public notice of a name's use.

The limited consequence of assumed business name registration for protection of exclusive rights is illustrated by 1962 federal litigation involving use of the name "Hot Shoppes," which more than one company believed to be a good name for a quick-stop restaurant. A company using the name "Hot Shoppes" began a restaurant business in Washington, D.C., in 1927 and opened locations in several other states on the East Coast.[11] In 1947, it registered the trademark "Hot Shoppes" with the N.C. Secretary of State, and, in 1950, it registered the name as a federal service mark. The Washington, D.C., company had not yet opened a restaurant in North Carolina

6. S.L. 1967-823.

7. Chapter 66, Section 68(a) (repealed by S.L. 2016-100) of the North Carolina General Statutes (hereinafter G.S.).

8. G.S. 66-68(f) (repealed by S.L. 2016-100).

9. S.L. 2016-100.

10. G.S. 66-71.12.

11. Hot Shoppes, Inc. v. Hot Shoppe, Inc., 203 F. Supp. 777 (M.D.N.C. 1962).

when, in 1951, a different proprietor opened a dinette known as "The Hot Shoppe" in Greensboro. In 1958, the Greensboro business incorporated in North Carolina with the name "The Hot Shoppe, Inc." The Washington, D.C., company filed legal action to bar the North Carolina business from continuing to use "Hot Shoppe" in its name. But under federal law, someone who was already using the name at the time of the federal registration may continue to use it in the same area. The court noted that several restaurants in North Carolina used the name "Hot Shoppe," or something similar to it, at least since the 1940s, and that the Washington, D.C., business was not known in the area. The court also found that the Washington, D.C., business did not acquire rights to a name with a protected "secondary meaning," which is based on the name's popularity and public acceptance in connection with the business. The outcome of the case was that the local North Carolina business could continue to use its name within its locale. As the federal court said in its opinion, "the law seems clear that state registration does not warrant any presumption of ownership or validity of the registered trade-mark. State registration affirms the common law and does not change it; state registration does not enlarge trade-mark rights without actual use of the mark within the state."[12]

Because a state trade name filing does not give exclusive rights to the name, someone who wants to claim such protection must follow other procedures. There are several possibilities, and determining which offers the best protection is a matter to be discussed with legal counsel. The following is a summary to give a sense of the complexity of business name protection and is no substitute for individualized legal advice.

To make a claim to exclusive use of a business name, the individual or entity claiming the name can file for trademark protection with the United States Patent and Trademark Office (USPTO). A federal trademark or service mark can be claimed for a name, word, symbol, or device that is used to identify and distinguish someone's goods or services. Words that are not distinctive—they are merely descriptive of goods or services or their characteristics—cannot be registered. Federal trademark registration gives public notice of the filer's claim of ownership of a mark and results in presumption of legal ownership nationwide and exclusive right to its use. Before filing a trademark registration application, the filer must search the national trademark database to ensure there is no registered mark used on

12. *Id.* at 781–782.

similar or related products or services. The national trademark database is the Trademark Electronic Search System (TESS), which contains "active" marks registered at the federal level with the USPTO. The USPTO does not police claims of rights to a filed trademark. The filer is responsible for bringing legal action if someone uses it without approval.

North Carolina state law also has a process for registering a name that is a trademark or service mark.[13] Someone who uses a mark, or who controls goods or services in connection with a mark used by another, may register the mark with the N.C. Secretary of State.[14] North Carolina law prohibits new registration of a mark that is likely "to cause confusion or mistake or to deceive" others about an existing mark or trade name that is in use in the state.[15] Before submitting an application for registration, therefore, the potential applicant must search for prior registrations, which include the N.C. Secretary of State's database of registered trademarks and service marks registered in North Carolina.[16] Potential applicants also must search the secretary's Business Registration division database for registered use of the name in corporations, limited liability corporations, partnerships, and other businesses. Someone considering state registration of a mark will therefore want to search the federal database. Registration of a mark is effective for ten years, renewable within six months of expiration for additional terms of ten years.[17] Someone who uses a registered mark without consent is subject to civil liability for damages, including lost profits and penalties, if the infringement was intended to cause confusion or mistake or to deceive.[18] Knowing and willful infringers are also subject to criminal prosecution.[19] The N.C. Secretary of State may cancel a registration if it is deceptively similar to a mark that a court determines was already filed with the USPTO.[20] In a modern environment in which sales of goods and services rarely are confined to a single state, someone wishing to protect exclusive rights to a name is unlikely to achieve much protection with state registration of a mark and will want to register the mark federally.

---

13. G.S. 80-1, -14.
14. G.S. 80-3.
15. G.S. 80-2(6).
16. G.S. 80-7.
17. G.S. 80-5.
18. G.S. 80-11.
19. G.S. 80-11.1.
20. G.S. 80-8(4)(g).

In the modern economy, presence on the Internet is important for most businesses. Accordingly, another form of protection that businesses might want to consider is the registration of an Internet domain name. The not-for-profit organization Internet Corporation for Assigned Names and Numbers (ICANN) manages the Internet's global Domain Name System (DNS). ICANN accredits domain name registrars that create registrations for available names. This registration system is intended to prevent unauthorized use of registered names on websites, including by someone known as a *cybersquatter*, who does not intend to use the name but rather to demand payment for its transfer. This can sometimes be seen when a name search leads to a site that has no content and only a proposal such as "this domain name for sale." The ICANN has an arbitration system for resolving domain name disputes. This alternative to litigation can result in a transfer of the domain name registration, but it does not offer monetary damage remedies if, for example, the rightful owner of the name has lost profits. Instead, those who have their names misappropriated have remedies under federal law. The federal Anticybersquatting Consumer Protection Act[21] authorizes a trademark or service mark owner to recover a name from someone who in bad faith with intent to profit uses the mark or something confusingly similar to it. The law allows up to three times actual damages.[22]

The availability of these remedies shows the importance of registering a business name as a trademark or service mark in the federal system for impactful legal protection against misappropriation. State registration of an assumed business name is not a substitute for such protection. It is for consumer protection. Registers of deeds play one part as a conduit in the array of legal obligations imposed on and opportunities available to individuals and entities that use assumed names in business.

21. 15 U.S.C. § 1125(d).
22. 15 U.S.C. § 1117.

8.2 Who Must File Assumed Business Name Certificates

To comply with North Carolina law, an individual or entity must file an assumed business name certificate with a register of deeds before engaging in business in the state using that name.[23] If business will be conducted in only one North Carolina county, the certificate must be filed in that county.[24] If business will occur in more than one North Carolina county, the certificate may be filed in any one of those counties, which gives notice in all counties by virtue of the N.C. Secretary of State's database into which the register of deeds enters the certificate.[25]

The assumed business name requirement applies when a human uses a name other than the individual's human name.[26] For example, if John Smith operates a café and uses the name "Heavenly Coffee," he must register an assumed business name certificate. It also applies when an entity such as a corporation or limited liability company uses a name other than its official entity name. For example, an LLC organized as Smith Coffee Shops, LLC, must file if it uses the name "Heavenly Coffee" rather than "Smith Coffee Shops, LLC."

The assumed business name filing requirement does not apply to entities that use the same name they declared in their organizational filings. For example, the requirement does not apply to a corporation named "Able Incorporated" if the corporation stated that name in its articles of incorporation filed with the N.C. Secretary of State. Similarly, the assumed business name filing requirement does not apply to the limited liability company's use of the same name stated in its articles of organization filed with the N.C. Secretary of State. In these cases, the name is not considered to be an assumed one, because use of the descriptors required for such entities (e.g., Inc., LLC, etc.) both define the legal status of the entity and can be seen in the entity's publicly filed organizational document. The statutes forbid use of any of such statutory entity terms or abbreviations in an assumed business name unless the entity is organized.[27] For example, someone may not use an assumed business name with "corporation" or

---

23. G.S. 66-71.4(a).
24. *Id.*
25. *Id.*
26. G.S. 66-71.3(1).
27. G.S. 66-71.5(b).

"inc." in the name without being a corporation that complies with North Carolina's organizational filing requirements for corporations.

The statute defines assumed business name to include "[i]n the case of a partnership other than a limited liability partnership or limited partnership, any name other than a real name of each of the general partners of the partnership."[28] This rule for general partnerships reflects their unique nature, in that they can be formed without any publicly filed organizational documents and each partner can bind the other partners. Using a general partner's name under such circumstances is therefore not considered deceptive for business name purposes, whereas using a name that is not the same as any of the partners might be considered misleading.

With respect to a trust, a name is an assumed business name if it is "any name other than the name specified in the trust instrument or, if the trust instrument does not specify a name for the trust, any name other than the name of the trustee and a designation of the trust for which the trustee is acting."[29] The statute also provides that an assumed business name is, "[i]n the case of any other person, any name other than a real name of the person.[30] The statute defines "person" to include "an individual, partnership, limited partnership, limited liability partnership, limited liability company, corporation, association, society, organization, joint venture, business trust, trust, governmental entity, or any other legal or commercial entity."[31] This broad definition captures use of any name used by any form of business entity other than that with which it is registered in organizational public filings.

Political committees and referendum committees do not file assumed business name certificates with a register of deeds. Committees for statewide offices must file such information with the State Board of Elections, and committees for county offices must file such information with the county board of elections.[32]

Someone who signs a certificate knowing it is false in any material respect, and intending for it to be filed with a register of deeds, is guilty of

28. G.S. 66-71.3(1)(b).
29. G.S. 66-71.3(1)(g).
30. G.S. 66-71.3(1)(h).
31. G.S. 66-71.3(2).
32. G.S. 66-71.4(c); G.S. 163-278.6(3); G.S. 163-278.7; G.S. 163-278.9.

a Class 1 misdemeanor.[33] Someone who fails to file a certificate or amend it as required has civil liability to anyone injured by the failure. Liability includes reasonable expenses and reasonable attorneys' fees incurred by the person for having to find out the required information needed for reasonable purposes.[34] The statute protects against liability for error or ambiguity in describing the nature of the business in an assumed business name certificate or amendment.[35] North Carolina law does not assign investigatory or reporting obligations on registers of deeds who suspect someone of making a fraudulent assumed business name filing. However, as a public official who takes an oath to support and maintain the law, a register who has such a suspicion should consider reporting it to the county sheriff or to the Consumer Protection Division of the North Carolina Department of Justice.

8.3 Register's Role in Assumed Business Name Filings

The North Carolina statutes designate the county register of deeds office as the place for individuals and entities to file a public notice that they are using an assumed business name within the state. In carrying out their administrative role in this system, registers should keep in mind that their entry of information presented to them into a statewide database is not an act that licenses or recognizes any legal rights to the names shown on the filings. Those who present assumed business name forms have the responsibility of complying with the statutory requirements and of taking other measures if they wish to protect a claim of rights to a name. As described in Section 8.1 of this chapter, even full compliance with the statutory requirements does not necessarily mean that the presenter acquired any legal rights to a name. Neither the register nor the N.C. Secretary of State searches to see if an assumed business name is unique or if someone else has already filed for the same name, and the fact that a certificate is entered into the system does not establish that the presenter has rights in the name that are superior to anyone else's. Registers cannot give advice to presenters about such rights, if there are any.

---

33. G.S. 66-71.14(a).
34. G.S. 66-71.14(b).
35. *Id.*

In reviewing assumed business name certificates presented for filing into the statewide database, the register's role is limited to ensuring that the document has the minimum statutorily required information for entry into the database. The register should not accept a presented submission missing any of the required elements. The statute requires that the following data be in the upload: "the assumed business name, the real name of each person engaging in business under that name, the type of certificate, the county in which the certificate was filed, and, in the case of a certificate of amendment or certificate of withdrawal, the identification number assigned to the assumed business name by the Secretary of State (SOS ID)."[36] The required components are further described in Sections 8.4 and 8.5 of this chapter. As noted in those sections, forms provided in the statutes are not required, but the information specified in them must be in whatever document is presented. Registers should have copies of the statutory forms on hand to facilitate their use, because they remind the preparer of the required elements and make it more efficient for the register to check to see that the required information is included. The register is not responsible for assessing the accuracy or truthfulness of the information. The presenter is ultimately responsible for failing to get the document into the system if the presenter used incorrect information.

Assumed business name filings may involve two different numbers assigned by the N.C. Secretary of State's office. When an entity, such as a corporation or limited liability company, files an assumed business name certificate, the entity must use the exact name used in its organizational filing with the N.C. Secretary of State's office as well as the office's identification number assigned for *that entity*. This number is a link between the organizational and assumed business name records. When anyone files an amendment or withdrawal of an assumed business name certificate, the individual or entity must include the identification number that the N.C. Secretary of State assigned to *the assumed business name*. A register may refuse to accept a presented assumed business name document if it is missing information required by statute, because a register takes an oath to execute "all things according to law."[37] The presenter, the register, and those who rely on the records will all benefit if the register brings detected

36. G.S. 66-71.10b).

37. G.S. 11-11; see Chapter 1, Section 1.4.1 of this book for a description of the oath.

missing or incorrect information, including with these identification numbers, to the presenter's attention.

The effective date of an assumed business name filing is the date that it is filed at the register of deeds office.[38] Within thirty days after accepting a certificate, amendment, or withdrawal, the register must forward a scanned image of it to the N.C. Secretary of State for its entry into the statewide database.[39] The statutes empower the N.C. Secretary of State to adopt rules for the database.[40] Registers should keep attuned to adoption or amendment of those rules.

Chapter 66, Section 71.10 of the North Carolina General Statutes requires that "the register of deeds of each county must index in accordance with Article 2 of Chapter 161 of the General Statutes every assumed business name with respect to which an assumed business name certificate, a certificate of amendment, or a certificate of withdrawal has been filed in that county." This means that the assumed business name filings should be indexed in the consolidated index similar to the manner in which assumed name certificates were indexed before the law required the centralized N.C. Secretary of State filing system, as described in Chapter 5, Section 5.4.5.4.

Someone who needs a certified copy of an assumed business name can obtain it from the register of deeds office where the information was filed. Someone claiming rights to a business name may have reason to enter evidence of a state assumed business name certificate or other filing in litigation, an investigation, or other official proceeding. The statutes provide that a certified copy of such a filing obtained from a register of deeds is "prima facie evidence of the facts required to be stated in the certificate."[41] This provision makes clear that a register need not be called to appear in a proceeding to authenticate the presence of the filing. Someone wishing to challenge the facts in the certificate or any rights claimed in connection with them may do so using other evidence.

38. G.S. 66-71.12.
39. G.S. 66-71.10(b).
40. G.S. 66-71.9(b).
41. G.S. 66-71.13.

8.4 Assumed Business Name Certificate Contents

The statutes contain a sample form with elements that will conform to the statutory content requirements for an assumed business name certificate.[42] The statutory form is not mandatory, but it is key to ensuring that the required elements are present for upload into the N.C. Secretary of State's database. Currently, assumed business name forms are made available on the Business Link North Carolina (BLNC) website, a service that provides business owners with information and resources available from state agencies. Registers who choose to make forms available in their offices or on their websites should endeavor to make sure they are up to date and be clear that the register is neither requiring use of the forms nor advising whether any particular form should be used or will be sufficient to achieve any particular legal objective.

To be recordable with the register for entry into the state database an assumed business name must have the following six elements:[43]

- **The assumed business name.** The register should not accept a certificate that does not indicate an assumed business name. The presenter—not the register—is responsible for ensuring that the name complies with the state legal requirements. Registers who detect a name that does not comply with the North Carolina assumed business name statutes should bring it to the presenter's attention and may refuse to record a certificate that clearly violates the requirements. Presenters are also responsible for complying with other federal and state laws about the use of names in business, such as federal trademark and state trade name and service mark laws.

An entity that has an entity name may file an assumed name certificate for a different name. For example, Jane Smith Corporation may file a certificate for "Jane's Wonders." The North Carolina assumed business name statutes prohibit use of an assumed name that has entity terms or abbreviations unless there is an entity registered in that name.[44] This language logically prohibits anyone who does not comply with the laws regarding formation of an entity from attempting to include entity types or their abbreviations

42. G.S. 66-71.11(a1).
43. G.S. 66-71.5.
44. G.S. 66-71.5(b).

that are restricted only to such properly formed entities. For example, an individual may not use an assumed name with "Inc." in it without filing articles of incorporation. This applies to the following:

- Unless the entity is a corporation organized under North Carolina law, the assumed business name may not include the following: corporation, incorporated, corp., or inc.
- Unless the entity is a limited liability company organized under North Carolina law, the assumed business name may not include the following: L.L.C. or LLC.
- Unless the entity is a limited partnership organized under North Carolina law, the assumed business name may not include the following: limited partnership, L.P., or LP.
- Unless the entity is a limited liability partnership organized under North Carolina law, the assumed business name may not include the following: limited liability partnership, registered limited liability limited partnership, or other similar abbreviation or form of those terms.

One certificate may include as many as five assumed business names.[45] The recording fee is not affected by how many assumed business names are listed (up to five for one certificate) or the number of counties in which business will be done.

- **The name of the person or entity engaging in business under the assumed business name.** North Carolina corporations, limited liability companies, and limited partnerships must provide the exact name registered with the N.C. Secretary of State's office and the Secretary of State identification number assigned to the entity at the time of formation.
- **The nature of the business.** The nature of the business may be identified by the type of service or product, as well as by the sector or area in which it is to be offered. This kind of information may be helpful to clarify when another's use of the same or a very similar name might cause confusion.
- **The street address of the principal place of business.** Although the statute does not require that the certificate contain a mailing

---

45. G.S. 66-71.4(b).

address if different from the street address, an address at which the name claimant can be contacted is important in case either the register or the N.C. Secretary of State needs to contact the claimant because there is a problem with entering the information into the system.

- **The counties where the assumed business name will be used to engage in business.** The certificate may list any number of counties individually, or it may indicate that business will be conducted in all 100 counties. The recording fee is not affected by the number of counties in which business will be done.
- **The signature of the person or entity who is claiming the name.** An assumed business name certificate must be signed. When the person engaged in business is a human, the certificate must be signed by the individual human.[46] A general partner must sign for a partnership or limited partnership.[47] An officer or other authorized individual must sign for a corporation, and a manager or other authorized individual for a limited liability company.[48] The statute also provides that for any other "person," which includes entities not specifically listed in the statute, "the certificate must be signed in the name of the person by an individual authorized to act for the person."[49] The register checks only for something that looks to be a signature by the individual in the individual's own behalf or by an individual in behalf of an entity. Nothing in the law requires the register to verify the actual authority of the officer to sign in behalf of the entity. Notarization is not required, and the register does not verify authenticity or originality. The signature can be in ink by hand, or it can be an electronic signature. As defined in G.S. 10B-101(6), an electronic signature can be anything that a signer applies intending it to be signature and that is logically associated with or attached to a document, including a digital image of a signature.

46. G.S. 66-71.6(1).
47. G.S. 66-71.6(2).
48. G.S. 66-71.6(3).
49. G.S. 66-71.6(4).

8.5 Amendment to and Withdrawal of Assumed Business Name Certificates

The statutes require assumed business name users to keep the information in recorded assumed business name certificates current. This means filing an amendment to the certificate if the user, assumed business name, or a county of use changes.

The statute imposes an obligation on the presenter of an amendment or withdrawal to provide the correct N.C. Secretary of State identification number (SOS ID) that was assigned to the assumed business name certificate. The SOS ID for the certificate is an important link in the N.C. Secretary of State's database between the original certificate and an amendment or withdrawal. Although ultimate legal responsibility for any harm resulting from an inability to correlate an amendment or withdrawal in the database with a certificate rests with the presenter, the register will avoid complications by ensuring that an apparently correct SOS ID appears on a presented amendment or withdrawal.

The statutes require that an amendment be filed with the register of deeds in which the assumed business name certificate was filed.[50] The presenter is responsible for filing an amendment within sixty days after a change in information on the recorded certificate.[51] The register is not responsible for checking whether this deadline has been met. There is a statutory form that, when completed, satisfies the statutory requirements, but use of that particular form is not mandatory.[52] To comply with the statute, the submitter must include the following information:[53]

- The assumed name as stated in the original certificate.
- A real name of the person engaging in business under the assumed business name as stated in the original, or most recently amended, assumed business name certificate.
- The book and page number of the original filing.
- The identification number assigned to the assumed business name by the N.C. Secretary of State (SOS ID).
- How the assumed business name certificate is to be amended.

---

50. G.S. 66-71.7.

51. *Id.*

52. G.S. 66-71.11(a2).

53. G.S. 66-71.7.

- The signature for the individual or in behalf of the entity that engaged in business with the name. An amendment must be signed in the same manner as an original certificate, as described in Section 8.4 of this chapter. The register checks only for something that looks to be a signature by the individual in the individual's own behalf or by an individual in behalf of an entity. Notarization is not required, and the register does not verify authenticity or originality.

Someone who stops using an assumed business name shown on a certificate that has been filed in the N.C. Secretary of State's database may withdraw that certificate by filing a certificate of withdrawal in the office of the register of deeds of the county in which the assumed name certificate was filed.[54] Withdrawals commonly are filed when someone sells a business associated with an assumed name, which occurs simultaneously with the buyer filing a new certificate for the same name.

No particular form is required for an assumed business name withdrawal. To comply with the statute, the presenter must include the following information in withdrawal:[55]

- The assumed business name being withdrawn.
- The book and page number of the original filing.
- The identification number assigned to the assumed business name by the Secretary of State (SOS ID).
- A real name of the person engaging in business under the assumed business name and that person's current address.
- A statement that the individual or entity has ceased engaging in business under the assumed business name.
- The effective date of the withdrawal if it is not to be effective upon the filing of the certificate of withdrawal.
- The signature for the individual or in behalf of the entity that engaged in business with the name. A withdrawal must be signed in the same manner as an original certificate, as described in Section 8.4 of this chapter. The register checks only for something that looks to be a signature by the individual in the individual's own behalf or by an individual in behalf of an entity. Notarization

---

54. G.S. 66-71.8.
55. *Id.*

is not required, and the register does not verify authenticity or originality.

Someone who has an assumed business name on file with a register of deeds that was recorded prior to the implementation of the statewide system on December 1, 2017, and who needs to amend the information in such a previously recorded certificate, must file a new certificate for transmission to the N.C. Secretary of State's central database. This requirement ensures that those using assumed business names include their certificates in the centralized database, rather than attempt to perpetuate a recording in a legacy system that by statute expires on December 1, 2022.

8.6 Expiration of Prior Assumed Name Certificates

Registers have in their records assumed business names that have been filed in different ways due to law changes. Prior to December 1, 2017, individuals and entities complied with the North Carolina assumed business name requirement by filing a certificate with the register of deeds in each county in which business was conducted. These certificates, filed before creation of the statewide database, expire on December 1, 2022.[56] Those who filed certificates before December 1, 2017, must file a new assumed business name certificate no later than December 1, 2022, for entry into the statewide database, to comply with the assumed business name filing laws. These newly filed certificates must contain the currently required information and must be amended and withdrawn according to current law. Any attempt to amend a certificate that was filed before December 1, 2017, is ineffective,[57] and the register should not attempt to transmit any amendment or withdrawal of those pre-December 1, 2017, records to the N.C. Secretary of State's database.[58]

Assumed name certificates, and records about their amendment and withdrawal, which were filed with a register before December 1, 2017, will continue to be in the register's records and indexed in the consolidated index. These records were not transferred or copied to the N.C. Secretary of State's centralized database. A certificate filed with a register of deeds

---

56. G.S. 66-71.15(a).
57. G.S. 66-71.15(e).
58. G.S. 66-71.15(f).

before December 1, 2017, can be withdrawn by filing with the same register of deeds.[59] The certificate that is the subject of such a withdrawal will not be in the N.C. Secretary of State's database and expires on its own account on December 1, 2022. One reason such a withdrawal might be filed is if the individual or entity using the name wishes to make record that it will be used by someone else, in which case the new user must file a certificate of assumed business name for entry into the new centralized database system.

---

59. G.S. 66-71.15(d).

Appendix 1

Fees

Recording Real Estate Instruments

Instruments except deeds of trust and mortgages . . . . $26 first 15 pages
$4 ea. add'l page

(S.L. 2016-23 provides that there is no fee for a Notice of Affected Parcel, recorded by the North Carolina Geodetic Survey, identifying property in the county along the reestablished boundary with South Carolina, pursuant to such session law.)

Deeds of trust and mortgages . . . . $64 first 35 pages
$4 ea. add'l page

Plats . . . . $21 ea. sheet

Highway right-of-way plan . . . .$21 first page, $5 ea. add'l page

Nonstandard document $25

Multiple instruments as one, each $10

Add'l assignment instrument index reference, each $10

Add'l party to index in excess of 20, each $2

Satisfaction instruments . . . . No fee

UCC Records

One or two pages in writing $38

More than two pages in writing . . . . $45 up to 10 pages
$2 ea. page over 10

Response to written request for information $38

Marriage Licenses

Marriage license $60

Delayed marriage certificate, with one certified copy $20

Application or license correction with one certified copy $10

Marriage license certified copy $10

Other Records

Recording military discharge . . . . No fee
Military discharge certified copy as authorized . . . . No fee
Birth certificate certified copy. $10
(register may waive for person over 62 years old)
Birth certificate after one year or more for same county, with one certified copy $20
Papers for birth certificate in another county one year or more after birth $10
Birth certificate for papers from another county one year or more after birth, with one certified copy $10
Death certificate certified copy $10
Birth record amendment. $10
Death record amendment $10
Legitimations $10
Certified copies unless statute otherwise provides . . . . $5 first page
$2 ea. add'l page
Uncertified copies. . . . . Cost as posted

Other Services

Notary public oath $10
Notarial acts . . . . $5 ea. signature
(not charged if performed with acts for which there is a fee except if fee is for registering instruments or plats)
Comparing copy for certification $5
State vital records automated search $14
State vital records automated search copy. $10
(register may waive for person over 62 years old)
Miscellaneous services . . . . Cost as posted

Appendix 2

Receipt Allocations

Deeds and Other Instruments (except plats, deeds of trust, and mortgages)

Register receipt (up to 15 pages)	$26.00
Less:	
1.5% Pension Fund	(0.39)
State Treasurer	(6.20)
Receipts retained by county	19.41
Less: 10% Automation Fund	(1.94)
Undesignated county register receipts	$17.47

Deeds of Trust and Mortgages

Register receipt (up to 35 pages)	$64.00
Less:	
1.5% Pension Fund	(0.96)
State Treasurer	(6.20)
Receipts retained by county	56.84
Less: 10% Automation Fund	(6.20)
Undesignated county register receipts	$50.64

Marriage Licenses

Register receipt	$60.00
Less:	
1.5% Pension Fund	(0.90)
Children's Trust Fund	(5.00)
Domestic Violence Center Fund	(30.00)
Receipts retained by county	24.10
Less: 10% Automation Fund	(2.41)
Undesignated county register receipts	$21.69

Other Fees Subject to Pension and Automation Funds

(not EBRS or excise tax)

Register receipt (example)	$10.00
Less:	
1.5% Pension Fund	(.15)
Receipts retained by county	9.85
Less: 10% Automation Fund	(0.99)
Undesignated county register receipts	$8.86

Index